COLONIAL
SMALL WARS

By the same author: BATTLES WITH MODEL SOLDIERS

COLONIAL
SMALL WARS
1837-1901

Donald Featherstone

David & Charles : Newton Abbot

0 7153 5711 5

Set in 11/13 IBM Press Roman
and printed in Great Britain
by W J Holman Dawlish Devon
for David & Charles (Holdings) Limited
South Devon House Newton Abbot Devon

Contents

Contents

Prologue

At 5 o'clock in the morning, shortly after daybreak on 20 June 1837, the Archbishop of Canterbury and the Lord Chamberlain went to Kensington Palace. Obtaining entry with considerable difficulty, they were shown to an ante-room, where they were kept waiting for many minutes. Told by an attendant that ' . . . the Princess is in such a sweet sleep I could not venture to wake her', they replied: 'We come on business of the State to the Queen, and even her sleep must give way to that.' It was the first occasion on which the princess had been called queen.

Within a few minutes, Victoria came into the room. Wearing slippers and a loose nightgown, she had a shawl thrown around her shoulders, over which her long hair fell. Although tears were in her eyes, she was perfectly collected and dignified.

Kneeling before the small slight figure, the Lord Chamberlain formally presented a paper announcing the king's death. The Archbishop stepped forward and added that he had been asked by Queen Adelaide to come to Kensington as it was thought that the Queen would like to hear how peaceful had been the end of the king.

There is no record of British soldiers fighting on any far-flung field at the time of Queen Victoria's accession. It was not until the latter part of 1837 that a small-scale revolt in Canada became the first of the many small wars that punctuated her long and glorious reign.

Introduction

Queen Victoria gave her name to an era which retrospect and nostalgia lead us to believe was a great and glorious period in British history. During the sixty-four years of her reign, British soldiers fought at least fifty campaigns, as well as dealing with the 'constantly running sore' of the north-west frontier of India. It was ' . . . an age in which, it almost seemed, any stray detachment of the British army could be relied on, should occasion demand, and almost as a matter of routine, to produce a junior officer capable of pacifying a frontier, quelling a rebellion or improvising and administering an empire'.

Colonial small wars, often begun as punitive expeditions, ended by bringing vast new territories under British rule in so colourful a manner as to conceal the price paid in British and native lives. Afghans, Africans, Afridis and Asians; Baluchis and Boers; fanatics and Fuzzy-Wuzzies; Kaffirs, kings, princes, rajahs and chiefs; Mahrattas, Maoris, mandarins, monks and mullahs; Pathans, Sikhs, Zulus, and even rebellious Canadian half-breeds, first defied and then accepted British rule.

This story of pacification and punishment in four continents could provide rabid anti-colonial propaganda. Hindsight indicates that right was not always on the British side: the politicians plotted, the soldier obeyed orders and played his role as unsung hero in a small war. He fought and died in many fierce and bloody campaigns in such alien country as the rocky hills of the North-West Frontier. The difference between outright success and stalemate was annihilation; capture probably meant being staked out, his mouth held open by a forked stick, the native women taking turns to squat and urinate upon him until the London cockney or the Highland laddie died by drowning.

Small expeditions, often unsuitably equipped, went out to take on superior numbers of warrior-races fighting on their own terrain. In red coats or dusty khaki, men from every British county marched in slow-moving columns where elephants jostled camels, bullocks plodded with donkeys and yaks, and mules carrying the little mountain-guns clattered and jingled. The enemy sometimes refused to fight, as he did in the Zhow Valley campaign of 1890, when a choleric commander made his impressive point by ordering the East Yorks Regiment to climb some hitherto unscaleable mountain. Sometimes the soldiers were accompanied by parties of boisterous straw-hatted sailors and marines landed from men-of-war. Under such dashing leaders as Lord Charles Beresford, the sailors dragged Gatling and Gardner guns through the sand of the Sudan, treating camels like boats, and caulking the animals' huge sores with pitch.

Each campaign was typical yet unique, most remarkable feature in all of them being the men who fought them — the common soldiers, the men in the ranks. Kipling conveniently left us Ortheris, Mulvaney and Learoyd to serve both as label and epitaph for them all. The names of their commanders are well known; they echo from country to country and from one war to another. Colin Campbell led an expedition against the Kohat Pass Afridis in 1850 and another in the Swat Valley in 1852; he was at the Alma, and he commanded the 'Thin Red Line' at Balaclava; later he relieved Lucknow and played a leading part in settling the Indian Mutiny. Frederick Roberts won the Victoria Cross at Delhi, had great victories in Afghanistan, and eventually commanded in the second Boer War. With the ubiquitous Sir Garnet Wolseley, he is the very epitome of the brave Victorian commander. Lesser lights abound — much-wounded Sir Charles Napier ('Old Fagin'), the conqueror of Sind, and his cousin Commodore Sir Charles Napier, RN who, in 1840, so obviously enjoyed land operations in the Levant, at the head of British sailors and marines, Austrian marines and Rocketeers, supported by Turkish infantry. Havelock, Hodson and Lumsden are part of the very fabric of British India; Cavagnari and the Battyes flamed brilliantly before laying down their lives. Even the doctors took up arms — Surgeon-Major G. Robertson was in the Chilas expedition in 1892 and, as British Agent, in command of the besieged fort at Chitral in 1895.

At times the British were brutal, prejudiced and ruthless; their native opponents showed on repeated occasions incredible courage and dignity while defending their homeland, in spite of invariably suffering at least a hundred casualties to every ten in the British ranks. Usually outnumbered, fighting in an alien climate, often physically inferior to his enemy, inadequately equipped for the prevailing conditions and not always well led, the British soldier was courageous in a quieter and more disciplined manner. To credit his successes to the Martini-Henry rifle and the mountain-gun would be both incorrect and unjust. Perhaps the shortcomings of both British soldiers and their native opponents are cancelled out by the noble virtue of courage.

The Crimean War, the Indian Mutiny and the second Boer War were, by the standards of their time, relatively major affairs, and so they fall outside the terms of reference of this book and are mentioned only in passing, for they are extensively documented elsewhere. Other relatively minor campaigns, such as the Lushai Expedition 1871, the Hunza Campaign 1891, the Niger Campaign of 1898 and the Ashanti War of 1900, have been excluded because there were no *British* units actually involved, the fighting being done by native units under British officers.

1 What Is a Small War?

Victorian small wars were expeditions and campaigns by disciplined soldiers against savage and semi-civilised races, undertaken to add the territory of barbarous races to the British Crown; suppress rebellion or lawlessness in a conquered or annexed territory; or to avenge a wrong, or wipe out an insult. They might also be punitive expeditions to overthrow a dangerous or troublesome enemy.

Campaigns of conquest or annexation were usually against the warriors, often irregulars, of some ruler or chief. Typical examples are the conquests of Sind and the Punjab, or the war against King Thebaw of Burma, all of which necessitated hard fighting against organised forces of considerable courage and ability. After organised resistance had been overcome, such operations frequently developed into campaigns of suppression involving ambushes and guerilla warfare, with the inevitable aftermath of stern and savage reprisals. Upper Burma was nominally annexed almost without a struggle, but British power there was only fully consolidated after several years of typical guerilla fighting.

Punitive operations entered upon to wipe out an insult or to chastise a troublesome tribe frequently developed into wars of conquest or annexation. Most of the punitive expeditions on the Indian Frontier may be included in this category and many of them resulted in annexation of the offending district. The Zulu War of 1879 is another example. The Abyssinian Expedition of 1868 was a campaign organised to avenge a wrong. Sometimes these expeditions became wars of expediency fought for political reasons, like the two Afghan Wars and the Egyptian War of 1882.

Because of primitive conditions, the enemy's mode of fighting, and the singular features of the theatres of hostilities, the conduct of Victorian small wars diverged widely from the regular warfare of the period. In regular warfare each side is well aware of what is to be expected from the enemy, and both adversaries are, to a certain extent, governed by specific common rules. But in small wars all manner of opponents were met, and all of them fought in different fashion.

For example, some Victorian small wars were against enemies trained and organised like regular troops, like the men commanded by Arabi Pashi in 1882, who were vastly different from the tribesmen of Africa and the North-West Frontier of India. When the enemy had been trained by instructors with knowledge and experience of European methods, the operations sometimes resembled the regular warfare of the day. The Zulus, for example, formed a well disciplined army with a definite organisation of its own, capable of carrying out manoeuvres on the battlefield with order and precision, although using primitive weapons. The Matabele, though organised on the Zulu model, were not such great warriors and lacked system. Both these races fought in a totally different fashion from the Chinese, the Afghans and the Egyptians, but they were none the less formidable on that account. The Sudanese and the Afghan Ghazis lacked the discipline of the Zulu, but fought with a bravery and recklessness that brought a return to old orders of battle, since tactics which were successful against forces armed with rifles and supported by artillery were useless against such foes as these. In the Kaffir Wars, an enemy deficient in courage and provided with poor weapons proved most difficult to subdue because he utilised his natural advantages of bush and jungle. The operations on the North-West Frontier of India in 1897 are an example of guerilla warfare, with the well-armed fanatical cut-throat of the hills fighting in a terrain peculiarly well adapted to his method of making war. But natives did not always fight in a manner which utilised the terrain of their country: in 1874 the Ashantis, for example, did not hesitate to risk a general engagement when they believed they had a chance of victory.

The methods of fighting in different small wars varied to such an extent that each presented new features which, if not foreseen, brought difficulty and even grievous misfortune to the regular troops involved. Isandlwhana, one of the worst disasters to befall British troops in Queen Victoria's reign, was directly attributable to a total mis-conception of the enemy's tactics, while the reverses in the first Boer War arose from a lack of cavalry, the one essential arm in this type of warfare. That was a period when, in three years and in one single quarter of the African continent, British troops came successively into conflict with the astonishingly different methods of combat employed by Kaffirs, Zulus and Boers. At exactly the same time, the regular army was heavily committed on the North-West Frontier and in Afghanistan.

Small wars were often complicated by the unexpected nature of the country and the routes over which the troops moved. The fighting qualities of the enemy and his method of warfare, his strength and weapons were all relatively unknown, as Napier discovered at Magdala in the Abyssinian War of 1868.

Generally speaking, small wars were campaigns against nature rather than against hostile armies; the health of the troops was affected by the climate which did not suit the trained soldier; movements and supplies were retarded by absence of communication; the jungle and the bush posed great difficulties for the commanders. Invariably, the losses sustained by the regular army were due far more to sickness than to fire and sword.

The strength of the forces of civilisation was also their weakness; the armaments and equipment which established their tactical superiority and eventually brought success also burdened them with non-combatant services and tied them to their base and lines of communication. Organised regular forces, backed by all the resources of science, wealth, man-power and navies, were at an undoubted strategical disadvantage in these small wars.

The conditions prevailing in a war against regular armies were quite unlike those in minor campaigns against natives, where material success was far more important than the moral effect of beating the enemy. This meant that the operations of small wars sometimes included depredations and havoc which the laws of regular warfare did not sanction. As Lord Wolseley said ' In planning a war against an uncivilised nation who has, perhaps, no capital, your first object should be the capture of whatever they prize most, and the destruction or deprivation of which will probably bring the war most rapidly to a conclusion. When the enemy could not be touched in his patriotism or his honour he was touched through his pocket by carrying off his flocks and destroying his crops.'

In a small war it was useless merely to drive the native enemy off the field without causing him very heavy casualties; once they had accepted combat, the natives had to be made to feel the real effects of battle against disciplined armies: hence the vast disparity in losses at such battles as Omdurman. The one great principle to be observed by regular troops during a small war was to hit the uncivilised enemy very hard by bold initiative and resolute action on the battlefield.

2 The Victorian Soldier

During the early part of Queen Victoria's reign, the British soldier 'existed in an unhappy vacuum' – an object of derision in an unpopular calling. In an age when hard living and harsh punishments were accepted, his calling stood out as one that put his life and limbs at risk without any compensations for its discomforts and hazards. The misery of his condition was never put forward as an excuse when the soldier was described as 'full of beer, beef and lust', and yet his vices were plainly no worse than those of the civilians of the period. Dogged by a reputation for violence and evil living, the redcoat was turned away at the door of music-hall or theatre and not every publican would admit into his bar a man wearing the Queen's uniform. The British public despised the apparently stupid, stolid soldier who only reacted when shouted at; it preferred the equally rough and hard-drinking navvy, simply because he lacked discipline and retained some vestiges of freedom.

The generally accepted view of the soldier as the scum of the earth tended to ostracise him and mould him into exactly that. His conditions of life encouraged him to drink heavily and to become involved in furtive and sordid sexual adventures that often ended in venereal disease. Probably a child of a large and poor family, he had almost certainly suffered from malnutrition and possibly rickets, so that his physique and ability to withstand hard conditions were impaired. Nevertheless, drilled into blind obedience by harsh discipline, the soldier displayed courage, endurance and humour, often under appalling conditions, in defeating superior numbers of naturally warlike races such as Sikhs, Zulus, Pathans and Dervishes.

Lacking a Waterloo to stimulate them, those in control of the army found it difficult to accept changes other than those arising from the glorious traditions of the past. For example, until the Mutiny, the army of the Honourable East India Company conducted its colonial wars in a far more practical manner than did the home army, yet its successes were in no way allowed to affect the moribund methods that passed for training in Britain. Success in Victorian small wars was gained through a constant emphasis on regimental honour, tradition and spirit and this, combined with high standards of duty, produced first-class morale and comradeship: everyone in the regiment, from commander down to drummer-boy, sought all possible opportunities to win new distinctions and reputations. The award of the Victoria Cross for acts of outstanding gallantry and sheer cold-blooded courage, although it had no military value beyond that of morale-raising, encouraged these qualities, and counteracted to some extent the slow-poison of home service, where even the ambitious, strong-minded officer or man could be drugged by stifling routine into an inertia born of the suppression of enterprise and responsibility.

Even if the British soldier was lacking in intellect and background, his undoubted constitutional courage and his burning desire for active service were unaffected. For officers, a reputation for personal courage was the key that opened the door to promotion. Looking on the fights against native foes as a dangerous form of sport, officers looked eagerly for transfers to the small colonial forces raised abroad and commanded by commissioned ranks from the regular army. But it was the officers and the country that benefited from colonial victories: the men in the ranks got nothing, while the officers, if they survived, won great rewards and public acclaim. When we sneer at 'colonialism' we should remember that the British soldier of this era organised and successfully maintained forces made up from the peoples inhabiting the recently conquered regions in Africa, India, Asia, Borneo and the West Indies; in every case these forces operated harmoniously and with loyalty.

In 1854, the year of the Crimean War, the British army consisted largely of hardened soldiers of the old school, some prematurely aged through the hard life of barracks, others undermined by drunkenness. Most of them were illiterate and constantly used coarse and blasphemous language, but they were stolid, shrewd, and long-suffering. They were commanded by officers who had fought under Wellington at Waterloo and in the Peninsula, and the moment for army reform was long overdue. Two reforming spirits, Secretary-at-War Sydney Herbert and Florence Nightingale, did much to change the old order and to introduce a milder atmosphere into the life of the army, and the long-service soldier faded from the scene, taking with him many of the old ideas.

As the Victorian era ran its course, the soldier spent less and less time in Britain, although he should have been five years at home for every ten overseas; this ideal could only be achieved by steadily reducing overseas garrisons, which meant that any threatening situation in India or Africa cut into already curtailed periods of home service. It was not until 1865 that, for the first time, one-third of the line battalions were actually in Britain. To the lengthy periods overseas must be added the months spent at sea on passage to and from remote parts of the Empire when, in the early days of steam, atrocious conditions had to be endured on the troopships.

Deeply conscious of her position as Queen-Empress and imbued with an unshakable concept of Empire, Queen Victoria was fortunate in having, throughout her long reign, a most remarkable assortment of strong-minded soldiers blessed with ability, as well as the good fortune to be invariably in the right place at the right time. Not only were they good soldiers; they also shared Victoria's faith in Britain's imperial destiny. Sir Garnet Wolseley had no humbug or hesitation about his imperialism when, writing to his wife in 1880, he said: 'l am a Jingo in the best acceptation of that sobriquet.' In 1882, he wrote: 'To see England great is my highest aspiration, and to lead in contributing to that greatness is my only real ambition . . . '

What made Victorian men 'take on for a soldier' when conditions were known to be so bad? The simple answer is: stark necessity — Jack Frost was the best recruiting-sergeant. When wages were good and employment abundant, army life did not present the same attraction to the young workman as it did in January 1853, for example, when the *Illustrated London News* reported that 'labour in the provinces being extremely down, owing to the continuous wet weather, scarcely a week has passed without large numbers of recruits coming forward for the army'. The recruiting-sergeant was perhaps not a true counterpart to the naval press-gang, but by painting a glowing and completely misleading picture of army life, he enticed many unsophisticated lads into the service. There was considerable attraction in the promises held out – a smart uniform, a horse to ride, a sword to wield, free meals, money to spend and an opportunity to see the world at Britain's expense. In some cases a cash bounty attracted a recruit, often a respectable and docile country boy raised by thrifty parents in a decent cottage home, who was the type most eagerly sought.

During the potato famines in Ireland, many young Irishmen discovered that the British army was their only means of obtaining food, clothing and a roof over their heads. Regimental rolls began to resemble Irish parish registers, and the onward march of the British Empire was milestoned by graves bearing Irish names.

In the early days of the era, the army became an asylum for the dregs of society as JP's gave prisoners the choice of prison, transportation or becoming soldiers, and once he had taken the Queen's shilling, the recruit was tamed and cowed into submission by savage drill and remorseless bullying by non-commissioned officers, and the process of 'breaking' men, often of poor physique and low health standards, coupled with unhealthy living conditions, gave the army a death-rate many times higher than that of the civilian population. The common punishment for even the smallest misdemeanour was 'pack-drill', often imposed so ferociously and for so long that the victim was reduced to a state of complete exhaustion. Men were punished for smoking, or for failing to keep in step whilst marching through the streets, and as late as 1840 the deserter was flogged and then branded with gunpowder massaged into the flesh to ensure that the letter 'D' remained indelible. The pressure of public indignation brought about the end of slavery at about the time that Queen Victoria came to the throne, but to the year 1881 it was still permissible to flog a British soldier, although from 1859 the punishment was strictly limited to certain classes of offence. The Mutiny Act of 1868 restricted corporal punishment to crimes committed on active service, but prolonged debates stretching through 1876, 1877 and 1879 failed to persuade the House of Commons totally to abolish flogging in the army and navy. A few men were flogged during the second Afghan War because they had rendered themselves unfit for service by looting brandy from medical stores. It would appear that the army, or the soldier himself, accepted flogging, old soldiers remarking: ' . . . serves him right . . . saves guards on him, too . . . ' In 1881, the Army Discipline Act abolished flogging and replaced it, on active service only, by the lashing of malefactors to a gun-wheel for a stated number of hours. Known as Field Punishment Number One, this method of disciplining the wrongdoer was still in use as late as the First World War.

When he was not spending countless hours on the barrack square being severely and tediously disciplined, the soldier lived in squalid barracks so overcrowded that he had less than three hundred cubic feet of space at a time when even a convict was allowed a thousand cubic feet. Such overcrowding and other bad sanitary conditions led to excessive mortality in the army – the Guards had 20, Line Infantry 18 and cavalry 11 deaths per 1,000 against 7½-9 deaths per 1,000 among the civilian population of military age. From tuberculosis alone, deaths were 18 per 1,000 as opposed to 3½ per 1,000 in the rest of the population. Even the much-vaunted barracks at Aldershot were damp, draughty and appallingly overcrowded, with iron cots almost touching each other; they were lit by smelly oil lamps, later replaced by flickering gas-jets. In the coldest of weathers, coal stoves in the centres of huts were lit, baking those near them whilst others on the outskirts shivered. Men washed in cold water in ablution huts which, with primitive latrines, were in the open outside the barrack-rooms. Tubs were placed in corners of the room at night for soldiers to relieve themselves during the hours of darkness. The men slept on iron beds that folded up during the day, and each man had a mattress with straw that was changed every three months, a pillow, four blankets and two sheets. The sheets were changed monthly, but the blankets were only washed when they were filthy. Life was a constant battle against fleas and lice.

Meals were eaten in the barrack-room on board-and-trestle tables set up in the narrow alley between the lines of beds on which the men perched: there were no chairs. The soldier provided his own crockery, usually a plate and a basin holding in turn soup, tea, coffee, beer and shaving-water. He had a daily ration of one pound of bread and twelve ounces of meat, including bone, fat and offal. Breakfast consisted of bread and 'hard-tack' (biscuits) soaked in coffee; this was known as 'slingers'. For dinner there were stews and a very occasional roast, with plenty of potatoes. White bread (provided from the canteen fund) and a basin of tea made up the last meal of the day. Until 1870, the soldier had sixpence a day deducted from his pay to cover his food – food which accounted for much of the sickness among troops serving abroad. Semi-rotten meat and bad vegetables were cooked outdoors, often by unwashed natives employed as cooks, over smoky fires in an atmosphere heavy with dust and flies. Whether it was provided by the authorities or bought from dubious private sources, the soldier's diet was abominable.

For the first forty years of Victoria's reign, her army proceeded overseas and went into action in full-dress uniform; the early part of the period found troops dressed as they were at Waterloo, in tight scarlet tunics with high leather stocks, trousers tightly strapped over Wellington boots, and shakos that gave no protection from the tropical sun. Those in control of the army would have considered it a startling heresy to suggest that men should wear loose, suitable clothing, boots stronger than those worn on ceremonial parades, and something more protective than a handkerchief hanging from the rear of a shako. After a few days in the jungle the gorgeous uniforms became tattered and the gold lace shredded; they had to be replaced with whatever came to hand. During the Kaffir War of 1852, men of the 6th Foot were described as being dressed in ' . . . red coats patched with leather, canvas and cloth of all colours, with straw hats, *wide-awakes*, long beards, tattered trousers and broken boots revealing stockingless feet'. It was as though nature had decided to play a part in adapting the men's clothing to suit her own stringent demands. In fact, fighting in the bush was nearly impossible until clothing was brought into this condition; parti-coloured garments made visibility less easy, and the outlandish head-dress afforded better protection from the sun than did shako or forage-cap. Colonel Michel, commanding one of the regiments during the operations, was said to have been seen in action with his shirt-sleeves tucked up to his elbows, his wide-awake cocked on one side, strong blucher boots on his feet and corduroy trousers on his legs. Hard wear and common sense sent clothing regulations to the wall.

Always more adaptable than the 'home army', the army in India had begun to make certain concessions to the climate during the second Sikh War and the Indian Mutiny ten years later. The officers, and sometimes the soldiers, were permitted to wear either a sun-helmet or a forage-cap with a pugaree (a thin muslin scarf) wrapped around it, the ends falling down behind to keep the sun off the back of the neck and spine. The time-honoured scarlet of the British army was slowly being replaced by uniforms of khaki — the Persian word for dust colour. A few British units during the Mutiny, among them the 32nd and 52nd Light Infantry, wore khaki, dyeing their own white clothing by using a variety of substances such as coffee, curry powder, and mulberry juice. This produced a number of different shades and some blotchy effects which made the soldiers of the period feel so scruffy, that they refused to 'walk out' in khaki, and spent their evenings in the canteen increasing the rate of drunkenness. After the Mutiny it was agreed that khaki was not smart enough and, except for use on the North-West Frontier by units such as the Guides, it went out of use for several years. White drill was the normal summer dress in India, but khaki returned for the Afghan War of 1878.

A British soldier landing in India during the Mutiny usually received light clothing, generally four white jackets and six pairs of trousers. In December 1857, when General Sir Hugh Rose assumed command of the Central India Field Force, one of his first measures was to provide the infantry with loose khaki clothing. Some authorities called it 'stone coloured'; others talked of 'khakee' and defined it as 'ash coloured'. Both stone and ashes vary in hue but the impression left is that khaki was originally less yellow and more grey than it was later; it is probable that the original khaki dye was curry powder.

Highlanders marched to Lucknow during the Indian Mutiny in feather bonnets and white spats; southern regiments were allowed the concession of a white cap-cover. Thus attired, these troops fought alongside the besiegers of Delhi, who were arrayed in khaki. In the Crimea, the kilt proved too cold in winter and eventually breeks were worn; as dress became more ragged, blanket gaiters and any tattered clothing that could be scrounged were the dress of the Highlander. In the Ashanti campaign of 1873, the

Black Watch wore sun-helmets and grey tweed tunics.

Old traditions die hard, and an officer of a Hussar regiment, writing of the Afghan War of 1878, stated that the men were so hampered by their leg-gear, overalls and tight riding-boots, that they kept in their saddles as much as possible. It is believed that the last occasion on which British troops went into action wearing red tunics was at the battle of Ginnis in the Sudan, fought on the last day but one of 1885.

Material conditions of the soldier's life changed very slowly during Queen Victoria's reign. In the early years, the Duke of Wellington opposed any increase in soldier's pay on the grounds that if the army became more costly the nation would resent the increase. In the Commons, Mr Windham was also against increased pay because, he said, more money would only make the army more licentious and more drunken; such a condition must end in a greater severity of discipline to act as a deterrent. In 1845 the principle of a grant of a penny a day as good-conduct pay for every five years' service was accepted and, in 1847, it was officially declared that no soldier should ever receive less than a penny a day in actual cash. In 1854, the daily stoppage made for a man's rations was reduced from sixpence to fourpence-halfpenny so that, at the outbreak of the Crimean War in 1854, the soldier received a minimum of a shilling a day and, in addition, a penny a day beer-money; from this total, fourpence-halfpenny was deducted for rations. This left the man with the sum of eightpence-halfpenny a day; from this were subtracted regimental stoppages and the cost of such necessities as cleaning materials.

In 1860 a new scale of good-conduct pay was introduced, ranging from a penny a day after three years' service up to sixpence a day after twenty-eight years' service. In 1865, the pay of a private of infantry of the Line was thirteen pence a day — one shilling for wages and one penny for beer-money. From this was deducted eightpence-halfpenny, a man had to pay for barrack damages, washing, renewal of his forage-cap, a shell-jacket, three shirts, a razor, brushes, soap, sponge and haversack. In 1867 an extra twopence was added to the soldier's daily pay, and recruiting improved at once. In 1870 good-conduct pay was set within the man's reach after two years' service; this was necessary in order to keep pace with the conditions of the new short service. In 1873, the free daily ration of food was introduced so that the daily rate of pay was raised to a clear one shilling a day; on the other hand, beer-money was abolished. Finally in 1876, a daily rate of twopence a day for deferred pay was brought in, with the idea of giving a man a start in civil life when he entered the Army Reserve; the total sum of the deferred pay would not be paid until he took his discharge. In 1898, new regulations assured the private soldier of his full shilling a day but, instead of the total sum of twopence a day deferred pay presented to the soldier on discharge, he was to get one pound for every year of service, up to a maximum of twelve pounds. But, at twopence a day, deferred pay over a seven-year period amounted to something like twenty pounds — so the soldier lost again!

Until the very end of the period, the soldier had few, if any, organised social amenities and recreational facilities. Even reading was denied to many because, at the time of the Crimean War, the line infantry regiments had a sixty per cent record of illiteracy. It is harrowing to consider the life of an illiterate private soldier in India, for example; for many hours during the hottest part of each day he was confined to his hut: no wonder there was a craving for active service, dangerous as it might be.

During the Duke of Wellington's years of influence over the army there was very little effort to educate the soldier, largely through fear of making him vulnerable to revolutionary propaganda, but from 1846 onwards, Sydney Herbert introduced educational reforms, in spite of a marked distaste shown by the average soldier for any form of 'book-learning', and as late as 1868 certain regiments provided financial inducements from regimental funds to persuade the men to attend school. In spite of a decree nine years earlier that no man should be promoted to corporal, except for good service in the field, unless he passed the lowest standard in the regimental school, it was not until the late 1880s that army education got very much under way.

Lacking social and recreational facilities and the education that might stimulate him to seek them, the soldier inevitably turned to drink as the means of blotting out the misery and squalor of his monotonous and bullied existence. The streets of garrison towns were nightly full of drunken, reeling men in black and ugly moods, spoiling for trouble. Dangerous antipathies existed between regiments, arising out of some obscure or fancied slight that had occured years before on active service — such and such a unit had not done its share on the rearguard during Moore's retreat to Corunna thirty-odd years before, or the 43rd Foot had not seen as much action at Waterloo as had the 92nd. These real or imaginary grievances survived in the form of feuds that shook garrison towns to their very foundations on pay nights, when grim purposeful mauls were fought out with bare fists, belts, bottles, sticks, stones and sometimes bayonets. Pay day usually saw these fracas because only then did the soldier have money to buy enough drink to get quarrelsome. To ensure that neighbouring units did not get drunk on the same night, a system of staggered pay-days came into being, and once the brawling had started the men were allowed to fight it out for a while so as to work off steam; then the hysterical trumpets would screech out in the nearby barracks and patrols armed with pickaxe handles would double out. As they were themselves sober, and had had their rest disturbed, these squads would not be too particular about the way in which they used their weapons, and so the men were dragged tottering back to the barracks, sometimes in handcuffs, and often badly beaten up.

All foreign stations had one thing in common — cheap drink, whether it brought profit to the government by being sold in the canteens or whether it was brewed under indescribable conditions by natives. Wood alcohol and berries were used to increase the potency of the liquor, and these native-brewed drinks brought with them blindness, gastro-intestinal irritation and pain, unconsciousness and tetanic convulsions probably leading to death.

The Victorian soldier spent far too much time in and around his barracks, grimy buildings often situated in the heart of crowded cities and towns, or else he garrisoned some ancient fort or castle. Because it interfered with farming and the grazing rights of common land, outdoor training was hardly ever considered. Happily, the North-West Frontier of India provided the perfect training-ground where belligerent, brave and tactically brilliant tribesmen gave every Victorian soldier much-needed experience of active-service conditions.

In an age of great change and advances in practically every other field, the British army changed very little, so that the line infantryman who fought at Mudki and Ferozeshah in 1845 would not have found it difficult to pull his weight at Omdurman in 1898. As the nineteenth century drew slowly to its close, along with the life of its queen, there was little that could shake the British belief that her soldiers were more than a match for any foreigners:

> *And when we say we always won,*
> *And when they ask us how it's done,*
> *We proudly point to every one*
> *Of the soldiers of the Queen.*

Even the disasters of the Boer War did not shake this confident attitude, this jingo-istic conviction — and it was certainly right that it should not do so. The man in the ranks, still a Victorian soldier for a few more months, fought the Boers and died well as he had always done when faced with Sikh and Zulu, Afghan and Fuzzy-Wuzzy.

3 The Weapons That Won an Empire

The twenty years that followed Waterloo saw few changes in the armaments of the British soldier, but from 1840 on new and superior weapons were placed in his hands every fifteen or twenty years. The flint-lock musket that had served the British infantryman for two centuries averaged 270 hits per 1000 shots and always threw the bullet high: Sir Charles Napier told his troops in Sind: 'The first duty of a soldier is obedience; his second — to fire low.' It was hardly worth firing at any targets smaller than the side of a barn if they were 100 yards distant. In 1840 the percussion-lock musket (later improved by being breech-loaded) began to replace the old 'Brown Bess' and, for the first time in the history of the British army, the calibre of muskets, carbines and rifles was the same so that one pattern of ammunition served for all. Within fifty years, the rifle was destined to bring greater changes to warfare than had taken place in the whole period between Naseby and Waterloo. The new weapon averaged 385 hits per 1,000 shots and misfires were reduced to 4½ per 1000 shots as against the 411 per 1000 of the flint-lock musket. The percussion-musket was first used in action by marines at the capture of Canton in 1841. Had the new musket reached India at the time it was first issued in England, the disastrous war in Afghanistan might well have taken a different turn, for both this campaign and the 1840 war in China were fought with the old flint-lock musket.

Early in 1852 Minié rifles were sent to South Africa for active-service trials against the Kaffirs. The Minié was a muzzle-loading weapon with a wide bore (7/10 inch); its three grooves with a spiral twist of one in seventy-two inches gave rotation to a heavy conical bullet possessing great smashing power. Sighted up to 900 yards, it was reasonably accurate and, although a muzzle-loader, it was a great advance upon the old smooth-bore musket. With a white target 6 feet high and 3 feet wide it was usual to achieve 2 hits out of 5 shots at from 500 to 800 yards, while at 900 yards 7 shots usually produced 1 hit. The initial distribution allowed for only six men in each company (usually the best shots) to be armed with this new rifle and on numerous occasions, at ranges of from twelve to thirteen hundred yards, small bodies of Kaffirs were dispersed and some killed. As it was a long rifle, it had the advantage of being effective with a fixed bayonet. In the same war, the King's Royal Rifle Corps used the Brunswick percussion-rifle, a weapon that took so long to load that each man was issued with a few rounds of smooth-bore ammunition for emergencies.

When the Crimean War broke out in 1854, the army was being re-equipped with the Minié rifle, but the war was fought primarily with the old smooth-bore musket. In use at the same time was the Enfield rifle, which ultimately superseded the Minié. Weighing only 8lbs 14ozs as against the 14lbs of the 'Brown Bess', the Enfield needed a far closer fit of cartridge and ball. In order to be quickly rammed down the 39 inch barrel, the cartridges were encased in greased paper and their ends had to be bitten off so that the powder could be poured down the barrel. The remainder, containing the wad and bullet, was then forced home with the ramrod, the bullet also having to be lubricated so that it could be driven down the rifle without undue effort. The Indian Mutiny is said to have been triggered-off because the caste-conscious sepoys of the Bengal army believed the cartridges to be greased with beef-fat or hogs-lard. Strenuous efforts equipped the British troops in the Abyssinian expedition of 1868 with the new Snider rifle, a breech-loader 72½ inches in length including the bayonet. By 1869, all the regulars and 16,000 militia had been so equipped.

In the same year the issue of improved equipment allowed the greatcoat (carried on the shoulders), and the two ammunition pouches (worn on the waist belt and each containing twenty rounds) supported by a pair of braces connected at the belt at both ends, to balance each other, although the haversack and water-bottles hung from separate slings still constricted the chest. From 1873-89, Slade-Wallace equipment was in use: here the valise or pack was carried in a curious manner, suspended on the buttocks, with supporting straps attached to the front buckles of the braces. Black pouches were worn on the white equipment, probably because the old cartouche box had been black so as not to show greasy finger-marks from the lubricant on the paper cartridges. When the Martini-Henry rifle was issued in 1871, an extra pouch carried another thirty rounds. Illustrations show the infantryman of the Egyptian campaigns of 1882-5 wearing his equipment of ammunition pouches, bayonet, haversack and water-bottle, with a mess-tin in a black cover on his back, strapped on where the braces crossed. Owing to the heat, packs were often not carried on the march and greatcoats were unnecessary in the Egyptian summer.

In 1869 trials began of a new hammerless .45 single-loader, the Martini-Henry, which ejected the cartridge case by a lever behind the trigger-guard; it fired a heavy bullet with great stopping-power. Its recoil was correspondingly violent and black powder was still used. Far superior to any arm previously issued to the British soldier, it was easy to operate, quick to reload and reckoned accurate up to 800 yards. It was 5 feet 11½ inches long, including the bayonet. First widely used on active service in Africa and Afghanistan, the Martini-Henry, a weapon with a small bore, great range, low trajectory and superior accuracy, has been claimed to be the earliest shoulder arm that could compete successfully with the longbow of the Hundred Years War so far as range, rapidity of firing and robustness were concerned. Every earlier firearm, even the famous 'Brown Bess', had been in some degree inferior to the master-weapon of Crecy, Poitiers and Agincourt.

At this time there were several types of sword-bayonet, some with long wavy blades, but the old triangular-bladed type still predominated. In 1878, a new and longer bayonet with a series of brass studs upon the scabbard, was issued to the infantry.

In 1881, the rifles used in the British service were the Martini-Henry and the Snider-

Enfield; the artillery carried carbines by the same makers, while the cavalry was equipped with the Westley-Richards carbine. With the new and improved firearms came a new system of drill described in *Field Exercises and Evolutions of Infantry*, specially issued in April 1877.

In about 1860, General Sir Samuel Browne VC, who had lost an arm and required a more convenient method of carrying his sword and revolver, invented the Sam Browne belt. It came into general use for British officers in the wars of 1870 and has been adopted by nearly all the armies of the world.

 Invented in 1889, the magazine Lee-Metford rifle, using smokeless cordite and with a magazine holding five rounds (which had to be put in separately) was the weapon used in Kitchener's Dongola Campaign, killing and wounding about 25,000 Sudanese at the battle of Omdurman, where not a single native closed nearer than 150 yards. This was in spite of the Lee-Metford bullet drilling a hole through a bone without bringing down or even stopping the rush of a fanatic Zulu, because of the pencil diameter of the bullet. Nevertheless, the Lee-Metford revolutionised warfare because it banished the old problem of the target being obscured by a cloud of black smoke after each volley while, at the same time, it revealed the position of the firer.

From about 1895 onwards, the .303 short Lee-Enfield rifle, with slight modifications, served the British soldier faithfully, right through the First and Second World Wars. British craftsmen can derive much credit from the production of a firearm that proved itself on many battlefields to be the best of its kind.

During the nineteenth century hardly any soldier, except an infantry private, could escape having to carry a sword of one pattern or another. In the British army, artillerymen, engineers, bandsmen, pioneers and even medical auxiliaries wore them. The Highland regiments had a special type, the broadsword. In 1853 it was decreed that all cavalry troopers should be armed with the same pattern of sword, imported from Germany. During the fierce battles in Egypt against the Mahdi and his Dervishes in the 1880's, many of these weapons completely failed their bearers — blades and hilts bent or even broke, not only in action but also through the ordinary wear and tear of campaigning. In the Boer War, the sword worn by the cavalry proved quite useless in action and it was not until after this period that a really first-rate weapon was designed and turned out in quantity.

The terrain and the conditions under which Victoria's small wars were fought allowed only the use of light artillery; Britain won her colonial wars with thirteen-pounder field-guns and mountain-guns carried in separate parts on mules. The hillmen of India's North-West Frontier said that what they feared was ' . . . not the child-rifle but the devil guns, which killed half a dozen men with one shot (shell) which burst and threw up splinters as deadly as the shots themselves'.

In the early colonial wars, gun-metal was often preferred for artillery used in tropical or mountainous areas. For the Bhutan expedition of 1865, three-pounder brass smoothbores, machined out to 3 inches in the bore and rifled on the French system, were issued as the seven-pounder Mk I. As they proved too heavy, a seven-pounder Mk II was produced and adopted by both army and navy. All brass guns were withdrawn from service in 1874. In 1881, breech-loading guns for the Royal Horse Artillery and field brigades were issued for service at Woolwich. These breech-loaders were, as far as was practicable, constructed on the model of the muzzle-loading thirteen-pounder considered to be the finest specimen of British ordnance. They were 3 inches in calibre at the bore and they weighed only 8½cwt. The gun was chiefly made of steel with bronze fittings.

Accounts of colonial small wars repeatedly mention the mountain batteries, who brought the use of mule transport to the point of perfection. Their officers claimed that they could take their guns anywhere a man could go, and they did so. Apparently blessed with hawk-like vision, they could pick out the lone Afridi sniper on the distant hillside. The mountain-guns used in Abyssinia in 1868 weighed about 150lbs but were later superseded by an almost identical piece weighing 200lbs with the barrel 3 feet 2 inches long. Two kinds of iron cradles were used, one taking the gun with its muzzle to the rear, and one the carriage, breast to the front. In 1880, the famous 'screw gun' was introduced: made in two pieces which screwed together, this gun was later immortalised by Kipling. The gun itself weighed about 400lbs and a mule could carry about 300 to 320lbs.

An early type of machine-gun, invented by Doctor Gatling of Chicago, was used in the Afghan War and also in Egypt. It consisted of a number of rifle-barrels bound together like a faggot and mounted on wheels, with a firing mechanism worked by turning a handle like that of a barrel-organ. It was not a great success, as it usually jammed at critical moments, as Sir Henry Newbolt wrote:

> *The sand of the desert is sodden red . . .*
> *The Gatling's jammed and the Colonel's dead,*
> *And the regiment blinded with dust and smoke.*

In 1880, the Admiralty decided to adopt the Nordenfeldt four-barrelled gun, which fired twelve solid steel shots per second, for use in the navy to repel torpedo-boat attacks. This weapon was selected, after a series of exhaustive experiments, in preference to the Gatling or Hotchkiss revolving cannon. In July 1883, the same five-barrelled Nordenfeldt gun, mounted on an ordinary infantry carriage, was adopted as an auxiliary weapon for infantry. The Gardner gun, another weapon of similar construction, was used during the Egyptian War. None of these 'machine guns' was particularly efficient until 1883, when the American Hiram Maxim invented the first automatic gas-operated machine-gun. Maxim was also the inventor of the Pom-Pom firing belts of one-pound shells, which was used in the second Boer War.

25

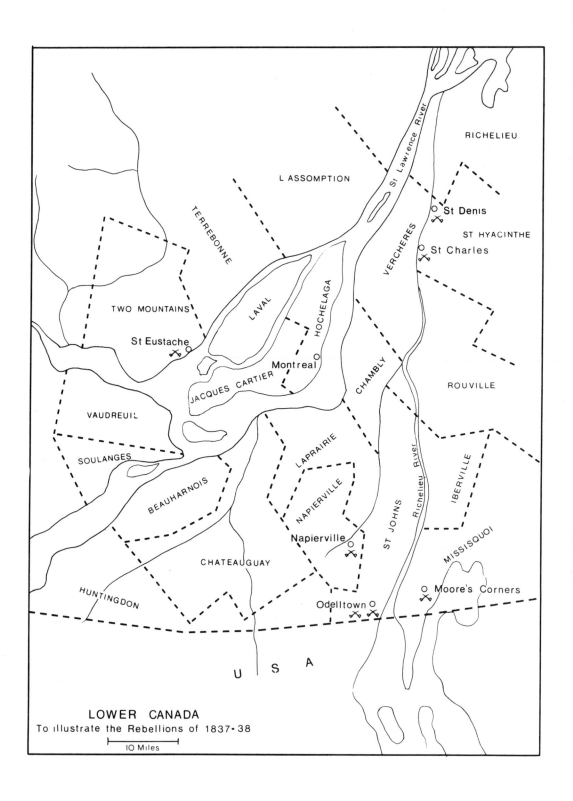

RICHELIEU

L ASSOMPTION

St Lawrence River

TERREBONNE

VERCHERES

○ ✗ St Denis

ST HYACINTHE

○ ✗ St Charles

TWO MOUNTAINS

LAVAL

HOCHELAGA

St Eustache
✗ ○

○
Montreal

CHAMBLY

ROUVILLE

JACQUES CARTIER

VAUDREUIL

Richelieu River

SOULANGES

LAPRAIRIE

IBERVILLE

BEAUHARNOIS

NAPIERVILLE

ST JOHNS

Napierville
✗

MISSISQUOI

CHATEAUGUAY

○ ✗ Moore's Corners

HUNTINGDON

Odelltown ○
✗ ✗

U   S   A

LOWER CANADA
To illustrate the Rebellions of 1837·38

10 Miles

4 Revolt in Canada 1837

During the latter part of 1837 colonists in lower Canada took up arms in open violation of the law. A revolt flared up, and the law officers of the Crown and the magistrates of Montreal appealed to the commander of the forces in Canada (Lieutenant-Colonel Sir John Colborne, afterwards Lord Seaton, GCB, GCH, at whose order the 52nd Regiment had charged down into the flank of the French Imperial Guard in the late evening at Waterloo — a move that many considered to be the turning point of the battle).

The ring-leaders of the rebellion were thought to be in the villages of St Denis and St Charles, and so detachments of the 24th, the 32nd, and the 66th Regiments under Colonel Gore, with a howitzer, were sent to St Denis. At the same time Lieutenant-Colonel Wetherall was directed to move from Chambly with four companies of the 1st Royal Scots and Captain David's troop of Montreal cavalry, together with a detachment of the 66th, and two six-pounders. This group advanced on St Charles, a timber-built village 17 miles from the ferry at Chambly. With each force went a magistrate to execute the warrant.

Impeded by the severity of the weather and the bad state of the roads, and informed that the rebels at St Charles had been reinforced, Wetherall's force halted at St Hilaire until a fifth company of the Royals came up. On 25 November the troops resumed their march and were fired on by insurgents from the opposite side of the river when they got within a mile of St Charles, where some 1,500 rebels were in buildings behind a wooden stockade. After an exchange of fire, the defences were carried by storm, costing 17 of the Royals and 4 of the 66th, while Lieutenant-Colonel Wetherall and Major Warde each had a horse shot from under him. Many of the rebels were shot or bayoneted and sixteen men were taken prisoner. On the following day the detachment fell back to St Hilaire.

On 28 November at Point Oliviere it advanced to attack another body of rebels entrenched behind an abatis of felled trees. After exchanging a few shots, the insurgents lost heart when they saw the soldiers form up for the attack; they ran from the field, leaving two cannon behind them. With twenty-five prisoners, the force returned with difficulty to Chambly in heavy rain, with frost and snow on roads knee-deep in mud.

Colonel Gore's force had suffered greatly from the severity of the Canadian winter and was forced to withdraw after a number of attempts to reach St Denis. The success of Colonel Wetherall at St Charles had not completely suppressed the rebellion and many soldiers were murdered by the rebels in the guerilla warfare that followed; in addition, the troops had many harassing duties to perform in the frost and snow of a severe winter.

On 13 December, Sir John Colborne marched out with every available man towards

St Eustache, a village on the Riviere du Chene, 15 miles from Montreal, to put down a revolt in the country of the Lake of the Two Mountains. Here insurgents, claiming control over a wide extent of territory, had driven the loyal inhabitants from their homes, exposing them to the rigours of winter. The Royal Scots, the Montreal Rifles and Captain Globinsky's company of Volunteers were formed into a single brigade under Colonel Wetherall. On the following day, the Volunteers were detached into the woods bordering the upper road leading to St Eustache, with the object of driving back and dispersing the rebel pickets, while the remainder of the brigade crossed the Ottawa Grande Riviere on the ice. Advancing upon St Eustache, the force entered the village at several points.

The Royal Scots and the Montreal Rifles seized the most defensible houses in the main street, but an officer going back with orders to bring up the artillery was prevented by the fire of the rebels in the village church from doing this. Entering the rear of the village, the artillery opened fire on the church but was unable to break down its strongly barricaded door. Companies of the Royals and the Rifles occupied the houses around the building and carried on a brisk exchange of musketry with the rebels inside. After a furious struggle a party of the Royal Scots got inside the presbytery and bayoneted its defenders; then they set it alight. The smoke from the burning building masked the church so that the rest of the battalion could advance unseen, covered by fire from the seigneur's house, which formed one face of the square in which the church stood. Lieutenant-Colonel Wetherall sent forward his grenadiers who carried the church by storm, killing several of the rebels and taking many prisoners. Meanwhile, other battalion companies, under Major Warde, fought their way into the church from the rear and drove out the garrison, bayoneting all who resisted. The building had been set on fire during the fighting and was now burning fiercely. In this attack the Royals lost only 5 men and took 118 prisoners. After an unopposed advance to St Benoit, the force returned to Montreal on 16 December with large numbers of prisoners. The rebels had unconditionally laid down their arms.

Almost exactly a year later, a second rising in Lower Canada was suppressed by Sir John Colborne who defeated the rebels at Napierville, and in order to strengthen the government of the colony, an Act of Parliament was passed in 1840 making Upper and Lower Canada into a single province.

5 The Capture of Aden and Operations against the Persians 1838

In 1838 the whole question of British communications with India and of the safety of India itself had to be most urgently considered by the British government, because Mohammed Ali, the Pasha of Egypt, by conquering most of Arabia and extending his empire from Khartoum to the Taurus range, controlled all possible routes, whether the development of steam navigation and of railways was to make the main route to India along the stream of the Euphrates, across the Isthmus of Suez, or even by the valley of the Nile to the Red Sea. The Pasha's belligerent public utterances alarmed the British government, which feared that France might befriend him, for, since Napoleon's expedition of 1798, she had felt that her influence should prevail in Egypt. Already she held Algeria and was looking greedily towards Tunis while, in the west, her puppet Don Carlos was on the throne of Spain. With the friendship of Mohammed Ali in the East, France could realise her dream of turning the Mediterranean into a French lake.

There were equally serious dangers on the very borders of India. In 1834, the Shah of Persia, friendly to England, had died and his son Mohamed Shah ascended the throne with the cordial assent of both Russian and British governments. At that time, Palmerston had warned him against allowing the Russians to push him into war against the Afghans, but, in the hope of recouping in the East his losses in the West, Mohamed Shah sent a Persian army, equipped with powerful artillery directed by Russian officers, to lay siege to Herat, an Afghan fortress, in November 1837.

The siege of Herat did not go well for the Persians, mainly because the direction of its defence was taken over by Lieutenant Eldred Pottinger of the Bombay Artillery, who was unofficially in the area to gather information about the Afghans. Nevertheless, feeble as were the operations of the Persians, they had violated the treaty under which Persia had pledged herself not to attack Afghanistan, and on 6 April the British Resident at Teheran, Mr McNeill, arrived at the Persian camp. His attempts to mediate were foiled by Russian officers freely distributing money, and on 7 June, after suffering many insults, he broke off diplomatic relations with the Shah and took his departure.

It was not only at Herat that a British Resident had been disrespectfully treated by the Persian authorities; the same thing had happened at Bushire. In May 1838, Lord Auckland, Governor-General of India, dispatched a small naval and military expedition to the Isle of Karak, north of Bushire in the Persian Gulf. The squadron reached its destination on 19 June; the troops (detachments of Bombay native regiments) were landed without opposition and Karak immediately surrendered.

Five days later, on 24 June, the most formidable Persian assault upon Herat was delivered and repulsed, mainly through the energy and example of Eldred Pottinger. Realising that rumour had magnified the strength and prowess of the expedition to

Karak, Mr McNeill judged it to be a favourable moment to demand a withdrawal of the Persian army from Herat. On 9 September 1838, Mohamed Shah and his troops marched back to their own country after a siege which had lasted for ten months and, which, despite Russian generals, artillerymen and engineers, had failed ignominiously. Pottinger asserted that a British army would have mastered the fortress within ten days.

In Kabul, a Russian agent was trying to tempt Dost Mohammed, the ruler of Afghanistan, into alliance with Russia and Persia. From Kabul it was no long journey to Peshawar, ruled by Ranjit Singh, an alliance with whom might allow Russian troops to appear upon the British frontier on the River Sutlej. It was a situation that was soon to bring about the first Afghan War, but for the moment, Palmerston met it by diplomatic remonstrance at the court in St Petersburg; in October 1838 the Russian agents in Afghanistan and Persia were withdrawn and the immediate danger on the north-west marches of India appeared to be diverted. More decisive action had to be taken to safeguard the route to India and, by a fortunate coincidence, at that very moment a quarrel arose between the Indian government and the chief of the Port of Aden over his ill-treatment of ship-wrecked British subjects. After protests, early in 1838 the Sultan of Aden ceded the port of Aden to the East India Company 'from friendly motives and of his own good will'. An expedition consisting of a wing of the 102nd Regiment (then the 1st Bombay Fusiliers) and a battalion of Bombay native infantry, under the escort of two of the Queen's ships and a squadron of the Indian navy, was sent to occupy the place. When they got there, the Arabs refused to allow the troops to land or to furnish them with water or supplies and so, under the cover of fire from the ships, the men were disem-barked and occupied the town. The Arabs took refuge in one of the forts and hung out a white flag. Except for a misunderstanding which cost sixteen British casualties while the Arabs were being disarmed, the capture of Aden was bloodless. In November 1838 and again in 1840 half-hearted attacks made upon the fortress were easily repulsed. By obtaining possession of this arid and forbidding stronghold, the southern gate of the Red Sea was secured.

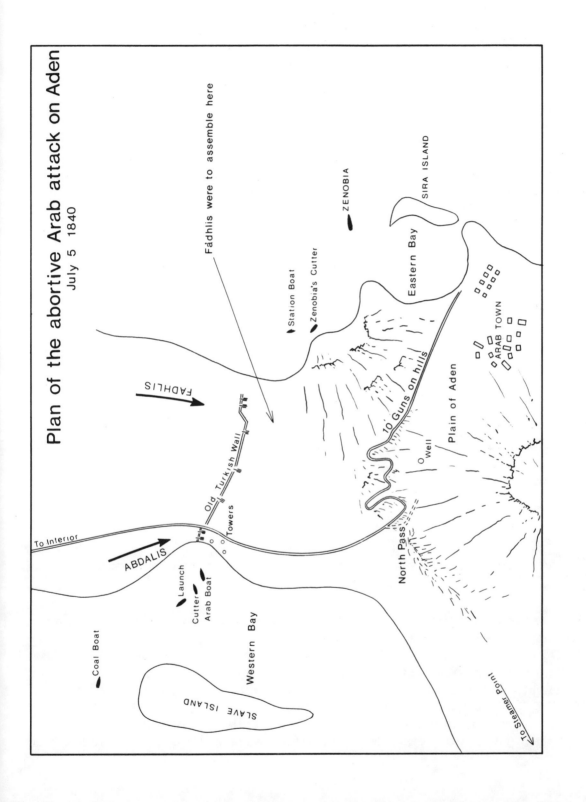

Plan of the abortive Arab attack on Aden
July 5 1840

Fádhlis were to assemble here

ZENOBIA

Zenobia's Cutter

Station Boat

SIRA ISLAND

Eastern Bay

FÁDHLIS

Old Turkish Wall

Towers

To Interior

ABDALIS

10 Guns on hills

Well

Plain of Aden

ARAB TOWN

North Pass

Launch

Cutter

Arab Boat

Coal Boat

Western Bay

SLAVE ISLAND

To Steamer Point

6 The First Afghan War 1838

When, in 1838, Dost Mohammed, ruler of Afghanistan, refused an alliance, the Governor-General Lord Auckland, decided to supplant him by a puppet-king, Shah Suja; by the autumn of 1838, this project had swollen into a large-scale invasion of Afghanistan. A Bengal division under Sir Willoughby Cotton was assembling in Ferozepore, while Sir John Keane led a division from Bombay. After a junction in the Indus delta the combined force had to march another 400 miles; a quarter of the distance was through rough mountain-passes.

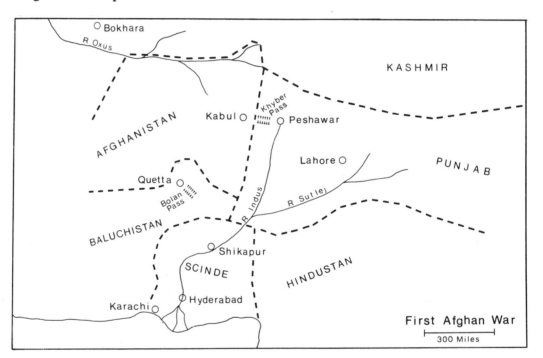

Cotton's force marched out from Ferozepore on 10 December 1838 in five columns which followed each other at intervals of a day, the supplies and stores coming last. The troops, who had to carry their packs instead of loading them on camels hired in the usual way, were hampered by 50,000 to 60,000 camp-followers and around 30,000 camels, but by March they had reached Baluchistan, where warlike mountaineers swooped upon them, cutting down followers, carrying off cattle and camels, and attacking hospital wagons. By great efforts and with heavy loss of transport-animals and baggage, the column got through the 60 mile long Bolan Pass and on 26 March Cotton arrived at

32

Quetta with his troops and camp-followers, on half and quarter-rations respectively. Harassed by tribesmen, men and animals dragged themselves along in a state of great distress in a temperature of over 100°F, the 16th Lancers walking and goading their horses forward with their lances. After marching just over 1,000 miles in 137 days, and on half-rations for the last 28 days, on 26 April the Bengal division marched into Kandahar. On 5 May, the Bombay division marched in, also suffering from the great heat, inadequate nourishment and dysentery.

On 27 June, Keane set out for Kabul, leaving behind his four eighteen-pounder siege-guns and on 21 July came in sight of the fortress of Ghazni, the only enemy stronghold on the way to Kabul. Occupied in some strength, Ghazni's strong walls and gates were impervious to Keane's light artillery; it was not possible to scale the 60 to 70ft high parapets, while mining was impossible because of a wet ditch. There was only three days food left; Ghazni had to be taken at once unless the army was to perish, and so Keane decided to blow in the Kabul gate and to carry the fortress by surprise, at the same time making a false attack on the southern face. Under the command of Brigadier-General Sale, the 240-strong storming party was composed of the light companies of the Queen's, the 17th and 102nd Regiments, and a flank company of the 13th Regiment, supported by the main attacking column of the Queen's and the 102nd, with the 17th in support and the 13th deployed as skirmishers on both flanks. At first streak of dawn, Captain Peat and Lieutenants Durand and MacLeod, carrying

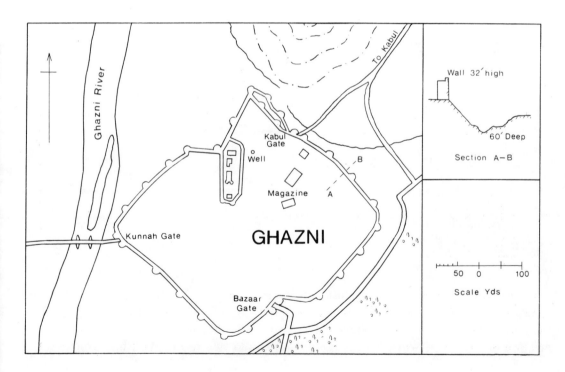

twelve bags of powder, crept towards the gate, to be discovered within 150 yards, when the Afghans opened a heavy fire by the light of blue flares. After Durand and his men had laid the 300lbs of powder against the gate and lit the fuse, Peat crawled forward to investigate a delay and was nearly killed when the charge exploded violently. Recovering himself, he returned to the column to report that he could not see daylight through the gateway. Sale ordered his buglers to sound the retreat, but this was soon changed to the advance when Major George Broadfoot reported that the gate had been breached. The advance party had mastered the defenders and were holding the breach. Reinforced by the main column, the stormers overcame all resistance and gained both city and citadel. Ghazni, impregnable by native tradition, had fallen at the cost of only 17 killed and 165 wounded, mostly British, from the storming-party. If Sale had not been so hasty in sounding the retreat, but had closely followed the storming party, the victory would have been even less costly.

On 30 July the force marched for Kabul, hearing that Dost Mohammed had fled, and on 7 August 1839, Shah Suja made his formal entry into the city, watched by a vast undemonstrative and unenthusiastic crowd.

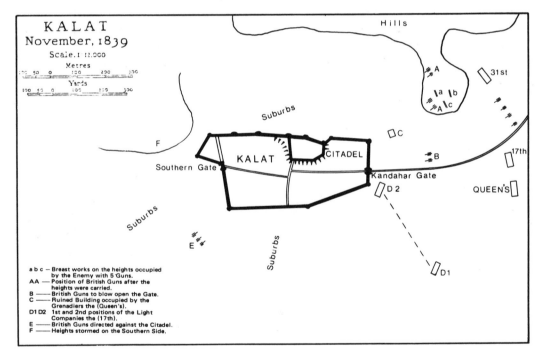

On 13 November, General Willshire and the Bombay Division (about 1,000 bayonets) came in sight of Kalat to find Mehrab Khan's Baluchi infantry crowded on three hills to the north-west of the fortress, sheltered by three redoubts and supported by five guns in position behind breastworks. Although outnumbered two to one, Willshire prepared to

storm Kalat in broad daylight. The assaulting columns advanced steadily, while the little six-pounder guns opened a very accurate fire of shrapnel at a range of about 700 yards on the men outside the fortress; these now attempted to withdraw inside the citadel, dragging their guns with them. Willshire ordered the Queen's and the 17th Regiments to rush the Kandahar gate at the northern angle and to try to enter it with the enemy, but the Baluchis abandoned their guns and secured the gate. Ordering his assaulting troops to take cover behind walls and ruined buildings, Willshire advanced his artillery to blow in the Kandahar Gate, allowing the storming columns to dash in against fierce resistance. Simultaneously, another force went round to enter the fort by a southern gate before the enemy could secure it. The stormers assaulted the citadel, where Mehrab was slain. The enemy troops then surrendered on condition that their lives were spared. It was a smart little affair, a more brilliant success than Ghazni, costing 31 killed and 107 wounded.

In October 1839, came the first of the major causes of impending British disaster when Keane withdrew from Kabul and Cotton was appointed his successor. He was in the unhappy position of being in nominal command, although the Shah's envoy, Sir William Macnaghten, had power to overrule his orders.

7 War in the Levant 1840

Because Russian intrigues with Egypt threatened Turkey, in August 1840 Commodore Sir Charles Napier was ordered to take a fleet to Beyrout with the object of throwing back a 15,000 strong Egyptian army under Souliman Pasha. On 10 September, a force of Turkish infantry and British marines was landed under the command of Napier himself; he settled himself in a church with a loaded cannon by his bedside. Refusing to accede to the demand for withdrawal, Souliman Pasha's troops came under heavy fire from the fleet, and two castles which they were defending were destroyed, but the Albanian garrison of an old castle in D'Jebaila easily repulsed a force of 220 marines and 150 native troops, so that Napier had to send seven of his warships to open fire on the castle whilst the marines, accompanied by armed Druses, landed on a beach to the south of the town. They too were turned back and the fleet resumed its pounding of the old walls without making any serious impression on the solid masonry. Next day the castle was abandoned by the Albanians who had lost only 1 killed and 2 wounded against 23 British dead.

On 22 September Sir Charles Napier, who seemed as much in his element when leading troops as on the quarter-deck, marched with one battalion of marines and another of Turks through rough country under a burning sun. The marines, unaccustomed to marching, suffered terribly during the journey. They came up to an entrenched camp of Albanians under Osman Pasha and, after waiting two days for reinforcements, Napier sent his men into the attack. Three Turkish battalions went along a deep ravine so as to arrive on the left of the enemy at daylight, while another battalion was sent across a bridge near the mouth of the river to occupy the heights on the opposite side, covering a battalion of Royal Marines and the Austrian Rocketeers crossing higher up and advancing towards the enemy. All went as planned and, finding their position turned, the Albanians abandoned the entrenchments and took up a new position on the heights of Ornagacuan. The red-fezzed Turkish battalions advanced with great spirit and gallantry against the kilted and shawled Albanians, who were soon routed with the loss of 400 prisoners.

Napier now went back to sea and led the fleet in an expedition against Sidon. At 11 am on 26 September the whole squadron opened their broadsides and sent shot and shell booming and whistling at the barracks and the castle to drive the Egyptian troops into shelter. After an hour and a half the cannonading ceased and boats shot away from the ships' sides, landing Turks close to the castle, while British and Austrian marines went ashore on a beach north of the town. Napier put himself at the head of this force which advanced, cheering, to break into the town and skirmish through the narrow winding streets until they seized the castle. The 1,000 strong allied landing-force killed or captured the entire garrison of 3,000, with a loss of 37 killed.

A few days later Sir Charles Napier personally led a force composed entirely of Turkish infantry to defeat the Egyptian troops of Ibrahim Pasha at Boharsof, and at the end of October, under the command of Admiral Sir Robert Stopford, he took a British naval squadron to bombard the town of Acre. For some hours the ships pounded away, under fire from shore batteries. At sunset, Admiral Stopford signalled the cease fire, but Napier, considering that this might encourage the enemy to re-man his guns, kept up his fire until dark when he was expressly ordered by the Admiral to withdraw. During the night the governor of Acre abandoned the town and on the following morning a large number of Egyptian soldiers surrendered. The fleet's losses were 1 killed and 58 wounded. A force was landed to garrison Acre and, after some more inland fighting between the Turks and the Egyptians and a considerable amount of diplomacy on the part of the allied powers, the war in Syria ended.

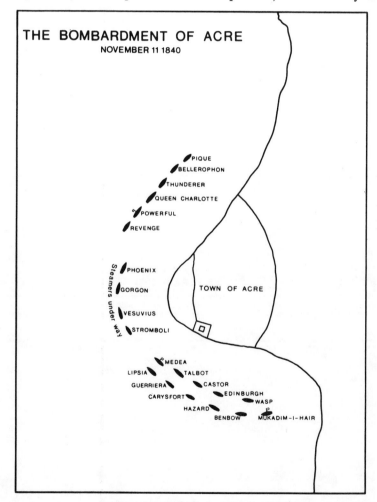

THE BOMBARDMENT OF ACRE
NOVEMBER 11 1840

PIQUE
BELLEROPHON
THUNDERER
QUEEN CHARLOTTE
POWERFUL
REVENGE

Steamers under way

PHOENIX
GORGON
VESUVIUS
STROMBOLI

TOWN OF ACRE

MEDEA
LIPSIA   TALBOT
GUERRIERA   CASTOR
CARYSFORT   EDINBURGH
                    WASP
HAZARD
BENBOW   MUKADIM-I-HAIR

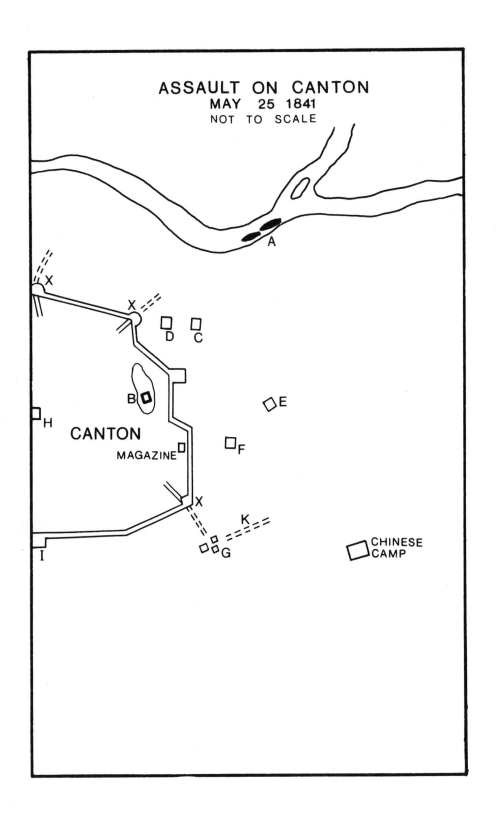

ASSAULT ON CANTON
MAY 25 1841
NOT TO SCALE

8 War in China 1840-1

In January 1841, during a disagreement between China and Britain, it became necessary to attack and destroy the lower forts on the Canton river, and an expeditionary force under Sir Hugh Gough, a veteran of the Peninsula, was assembled. It was composed of the 18th (Royal Irish); the 26th (Cameronians); the 49th; the 55th; and other British and Indian troops who had been in the country for some time. On 25 March, Gough's land forces took the heights commanding Canton and, while British light frigates anchored in the river, the British occupied the city, and the Chinese agreed to pay six million dollars ransom.

On 20 August 1840 orders were given to attack the rocky island of Amoy, and the British squadron sailed from Hong Kong. It consisted of 2 line-of-battle ships, 3 heavy frigates, 2 eighteen-gun sloops, 2 sixteen-gun brigs, 4 armed steamers, and 22 transports. As the force sailed into the outer harbour of Amoy a few days later, some shots were fired from the batteries at the harbour mouth, but the fleet did not return the fire.

The harbour of Amoy was formed on one side by an island defended by a number of batteries, one reputed to be of 100 guns. On the other side a string of semi-fortified islands formed the limits of the bar and there was at least one eighteen-gun battery bearing directly on the harbour. The British warships took up their stations at noon on 26 August and in quick succession the seventy-four guns of the warships belched out their iron-shot at close range, to be answered by repeated gun-flashes from the old dark walls. The exchange of fire continued for two hours and did not cease until the troops who had been landed began to take the batteries in flank.

The decks of the two steamers and the towed transport-boats were crowded with soldiers who landed on a fine sandy beach without the loss of a man. Beyond the beach a high wall connected the long lines of gun-batteries with some rocky heights in the rear. Chinese troops manned the wall and poured a heavy fire into the troops who were being formed up for the attack. Without orders, the captain of one of the steamers led a few seamen in a rush that took them up on to the wall. The soldiers could be held back no longer; they broke from their ranks and rushed forward cheering. A colonel of the Cameronians was the first to lead his men over the wall, to fling open a gate for the advancing troops and the rest of the landing-party poured through the gate while the 49th Regiment swarmed over the ramparts nearest the sea. The Chinese broke ranks and fled and in a few minutes not an enemy soldier was to be seen except for a few dead and wounded. The British troops ascended the heights in the rear of the wall and, after a little skirmishing, occupied the populous town of Amoy.

On 10 October the British force stood before the towering defences of Chusan, a quaint city surrounded by walls 30ft high, strengthened every 300 yards by great square

39

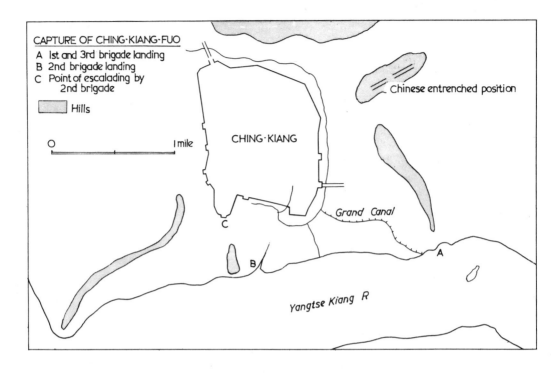

CAPTURE OF CHING·KIANG·FUO
A 1st and 3rd brigade landing
B 2nd brigade landing
C Point of escalading by
    2nd brigade

Hills

0   1 mile

CHING·KIANG

Chinese entrenched position

Grand Canal

A

B

C

Yangtse Kiang R

stone towers. Here the troops encountered some of the smartest fighting they had yet seen, against troops so resolute that they stood until every man of them was shot down or bayoneted. Chinese fire was very heavy but British losses were small. The force was, however, decimated by disease, so that when Chusan was taken, there were barely 600 privates, exclusive of artillery and sappers, available for duty in a city of 300,000 inhabitants. The mob followed the custom of looting as soon as the city fell.

Chapoo, a large town 75 miles from Chusan, was quickly taken by Gough on 18 May 1841. On 21 July, he advanced on Ching-Kiang-fuo, a walled town situated on a river, with a hidden Tartar garrison. Gough did not expect very much opposition, but the Tartars, armed with matchlocks, swords, bows and arrows, and wearing helmets of hammered iron, proved desperate antagonists and caused heavy losses to the British force. Most of the Chinese soldiers were robust, muscular and brave, but usually ineffectual because of their lack of discipline.

Gough advanced against the principal gate and blew it open, whilst an infantry brigade made a diversion eventually converted into a real attack which assailed the enemy simultaneously in front and rear. Finding the struggle hopeless, the garrison eventually retired, but not until they had murdered their families by cutting the throats of their wives and flinging their children into wells. Chinese peasants surged into the town as soon as it fell, sacking the place until it was completely gutted and destroyed.

Gough took his force off to capture Nankin, but further operations were suspended by the arrival of peace envoys from Peking, and a treaty was formally signed on board HMS *Cornwallis*. It allowed British subjects to reside at Canton and four other ports; Hong Kong was ceded in perpetuity to Britain and large cash indemnities were extracted from the Chinese.

Far greater numbers of British troops died by disease and exposure than were lost in battle. At Chusan in the six months leading up to 31 December 1840 the 3,000 British troops suffered 450 deaths and had more than 500 admissions to hospital. They were debilitated by intense heat and fatigue; their provisions were often putrid; men died like flies from fever and dysentery. Within six weeks of landing, the 26th, a magnificent battalion more than 900 strong, was reduced to a bare 110 men fit for duty.

9 Afghanistan: The Destruction of an Army

Everything was so quiet in the two years that followed the occupation of Kabul that wives and families joined their soldier-husbands and social events took place daily in and around the almost defenceless cantonments. In 1841, the British force consisted of 4 infantry regiments; 2 batteries of artillery; 3 companies of sappers; a cavalry regiment and some irregular horse, all well equipped and in good order. Towards the end of that year trouble began when Sale's regiment, the 13th, was attacked by tribesmen while marching towards Jalalabad, losing 124 men under rather ignominious circumstances. In Kabul the mob murdered Sir Alexander Burnes and then ran riot, plundering, burning and massacring. Outlying detachments were attacked and, through a misunderstanding, a fort in which the food supplies were stored was abandoned, leaving the garrison with only two days' rations. General Elphinstone, the British commander, was a sick man and Brigadier Shelton, his deputy, did not believe that the cantonment could be defended. During the rioting he almost lost his life when the 44th Regiment was attacked and, refusing to obey his orders, fled back to the cantonments.

Negotiations with the Afghan leader Akbar Khan began and on 23 December, at one of the meetings, Sir William Macnaghten, the British Envoy in Kabul, was murdered. Since there seemed to be no possible alternative, it was agreed to accept the degrading conditions demanded by the Afghans: to abandon Kabul and withdraw the entire force. Preparations for withdrawal began as snow fell with ruthless persistence, but the departure was repeatedly delayed by Afghan pretexts so that it was not until the dreary winter morning of 6 January 1842 that the column moved out from the cantonments. In addition to 690 British infantry, 2,840 native infantry, and 970 native cavalry under General Shelton, there were large numbers of women and children and sick and wounded, together with a huge crowd of panic-stricken camp-followers with their baggage. The column was attacked as soon as it left the cantonment, the Afghans closing in on the rearguard, killing more than 50 men and causing two guns to be abandoned. After covering only 6 miles, with the Afghans plundering, hacking and slaying throughout, the column camped in the deep snow without wood, fire or shelter, and then a disordered mob, it struggled sluggishly on for three days with the Afghans slaughtering and looting, sometimes charging their horses right into the heart of the slowly-moving mass. Five of the seven guns were lost, but with those that remained a small detachment held back the Afghan pursuit at the Khoord-Kabul Pass and so gave the fugitives a few hours' grace.

Daily Akbar Khan rode into the camp to offer advice and encouragement. Pottinger and two other officers were taken as hostages, together with the women and children and the married officers – 'for protection'. On the fourth day, they had to traverse a

42

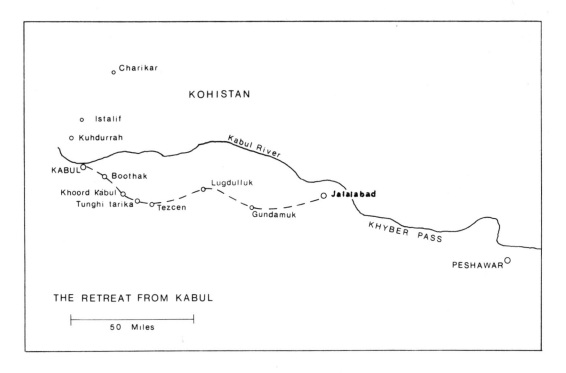

THE RETREAT FROM KABUL

deep gorge barely 10ft wide; the Afghans lined its sides and fired into the struggling mass below. After running this gauntlet, there remained only 70 men of the 44th, 100 troopers, and a detachment of horse artillery with a single gun. The sick and wounded had to be left. On the afternoon of 11 January the men reached Lugdulluk and bivouacked under heavy fire that only ceased when Akbar came into the camp to take General Elphinstone and Brigadier Shelton as hostages. He assured the survivors that they would be allowed to march unmolested to Jalalabad, but next morning, when the march was resumed, the tribesmen harassed the small party, slashing and hacking with their deadly knives.

On the morning of 13 January, only 20 officers and 45 British soldiers remained. Unable to go any further, they took up a defensive position on a hillock surrounded by Afghans. When the ammunition had gone, the small force fought on with sword and bayonet until finally overwhelmed. One officer escaped to Jalalabad as the sole survivor of the British army that had quitted Kabul a week before.

Akbar Khan with 5,000 men then besieged Jalalabad and offered safe conduct to the garrison. After some discussion it was refused and Sale led out three attacking columns, with Havelock commanding the right. Coming to the front at a gallop, the guns poured fire into the massed Afghans, while the three columns deployed into line and moved forward at the double. In the face of heavy fire, they swept the enemy clean out of his position, captured his artillery, set fire to his camp and put him to rout.

A fortnight later, after forcing the Khyber Pass by outflanking and thoroughly defeating a strong force of Afghans, General Pollock arrived with 8,000 men. There was a frustrating delay whilst he reorganised and trained his troops, but he left Jalalabad on 7 September, and drove the tribesmen from the Jugdulluk Heights, and then took on Akbar and 15,000 Afghans among the ravines and precipices beyond Tezeen. The Afghans fought desperately, but they were chased from crag to crag in a merciless pursuit. Marching over the same route as the retreating army had taken, Pollock's force arrived in Kabul on 15 September. At the head of another British force, General Nott had been successfully holding his own in the area around Kandahar where he had decisively beaten an army of 10,000 Afghans. Moving forward, he drove them from Ghazni and then won a final victory within a few marches of Kabul, which he reached on 17 September 1842.

After destroying the bazaar of Kabul and defeating the remaining Afghans in the area, the combined force marched out of the city on 12 October, and Dost Mohammed moved back to reoccupy the country from which he had been driven three years previously. So ended the first Afghan War, its only redeeming features being the defence of Jalalabad and the dogged determination of Nott and Pollock.

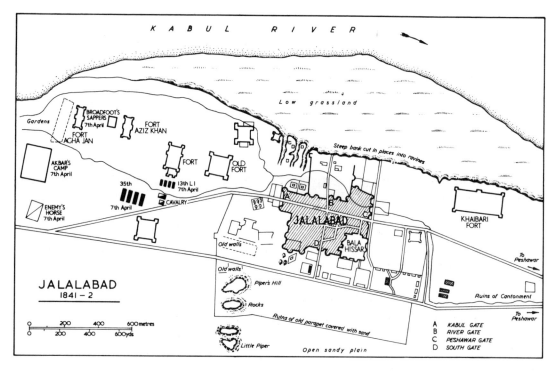

10 The Conquest of Sind 1843

In order to discourage the Amirs of Sind, Sir Charles Napier decided to seek out and destroy the reputedly impregnable fortress of Emaum Ghur, although he knew nothing of its location except that it was at least 100 miles (eight marches along vague and ill-defined tracks in the Great Eastern Desert. He set off on 5 January 1843 at the head of 350 men of the 22nd Regiment (two soldiers to a camel), 2 twenty-four pounder howitzers and 200 troopers of the Sind Horse. Eight days later they came upon the fortress, abandoned by its garrison who had marched out a few hours before. After razing it to the ground. Napier's men retraced their steps.

Hearing that 25 to 30,000 Baluchis were entrenched in a dry river-bed at Meani on 17 February 1843 Napier marched out with 2,200 men, including 500 British infantry, mostly Irishmen. Under heavy artillery fire, his small force assembled in echelon of battalions with his twelve guns on the right, flanking the 22nd Regiment under Colonel Pennefather. The Baluchi line could be seen in a dry river-bed about 1,000 yards away and so Napier gave the order to attack the enemy centre, going forward with his staff, under heavy fire from the enemy's guns, to join the skirmishers. In columns of regiments, the troops advanced to within 200 yards of the enemy, when they deployed into line and charged. At the river bank, the 500 men of the 22nd, after halting momentarily at the sight of 20,000 Baluchis waiting to receive them, flung themselves into the turbaned mass. The Baluchis held their own and, by sheer weight of numbers, even pressed back Napier's small force in a struggle that lasted for more than three hours. In desperation, Napier ordered Colonel Pattle and his Bengal cavalry, together with Jacob's Sind Horse, to charge the enemy's right. Crashing through the Baluchi guns, the cavalry crossed the river-bed and thundered over the plain beyond into the rear of the Baluchi mass, causing them to falter. The 22nd and the native infantry redoubled their efforts and soon the Baluchis were slowly and reluctantly retreating on all sides.

In this 'soldier's battle', Napier lost 20 officers and 250 men against the Baluchi losses of about 7,000. At one period of the battle, Sir Charles Napier was alone for several minutes in the midst of the enemy but so overawed were they by this strange, loudly swearing figure with long flowing hair, whiskers and beard, wearing a huge helmet and gigantic spectacles, that no one lifted a weapon against him.

Reinforced, on 24 March Napier marched 10 miles at the head of 5,000 men and 19 guns to attack 26,000 Baluchis in a skilfully chosen position with their right in an unturnable flank resting on the river Fullailli at the village of Dubba, and their left on a wood 2 miles away. Seeing that the cavalry had prematurely charged off on his right, Napier ordered the 22nd Regiment to attack the village of Dubba. Supported by artillery fire and with Napier himself at their head, the cheering infantry swept forward into the Baluchis. In the struggle that followed, the tribesmen were forced back from

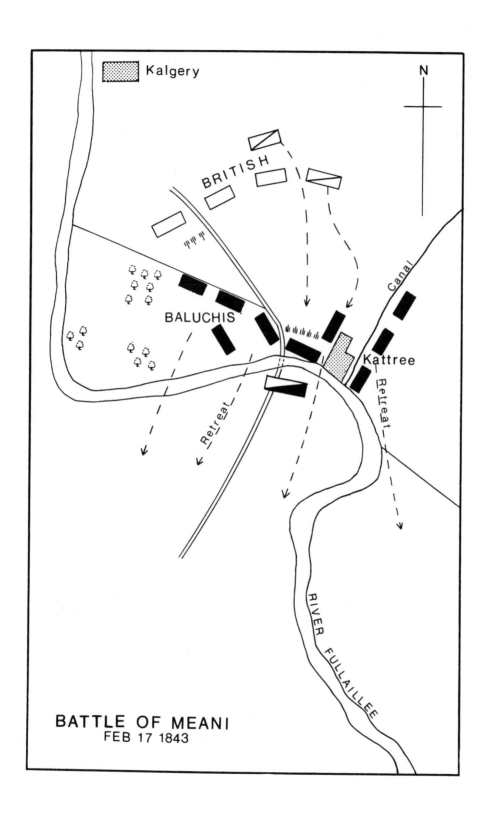

Kalgery

N

BRITISH

Canal

BALUCHIS

Kattree

Retreat

Retreat

RIVER FULLAILLEE

BATTLE OF MEANI
FEB 17 1843

one nullah into another and then out into the open where they were repeatedly charged by cavalry and horse artillery. In this battle Napier lost 270 officers and men (147 of the 22nd Regiment) against 5,000 enemy dead. This closed the campaign and never again were the British troubled by the Baluchis.

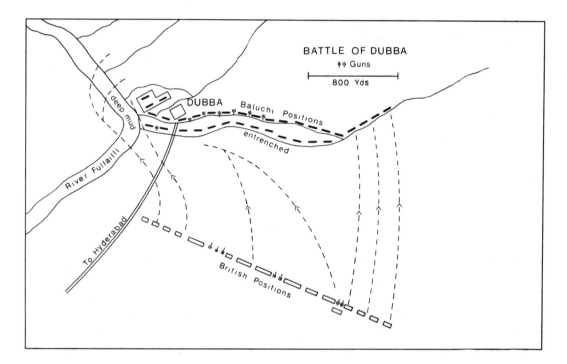

BATTLE OF DUBBA

11 The Gwalior War 1843

To prevent a combination of Sikhs and Mahrattas which would have brought 120,000 men and 500 guns into the field against the East India Company, it was decided that the Mahrattas should disband their army. As it was believed that this object could be attained, without recourse to arms, by a march of the Company's army on Gwalior (the capital), the heavy guns were left at Agra and officer's ladies were permitted to accompany the army into the field. In December 1843 Sir Hugh Gough, at the head of 12,000 men and 40 light field-pieces, marched towards the Mahratta capital from the north, while General Grey with 4,000 men crossed the River Jumna at Calpi and advanced against the city from the south. With two small British armies converging from opposite directions and acting quite independently of each other, the Mahrattas should have concentrated their forces and attacked either in detail, but they neglected this opportunity and dispatched 14,000 infantry, 3,000 cavalry and 100 guns to oppose Gough, while another force of 12,000 men and 40 guns marched southward to meet Grey.

Although his advance guard had already been under heavy gunfire during the previous day, on 29 December Gough marched his army at ease in three parallel columns with a long baggage-train slowly struggling in the rear. Lady Gough and Sir Harry Smith's wife, together with the wives of several other officers, mounted on elephants, were actually riding at the head of the army to avoid the dust! Gough lacked reconnaissance, and was unaware that a large Mahratta force with 28 heavy guns had taken up a strong position in and around the villages of Maharajpur and Shikarpur. He issued rapid orders; trumpets and bugles sounded; the regiments deployed into line and took station under a well-directed fire. The six- and nine-pounder guns of a British Horse Artillery battery that had gone to the front to silence the enemy guns were completely outweighed by the superior metal of the Mahratta eighteen-pounders, and suffered heavy losses.

Between the British force and the enemy stretched what appeared to be a level green plain, but when the British troops began to advance they found that it was intersected with ravines, while on the smoother stretches there was not a rock or shrub to give shelter from the withering artillery fire that swept the ground. The men had nearly a mile to go under heavy fire to reach the enemy lines; they were well out of musketry range and men were falling fast on all sides from the fire of heavy guns which the British artillery had been unable to silence. General Gough had to make a quick decision — characteristically he gave the laconic order 'On and at them!'

The advancing line consisted of General Littler on the left with the 39th Foot and the 56th native infantry; Brigadier Wright in the centre with three Sepoy battalions; and

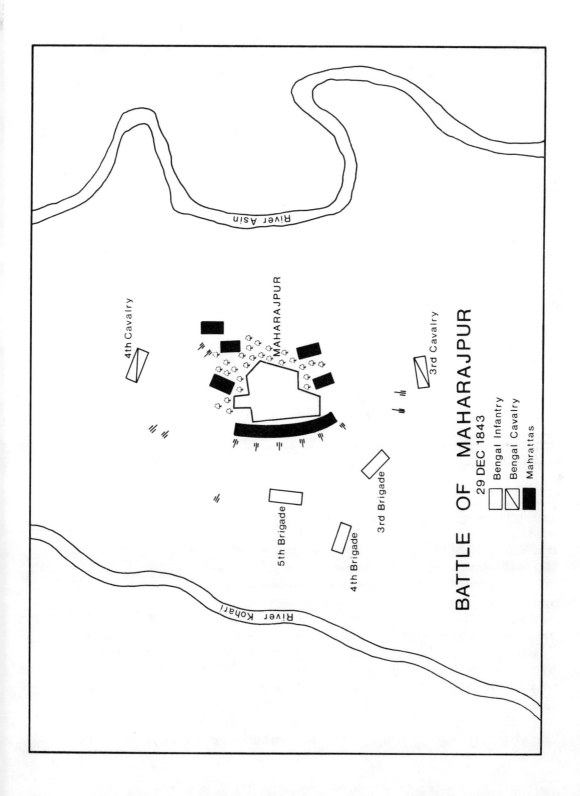

River Asin

River Kohari

4th Cavalry

MAHARAJPUR

3rd Cavalry

5th Brigade

3rd Brigade

4th Brigade

BATTLE OF MAHARAJPUR
29 DEC 1843

Bengal Infantry

Bengal Cavalry

Mahrattas

General Valiant on the right with the 40th Foot and the 2nd and 16th Grenadiers, two fine native regiments. Their order broken by their climbing in and out of ravines, the infantry struggled forward, with the 39th on the left outstripping the others. In spite of heavy losses, the infantrymen did not pause until they were within 60 yards of the enemy position, when the order was given to fire a volley; then, with a somewhat breathless cheer, they charged forward. As they did so, seven Mahratta regiments swarmed out in front of their guns to meet them. At first, the 39th bore the brunt of the fighting and then, as the other battalions came up, the Mahrattas were gradually pushed back, fighting every step until a final furious rush sent the 39th and 56th into the enemy entrenchments, where they bayoneted the artillerymen at their pieces and carried the battery.

On the right, General Valiant's brigade had stormed the village of Shikarpur with equal success; it then wheeled round to attack Maharajpur in reverse, with the 40th Regiment leading. The British attack closed in on front and flank, amid scenes of confusion as smoke from the burning village enveloped everything. In a tangled mêlée, Valiant's brigade crossed Littler's line and when it emerged the positions were reversed, Valiant now being on the left and Littler on the right.

Although a strong position had been stormed and 28 guns had been captured, it was only one of three that had to be taken; 1,200 yards behind the village another formidable battery of 12 guns was posted. No sooner had Gough's troops emerged from Maharajpur than the 12 gun battery opened a brisk fire on them. Still in disorder, the men halted, under a galling storm of shot from the excellently served Mahratta guns. Then, with heads bowed, they advanced to the attack again over ground even more difficult than before, littered with carts, baggage and other impedimenta abandoned by the retreating enemy. Men fell fast as the leading regiments pushed on to force their way through the earthworks and into the position, driving the Mahrattas out with bayonet and clubbed muskets.

Without pausing for rest, the line again re-formed and moved against the enemy's main camp at Chaunda, some two miles away. When the attackers came within range they were greeted by a hail of artillery fire and volleys of musketry from massed Mahratta infantry regiments. Exhausted after fighting for three hours, Gough's infantry shambled forward, encouraged by Grant's battery of horse artillery that unlimbered and opened fire. As they came up to the enemy position, the Mahrattas came sallying out to meet the attack and for a few minutes held their own, but slowly and irresistibly the British and native infantry forced them back until suddenly they broke and ran.

Maharajpur was a 'soldiers' victory won by the bayonet without the benefit of tactics, strategy or manoeuvring. Gough displayed no generalship whatsoever and gave but one order, 'On and at them', to send his infantry at three formidable lines well defended by competent infantry. The generals of brigade, Littler, Valiant and Wright were all wounded; the 39th lost 12 officers and 177 men; both the 56th and 16th Grenadiers left over 100 men on the field, to make Gough's total casualties exceed 800.

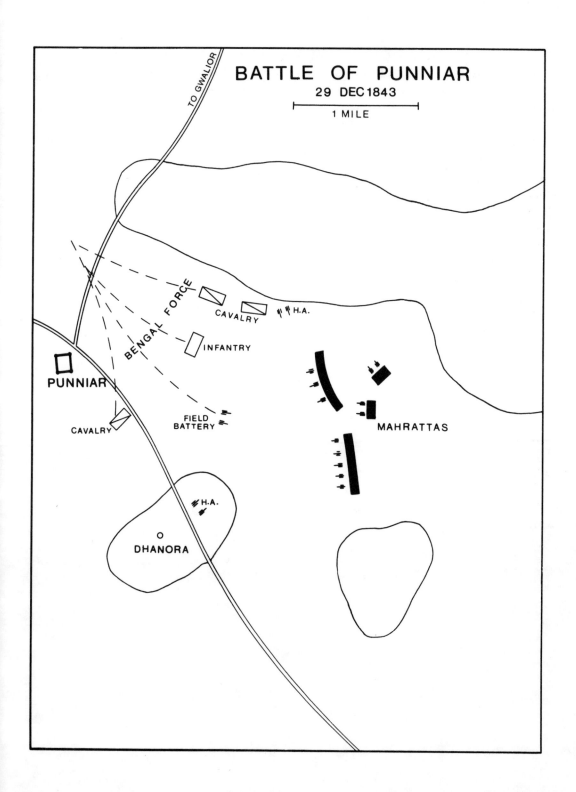

BATTLE OF PUNNIAR
29 DEC 1843

1 MILE

TO GWALIOR

BENGAL FORCE

CAVALRY   H.A.

INFANTRY

PUNNIAR

CAVALRY

FIELD
BATTERY

MAHRATTAS

H.A.

o
DHANORA

The Mahrattas were reported to have lost over 3,000 with 56 guns.

By a strange coincidence almost unique in British military history, the Mahrattas sustained another defeat at British hands on the same day. Some twelve miles south of Gwalior, General Grey reached the village of Punniar on 29 December, with the Mahrattas making a parallel movement on the farther side of a range of hills, hidden from his view. Suddenly they attacked the long baggage-train straggling in the rear of the army; instead of returning to its aid, Grey sent back half his horse artillery and some cavalry, who saved the baggage. But at half-past three in the afternoon, the Mahrattas took up a threatening position on a chain of high hills to the east of the British position. Grey sent the 3rd Foot (the Buffs) and some Sappers and Miners to attack their front, with the 39th native infantry to turn their left flank, holding in reserve the 2nd Brigade, consisting of the 50th Foot and the 38th and 50th native infantry. In the teeth of heavy fire the 3rd Regiment climbed up the steep hillside and, reaching its crest, drove the Mahrattas from height to height in a succession of gallant rushes, capturing 11 of their guns. At the same time, the 39th occupied the summit of a hill commanding the enemy's left and, after pouring a destructive fire on them rushed down and captured a battery of two guns which they turned to fire upon their late owners. The 2nd Brigade now made a determined attack on the enemy's right flank where 11 guns were firing upon them, and carried it after a short but spirited struggle. Then the whole line advanced and, completely outmanoeuvring the Mahrattas, sent them fleeing from the field with their 16 remaining guns, leaving 1,000 casualties behind them.

In sharp contrast to Maharajpur, the Battle of Punniar was won by skilful general-ship and a striking demonstration of co-ordinated action on the part of all units concerned, although, in fairness, it must be admitted that the resistance was not nearly so fierce as at Maharajpur. A few days later, the Company's two victorious armies united at Gwalior where Lord Ellenborough, the Governor-General, dictated terms of peace which included the disbandment of the Mahratta army.

12 The First Sikh War 1845-6

Early in the nineteenth century, Ranjit Singh their shrewd and dynamic leader, welded the Sikhs of the Punjab into the most formidable fighting force that India had ever known, using the training methods of the British East India Company and employing European mercenary soldiers to produce a highly disciplined army with probably the best artillery arm in the world at that time. When he died in 1839, Lal Singh and Tej Singh, the two men who emerged from the welter of murder and intrigue that followed, found their ambitions hindered by the militant strength of the Sikh army, the Khalsa. Believing that the British could smash the Khalsa, the two Sikh leaders incited their army to invade British territory, at the same time reporting their intentions and plans to the British throughout the war that followed!

The Sikh army crossed the river Sutlej on 11 December, 1845 and immediately came up against the British frontier post of Ferozepore, garrisoned by 10,000 men under Sir John Littler. The armies faced each other for a week. Sir Hugh Gough, accompanied by Sir Henry Hardinge, the Governor-General, led his army out from Ambala (160 miles from Ferozepore) on 12 December; marching more than 100 miles in five days over exceedingly trying country, it shambled wearily into the mud village of Mudki at noon on 18 December, after trudging 21 miles since dawn through ankle-deep sand. Without food since the previous day, the exhausted British and native soldiers sprawled on the dusty ground to await the arrival of the baggage-train left far in the rear. Suddenly Major Broadfoot, the political agent, galloped wildly into the camp shouting: 'Your Excellency! There is the Sikh army!' Sir Hugh Gough had allowed Lal Singh to come upon him with an army of 22,000 men and 22 guns! Strident bugles brought the weary troops to their feet and officers and sergeants pushed and bullied them into the ranks, buttoning up their jackets and buckling on equipment. With Sir Hugh Gough waving them forward, they marched out to the last of the wars fought by the British army in the manner of Waterloo and the Peninsular, going into action in an Order of Battle, with the infantry in line-of-column, the cavalry on their flanks, and the artillery in the intervals. Their uniform and weapons were the same as those used at Waterloo in 1815 and their commanders were veterans of the Peninsula War of forty years back.

The Sikhs quickly and efficiently positioned their numerous guns so that they were semi-concealed in dense, low jungle, with their infantry in the intervals and strong bodies of mounted cavalry on their flanks. In a headlong gallop, the Bengal Horse Artillery bumped and jingled towards the enemy to unlimber in line and open fire with its light six- and nine-pounder field-pieces at the heavier Sikh twelve- and eighteen-pounder guns which were detectable only by the gouts of flame from their muzzles as they replied with devastating effect.

53

BATTLE OF MUDKI, December 18, 1845

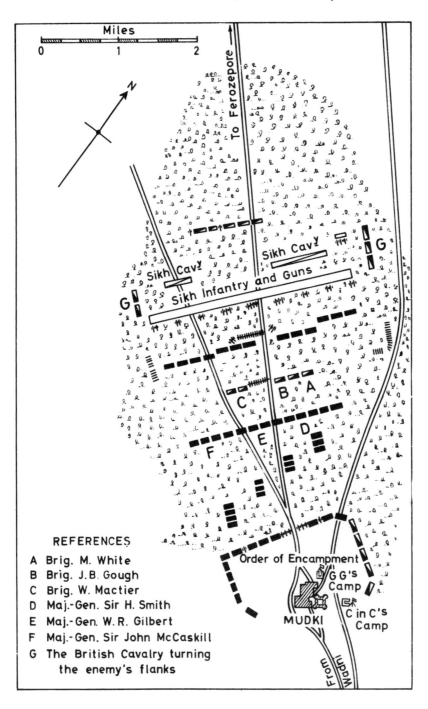

Miles
0   1   2

N

To Ferozepore

Sikh Cavy

Sikh Cavy

Sikh Infantry and Guns

G

G

G

C B A

F E D

Order of Encampment

GG's Camp

MUDKI

C in C's Camp

From Wadni

REFERENCES

A Brig. M. White
B Brig. J. B. Gough
C Brig. W. Mactier
D Maj.-Gen. Sir H. Smith
E Maj.-Gen. W. R. Gilbert
F Maj.-Gen. Sir John McCaskill
G The British Cavalry turning
    the enemy's flanks

Just before four o'clock, with only an hour of daylight remaining, the scarlet and blue lines of the British and native infantry moved forward in echelon of lines. Despite heavy casualties inflicted by the well-handled Sikh artillery, the British infantry closed doggedly with the enemy, but the native Sepoy regiments held back, panicking and firing into the backs of passing British regiments. Sir Hugh Gough sent his cavalry division, led by the 3rd Light Dragoons, out to meet a threatening out-flanking movement by the Sikh cavalry, and dispersing the native cavalry, they charged the Sikh batteries, taking heavy losses as they galloped through dense jungle to sabre the gunners. The British infantry got among the Sikh positions and began to dislodge the enemy from the thick scrub of jungle that bordered the sandy track, capturing gun after gun – almost to a man, the Sikh gunners died gallantly defending their beloved cannon. Eddying clouds of smoke and dust choked the combatants so that they were unable to distinguish friend from foe. The battle continued in darkness for another hour and a half, with men on both sides blazing away at each other or at nothing.

Only the coming of night saved the Sikh army from a great disaster as, disputing every inch of the ground, they retired steadily with their faces turned towards the enemy. In the sharp and bloody battle their losses were heavy, and included fifteen pieces of artillery; Gough's army lost 872 men killed and wounded, among them Generals Sir Robert Sale and Sir John McCaskell.

After two days spent resting and burying their dead, the British moved out at 3 am on 21 December, looking for the enemy who, after the defeat at Mudki, had retreated to Ferozeshah to join a large Sikh force in an entrenched camp. Gough's force, after a tiring march through heavy sandy ground, halted in the middle of a broad expanse of level plain dotted with thorn-jungle, before a Sikh army of 35,000 infantry and 73 guns in a formidable defensive position protected by breast-high earthworks a mile long by half a mile broad. Orders had been sent to Sir John Littler at Ferozepore to leave his camp standing and join the main army, but Gough found the waiting intolerable and at eleven o'clock confronted the governor-general: 'Sir Henry, if we attack at once I promise you a splendid victory!'

Hardinge, who had offered to serve as second-in-command to Gough, was not prepared to assault the Sikh positions without Littler's 10,000 men and said: 'Sir Hugh, I must exercise my civil powers as governor-general and forbid the attack until Littler's force has come up.'

Although Littler arrived at 1. o'clock it was not until 3. o'clock on the shortest day of the year that the battle began, allowing only two hours of daylight for Gough's army to defeat a disciplined and confident force nearly twice its own strength and entrenched in a strong position. The light guns of the Horse Artillery clattered to the front and opened fire, but they made little impression upon the enemy's entrenched batteries. Then Littler's men went forward to assault the strongest face of the entrenchment, to be met by showers of grape and canister at under 300 yards range. At first they halted; then they turned back: the force for which Gough had been waiting half

BATTLE OF FEROZESHAH, DEC. 21 AND 22, 1845.

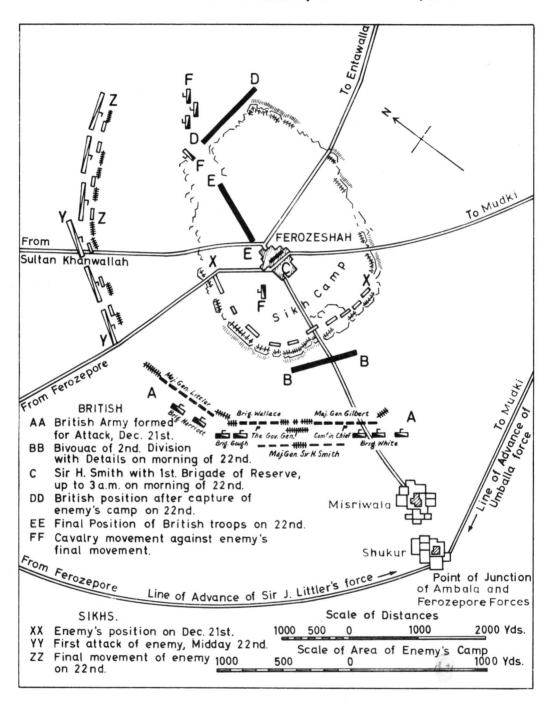

To Entawalla

N

To Mudki

From Sultan Khanwallah

FEROZESHAH

Sikh Camp

From Ferozepore

To Mudki

Line of Advance of Umballa force

Maj. Gen. Littler

BRITISH

Brig. Wallace   Maj. Gen. Gilbert

Brig. Harriott   The Gov. Gen.   Com'n in Chief

Brig. Gough   Maj. Gen. Sir H. Smith   Brig. White

AA British Army formed for Attack, Dec. 21st.

BB Bivouac of 2nd. Division with Details on morning of 22nd.

C Sir H. Smith with 1st. Brigade of Reserve, up to 3 a.m. on morning of 22nd.

DD British position after capture of enemy's camp on 22nd.

EE Final Position of British troops on 22nd.

FF Cavalry movement against enemy's final movement.

Misriwala

Shukur

Point of Junction of Ambala and Ferozepore Forces

From Ferozepore   Line of Advance of Sir J. Littler's force

SIKHS.

XX Enemy's position on Dec. 21st.

YY First attack of enemy, Midday 22nd.

ZZ Final movement of enemy on 22nd.

Scale of Distances

1000 500 0 1000 2000 Yds.

Scale of Area of Enemy's Camp

1000 500 0 1000 Yds.

the day took little further part in the battle.

In the centre and on the right, under a heavy fire from Sikh guns served with extra-ordinary rapidity and precision, the infantry pressed forward in echelon of regiments. As at Mudki, the Sepoys hung back so that the bulk of the work fell upon the British battalions. At considerable cost, a footing was secured in the entrenchments and, at bayonet point, the Sikh batteries were captured one by one; then the village of Ferozeshah itself was stormed and cleared of the enemy. Ordered to charge a battery of guns, the 3rd Dragoons took severe losses in capturing them. A vast cloud of smoke hung over a battlefield lit by the lurid glare from burning tents and houses. Separated from their regiments, men in small groups moved about aimlessly under a demoralising fire from the Sikhs, and when darkness fell, only a part of the Sikh entrenchments had been carried. Even the redoubtable Gough realised that there was no hope of success that night, and so he ordered his troops to withdraw 400 yards to the south. Returning to their batteries, the Sikhs turned the recaptured guns on Gough's force and through-out the long night shot and shell whistled continuously overhead and exploded with crashing roars among the unhappy men crouching on the bare plain, the white covers taken off their caps so as not to afford a mark for the enemy. Disappointed, hungry, thirsty and exhausted, the British force was in a sore plight, isolated in three divisions cut off from each other. Gough and Hardinge moved continuously among their men, comforting and encouraging: they had no other thought but to resume the attack in the morning.

With daylight came a watery mist. Dew fell on the metal parts of weapons, and was licked up by the thirsty soldiers. Cold, hungry and exhausted after the long sleepless night, they still found heart enough to raise cracked cheers as, under heavy fire, Gough marshalled them into two divisions — one led by himself and the other by Lord Hardinge. Just as they were moving off, Sir Harry Smith rejoined the force with his division, having fought his way back during the night from the far side of the Sikh position. In the face of shot and shell, the force moved stiffly forward in a determined onslaught that rolled over and through the Sikh entrenchments, carrying battery after battery at the point of the bayonet. Changing front to the left, the men drove the enemy helter-skelter from Ferozeshah, and soon the Sikhs were running in all directions, leaving behind them 78 guns. It was a feat of arms worthy of the best traditions of the British army, made even more memorable by contrast with the serious repulse of the previous evening.

As the exhausted but victorious British stood resting on their arms, Tej Singh arrived from Ferozepore with 30,000 fresh Sikhs and, driving-in the British cavalry, whose weary horses could not muster even a trot, the Sikh artillery unlimbered their 70 guns and opened fire. The British artillery, its ammunition exhausted, fired an occasional blank charge in a vain attempt to deceive the enemy. Then, because of a misinterpreted order, the cavalry and half of the Horse Artillery rode from the field. The dauntless Sir Hugh Gough rode forward in his white fighting-coat, unaccompanied except for his personal aide, to draw the enemy's fire from his men, and at 3 o'clock in the afternoon with the battle in their grasp the Sikhs retired, leaving Gough master of the field at a cost of 2,400 men. Later it was said that Tej Singh had withdrawn because he did not wish to defeat the British, but he claimed that he believed the mis-ordered retreat of the cavalry and artillery past his right flank was a tactical movement designed to turn his flank and interpose between him and the River Sutlej. Sir Henry Hardinge, talking of the battle to Colonel Havelock, remarked: 'India has been saved by a miracle . . . another such victory will cost us the Empire.'

For a month the British reorganised, whilst the Sikhs, still strong in artillery and men, withdrew to the west of the River Sutlej. Reinforced by the arrival from Meerut of Sir John Grey with 10,000 men, Gough waited for the heavy guns slowly moving up from Delhi in a column that covered 10 miles of road. In the middle of January a Sikh force of 20,000 men and 70 guns under Ranjur Singh crossed the River Sutlej some six miles north of Ludhiana, to threaten the column coming up from Delhi.

Gough dispatched Sir Harry Smith with 10,000 men and 32 guns to cope with this threat. The force had to fight its way through to Ludhiana, losing the greater part of its baggage, but Harry Smith caught the Sikhs on 28 January 1846, in an entrenched position at Aliwal with the Sutlej River in their rear. In the face of heavy fire, the 53rd Regiment stormed the earthworks and captured Aliwal, the key to the enemy's position. Galloping up to within close range of the Sikh guns, the Horse Artillery unlimbered;

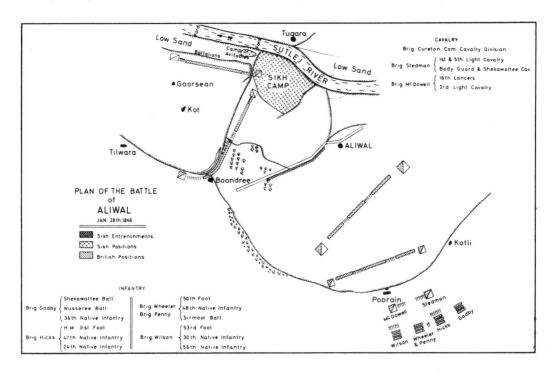

their well directed fire caused the Sikh artillerymen to quit many of their pieces. Next, Smith sent his cavalry forward in several daring and effective charges at the left and centre of the Sikh line, the 16th Lancers repeatedly smashing their way through formed squares of the crack Sikh infantry. Three times the Lancers charged, losing more than a hundred of their number and nearly one-fifth of the total British casualties in this action.

The British infantry stormed and took the Sikh batteries one after another until the Sikhs were driven to the bank of the Sutlej, scrambling across in confusion under heavy artillery fire, to stream away, leaving camp-stores, baggage and every one of their guns. Sir John Fortescue wrote that Aliwal was 'a battle without a mistake' — it was a brilliant little action in which the combined powers of infantry, artillery and cavalry were successively and successfully brought into play.

After Aliwal, the Sikhs abandoned all their posts south of the Sutlej except a vast semi-circular entrenchment at Sobraon, bristling with triple rows of guns and much stronger in design than the earthworks of Ferozeshah. Connected by a bridge of boats to the far bank of the river, it was defended by 120 guns and 30,000 picked troops. Gough decided first to hit the enemy with the heavy guns which had arrived from Delhi and then to storm the right flank and sweep the camp from right to left. His force totalled 15,000, two-thirds of them native troops. At 7 o'clock in the morning of 10 February 1846, a hundred guns, formed in an extended semi-circle around the Sikh position, began the bombardment, but made little impression upon the 16ft thick enemy earthworks. After two hours of ineffectual pounding, ammunition ran out and Gough exclaimed with delight: 'Thank God! Now I can be at them with the bayonet!'

After being halted by withering fire 300 yards from the Sikh heavy batteries, Sir Robert Dick's brigade rallied and rushed on to gain a footing in the earthworks. Gilbert's division, together with Harry Smith's division, went forward to storm the entrenchments and batteries directly facing it. Taking a diagonal course and unsupported by cavalry or artillery, Gilbert's leading brigade missed its objective and arrived in front of the strongest point of the enemy's defences. Three times the British were repulsed and compelled to retreat across the moat; on each occasion they were followed to its edge by the Sikhs who spared none of the wounded. Rallying, they returned to the assault on the high embankment to burst at last into the centre of the Sikh camp just as General Dick's division made good its footing on the left. Sir Harry Smith's division on the right had been temporarily checked before finally carrying the defences, and the cavalry, ordered to its assistance, performed the astonishing feat of breaking through field-works, passing singly through an opening made by the Pioneers in the thick earthworks, to re-form inside and then to charge over trenches and batteries, cutting down the Sikhs as they served their guns.

The three divisions of the British force converged on the head of the bridge of boats, defended with great bravery by the Sikhs in a fierce hand-to-hand struggle. Presumably in order to prevent surrender, the Sikh commander had the two centre boats of the bridge cut adrift so that the tightly packed Sikhs fought desperately to avoid being pushed into the water. The overladen bridge inevitably parted from its moorings and broke up, choking the waterway from bank to bank with guns, men and horses on to which the Horse Artillery played grapeshot until the river was bridged with bodies.

In the two hours of battle at Sobraon the British lost 2,383 men killed and wounded. Sikh casualties were estimated to be between 8,000 and 12,000 and all their guns fell to the British. Heartened by the victory at Aliwal, the Sepoys fought manfully alongside their British comrades. Completely shattered, the Sikh army dispersed, and a peace treaty was signed at Lahore on 8 March 1846.

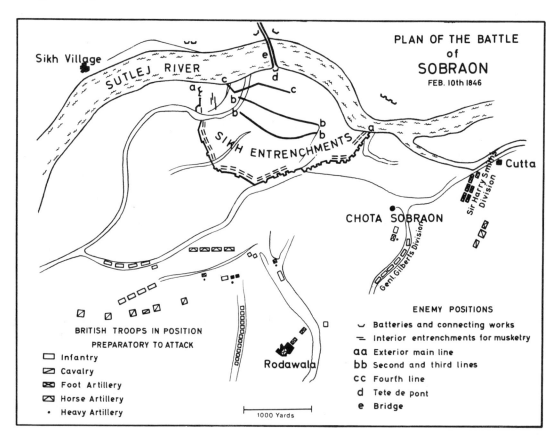

PLAN OF THE BATTLE
of
SOBRAON
FEB. 10th 1846

Sikh Village

SUTLEJ RIVER

SIKH ENTRENCHMENTS

Cutta

Sir Harry Smith's Division

CHOTA SOBRAON

Genl. Gilberts Division

Rodawala

ENEMY POSITIONS

⌣ Batteries and connecting works
≖ Interior entrenchments for musketry
aa Exterior main line
bb Second and third lines
cc Fourth line
d Tete de pont
e Bridge

BRITISH TROOPS IN POSITION
PREPARATORY TO ATTACK

☐ Infantry
▨ Cavalry
▧ Foot Artillery
▧ Horse Artillery
• Heavy Artillery

1000 Yards

13 Campaigns against Boers and Kaffirs in South Africa 1838-52

Throughout the early days of Queen Victoria's reign there was continuous unrest in South Africa as the Kaffirs made raids across the border to carry away cattle, whilst the Boers migrated north and north-east to seek new homes free of British control.

In 1838 and 1839, Governor, Sir George Napier, made some not-too-successful attempts to control the raiding of Kaffirs into Cape Colony and, in an effort to stem the Boer emigration, in November 1838 he sent troops and artillery to Port Natal to cut off their supplies of arms and ammunition. In May 1842 the Boers attacked a force of British troops in Natal, capturing 2 guns and causing 49 casualties. But the weight of British reinforcements prevailed: the Boers capitulated in August 1843, and Britain assumed sovereignty of Natal.

Napier resigned and was replaced by Sir Peregrine Maitland, another Peninsula veteran. In mid-1846, after trouble with Chief Sandile's Kaffirs, a large British force numbering 2,600, assembled, it included the 90th Regiment; the 7th Dragoon Guards; the 27th Regiment; the 1st/45th Regiment; the 90th Regiment; the 91st Regiment, and detachments of Royal Artillery and Royal Engineers. Early operations brought little result and in September the 45th and 73rd Regiments arrived, together with the 1st Battalion Rifle Brigade and the 6th Foot. By now Kaffirs were anxious for peace and chief after chief offered submission.

In June 1847, Maitland's replacement, Sir Henry Pottinger, sent out a flying column to harass Chief Sandile's tribesmen, and after five weeks of such operations Sandile surrendered. Then, on 1 December 1847, Pottinger was replaced by Sir Harry Smith who, in July 1848, proclaimed the Queen's sovereignty over all the territory between the Orange and the Vaal Rivers. This provoked a large-scale Boer revolt. Dressed in civilian clothes, on 29 August 1848 Sir Harry rode forward with a small escort to reason with rebels at Boomplatz but he was met by a volley which brought down an officer and three men of the escort. The low hills in the area were lined with Boers who opened a brisk and regular fire. The guns were brought to bear upon the enemy, and the waggons were withdrawn to the rear and laagered. The infantry was deployed into line and the Rifle Brigade was sent to skirmish over the hills to the right, with the 45th to the centre. The Boers were advancing in skirmishing order to get round to the British rear, but they were turned back by artillery fire and by the Cape Mounted Rifles, who swept round to the left. In about twenty minutes the first range of hills was cleared and the Boers reformed at a farmhouse below, only to be driven out when the artillery managed to advance the guns over a rocky hill. In disorder, the Boers spread across an open plain and then through a neck between two hills, where they made a last brief stand before dispersing over the plain beyond. They had fought a series of typical rear-guard actions,

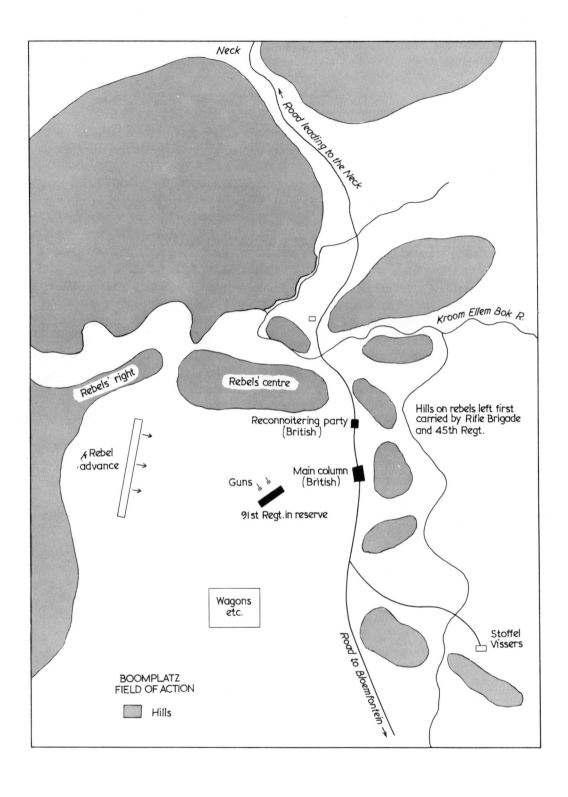

Neck

Road leading to the Neck

Kroom Ellem Bok R.

Rebels' right

Rebels' centre

Reconnoitering party
(British)

Hills on rebels left first
carried by Rifle Brigade
and 45th Regt.

Rebel
advance

Guns

Main column
(British)

91st Regt. in reserve

Wagons
etc.

Stoffel
Vissers

Road to Bloemfontein

BOOMPLATZ
FIELD OF ACTION

Hills

holding their ground while they could be sure of getting safely to their horses at the foot of the hill behind them, and then retiring to another hill or defensive position in their rear in order to repeat the operation. The British lost 7 officers and 47 men whilst the Boers are reported to have had 9 killed.

Early in 1851, the Kaffirs showed signs of unrest and there were mutinies among the Kaffir Police; even the Cape Mounted Rifles were disturbed. At his disposal Sir Harry had the 60th, the 45th, the 73rd, the 91st and the Cape Mounted Rifles with 400 Kaffir Police — the entire force did not amount to 2,000 men. Soon the country from Grahamstown to the Orange River was almost a desert. Homesteads were abandoned, flocks and herds were either driven to safety or captured, while attacks were made on British columns, and two small forts were besieged by Hottentots and Kaffirs who swarmed across the frontier.

The 15 to 20,000 brave and cunning Kaffirs were well armed, through theft and gun-running. They holed-up in the almost inaccessible forests among the Amatola Mountains, where they were infinitely superior to the British soldier in mobility, swiftness and woodsmanship. Sir Harry conducted operations with his customary vigour although it was not until March — when he had assembled 9,000 men including 3,000 regular troops — that he felt the time was ripe for offensive operations. During the second half of March, April and May, his four columns never gave the tribesmen a moments rest, and constant skirmishes took place. Casualties were few but fatigue and hardship took a heavy toll.

In June, operations took place in the Amatola Mountains, culminating in three days sharp fighting, 2,000 cattle captured, and large stores of enemy grain destroyed. In July, operations in the Waterkloof involved arduous marches over rough country, with invisible foes harassing the column at every step. From August onwards the Kaffirs became daring and aggressive, making a succession of plundering raids from the almost impenetrable forests and mountains of the Kroome range, with its offshoots of the Blinkwater and the Waterkloof and, in the south, from the rough country between the Fish and Keishamma Rivers. Smith realised that he had not only to expel the Kaffirs from these strongholds; he also had to garrison them in order to prevent the natives from returning.

In October he had about 6,600 regular troops to carry on a war against a numerous enemy over an area twice as large as the British Isles. His men included the 12th Lancers; the 2nd Queen's; the 6th Foot; the 12th Foot; the 45th Foot; the 60th Foot; the 73rd Foot; the 74th Foot; the 91st Foot; detachments of the Royal Engineers and Royal Artillery; and 900 men of the Cape Rifles. Moving from different directions, two columns began to operate in the Kroome Range, the infantry working to drive the enemy into marked positions where they were shelled by the artillery. By 9 November most of the enemy had been cleared out of the Waterkloof although they still held a few strong points in the Kroome Range. In these operations the troops suffered much hardship, privation and fatigue, frequently having to bivouac in a sea of mud after hours of rain, so that fever, dysentery and muscular pains affected everyone. Progress was very laborious through the dense forests, with their interlaced creeper and vines, dotted with enormous rock masses; the dense thorny undergrowth concealed dangerous crevices, and hooked thorns tore flesh and clothes. In their ridiculous coatees, carrying heavy muskets, bayonets, water canteens and three days' rations, the British soldiers had a hard job to force their way through the difficult terrain. It was essential to maintain contact and to avoid ambush; a lingering death by torture awaited the unfortunate man taken prisoner.

By the beginning of January 1852, Smith was able to report many Kaffirs slain and 30,000 cattle captured; nevertheless an impatient government in England considered that the operations were unduly prolonged and on 14 January Lord Grey sent a despatch recalling Sir Harry Smith — who, after reading the document said 'I think it is my duty to continue operations.'

On 10 March 1852 the Waterkloof was simultaneously attacked by three columns from different directions. With immense difficulty guns were brought up precipitous ascents to commanding positions and each stronghold was heavily shelled before being stormed. In these operations the 74th Highlanders particularly distinguished themselves: in one action they had to crawl up a bare grassy slope, steep as the roof of a house, to reach the natural rock citadel that crowned its summit. From this fortress the almost invisible Kaffirs, only their black woolly heads and the muzzles of their muskets showing, swept with fire every inch of the steep approach. Reaching the top of the slope and climbing from crag to crag, two companies of the 74th crowned the ridge, closing in with fixed bayonets to send the natives fleeing to a dense forest in the rear of their position. Following them into the gloomy woods, the Highlanders came under heavy fire from an unseen enemy, but continued to drive the Kaffirs headlong before them until they disappeared into inaccessible retreats among the extensive forest clothing the upper reaches of the area.

The naked, grease-covered Kaffir, strong, active and lightly armed, had a great natural advantage over the heavily accoutred soldier. The British troops struggled over rough and tangled ground, fighting their way forward, exchanging shots with Kaffirs perched high up in the trees. Although forced to abandon their strongholds, the natives were still full of fight and invariably attacked the columns when they withdrew for revictualling, but eventually the mountain mass was cleared and the Kaffirs fled in all directions, the 12th Lancers and other mounted troops clearing up many of the fugitives.

On 18 March, Sir Harry Smith marched to the Amatolas and for four days the column scoured the country, driving the Kaffirs before them. When, on 8 April, Sir George Cathcart, Smith's successor, reached South Africa the back of the Kaffir resistance had been broken; they had lost 6,000 warriors, including 80 chiefs, and over 80,000 cattle. There was little for Cathcart to do but to mop up, and, by constant patrolling, to prevent the reassembly of the enemy.

14 The Second Sikh War 1848-9

In the spring of 1848, with the connivance of Mulraj, the deposed governor of the Province of Multan, Vans Agnew of the Bengal Civil Service and Lieutenant Anderson of the Bombay army were murdered. Mulraj then placed himself at the head of a Sikh insurrection. Lieutenant Herbert Edwardes, a Political Officer, gathered together 1,500 wild and undisciplined natives from Bunnu and, with a couple of guns, marched towards Multan. He was joined by Colonel Cortlandt with 2,000 Pathans and 6 guns and, on 20 May this scratch force defeated Mulraj's 6,000 strong army. In June and July, they again defeated Mulraj at Kinairi and on the Plain of Sudusain, driving him into his fortress of Multan.

In response to Edwardes's fervent appeals, General Whish was sent with a force of 7,000 men and a siege-train to besiege the fortress. In mid-September a Sikh force under Shere Singh, allied to the British, deserted to the enemy and so Whish withdrew. The siege was not reopened until late in December. In October 1848, Shere Singh quarrelled with Mulraj, left Multan and marched northward in the direction of Lahore with a force of 5,000 men; the warriors of the old Khalsa flocked to his standard and turned the local outbreak into a national revolt. Lord Gough came into the field in mid-November with four British and eleven native infantry regiments, a cavalry force of three English regiments, five native Light Cavalry and five corps of Irregular Horse, with sixty horse and field guns, eight howitzers and ten eighteen-pounders. Gough arrived at Ramnuggur on the River Chenab on 22 November. The British Horse Artillery unlimbered in the sandy area bordering the river bed and, when forced to withdraw by the heavier weight of the Sikh artillery, found that some of their guns were bogged down so that two had to be abandoned. The Sikhs rushed forward to take over the guns, and the British Light Cavalry dashed impetuously forward to flounder through sand and water with horses and men wallowing helplessly under heavy fire from the Sikh guns. In a few minutes they had lost 90 men, including Colonel Havelock (brother of Henry Havelock) and, most important, General Charles Cureton, the Adjutant-General of the army, who had ridden out to check the charge.

Realising that a direct assault across the river was impracticable, Gough sent a part of his force under Sir Joseph Thackwell up the river on a 50 miles' march, to cross by a ford and come down on the other side, so turning the enemy's flank. The Sikhs abandoned their position and the main British force crossed the river.

Inadequately reconnoitring the ground ahead, Gough suddenly came upon the Sikhs formed behind the village of Chillianwalla on the left front of the British line of march. At 2 o'clock in the afternoon of a short winter day, across a belt of low, dense jungle bushes and thorny mimosa, Gough saw the Sikh army drawn up in battle array. With

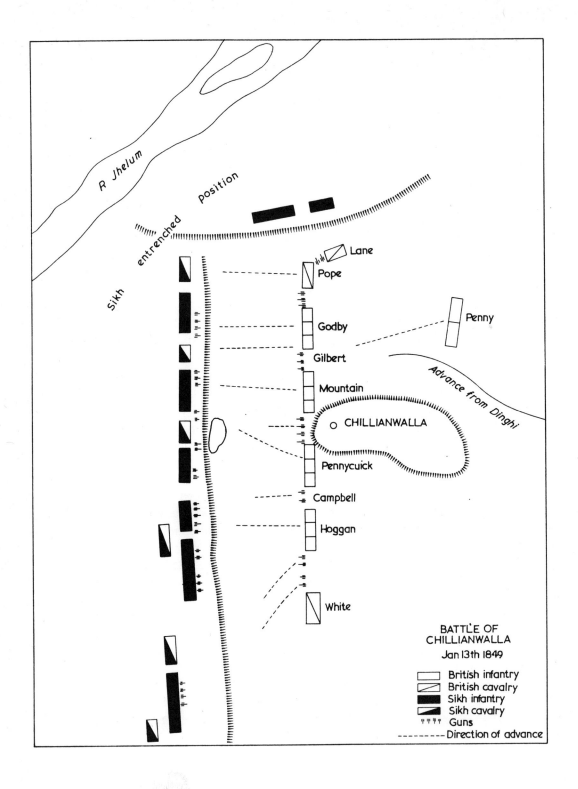

R Jhelum

Sikh entrenched position

Lane

Pope

Godby

Gilbert

Mountain

O CHILLIANWALLA

Penny

Advance from Dinghi

Pennycuick

Campbell

Hoggan

White

BATTLE OF
CHILLIANWALLA
Jan 13th 1849

☐ British infantry
◩ British cavalry
◼ Sikh infantry
◣ Sikh cavalry
ᵼ ᵼ ᵼ ᵼ Guns
------- Direction of advance

memories of Mudki and Ferozeshah, and conscious that his troops had been under arms since daybreak, he reluctantly decided to wait until the next day, but a few Sikh cannon-balls whistling overhead provoked him into ordering an immediate attack.

Badly affected by the dense jungle, the British infantry pressed forward in lines, masking their own guns so that they were only able to get off a few rounds. On the British left, the first to be engaged were Campbell's infantry division formed of two brigades — Pennycuick's on the right and Hoggan's on the left — with a field battery moving in the interval between brigades. Pennycuick's brigade (24th Foot; 25th and 45th Native Infantry regiments) suffered cruelly from a battery of 18 guns directly to their front and from the masses of Sikh infantry positioned around the guns. Pennycuick was killed together with his young son; 13 officers were killed and 9 wounded, with 203 men killed and 266 wounded. Unsupported by the native regiments, the heavily hit 24th were now charged by cavalry so that they broke in disorder and, pursued and harried by the Sikh horsemen, fled almost to their original position.

Hoggan's brigade (61st Foot; 36th and 46th Native Infantry Regiments) advanced into a hail of fire from four Sikh guns. To their front they could see a large force of enemy cavalry and dense infantry formations. Shaken by the heavy fire, both the native regiments gave way and retreated, but the 61st advanced in line firing steadily (a manoeuvre constantly practised by Campbell), putting the Sikh cavalry to flight. The enemy pushed two guns to within 25 yards of the right flank of the 61st and began to tear great holes in their ranks with grape shot; Campbell wheeled the two right companies of the 61st and headed their charge on the guns, which were captured. After turning the Sikh right flank, the 61st then encountered a strong enemy infantry mass with two more guns. Again Campbell led his men to capture the guns and disperse the infantry, and then proceeded to roll up the enemy's line until he had taken 13 guns, all captured by the 61st at the point of the bayonet.

This success would not have been attained but for Thackwell who, out on the left, prevented the Sikhs from harassing Campbell's flank and rear. In this action, the three troops of horse artillery expended 1,200 rounds of ammunition, whilst the 3rd Light Dragoons repeatedly charged strong bodies of Sikh infantry in defensive formations. Even so, at one period Campbell found himself engaged simultaneously in front, flank and rear, and was only saved by the staunchness of the 61st Foot.

On the right of the British line, Gilbert's infantry division began with an attack by his left brigade under Mountain (29th Foot; 30th and 36th Native Infantry Regiments). With a loss of 200 men, the 29th stormed the Sikh entrenchments, routed the enemy, and captured the batteries. The 36th Native Infantry was shattered by repeated charges from Sikh cavalry, losing 6 officers killed and 316 men dead or wounded. Both colours were captured. The 30th Native Infantry also lost a colour, but maintained its ground alongside the 29th in spite of heavy losses.

On the extreme right Gilbert's other brigade, under Godby, came up against some very hard fighting as the 2nd Europeans swept forward through the jungle with the

31st and 70th Native Infantry Regiments on their left. Suddenly finding themselves surrounded by overwhelming numbers of Sikh infantry, the native infantry formed square while the 2nd Europeans rear ranks faced outwards in a fierce conflict that lasted for three hours before their opponents were driven off the field, leaving their guns behind.

On the right, the British Cavalry brigade, masking their own guns, had their formation broken up by the jungle and halted to re-form ranks. Suddenly the order 'Threes about' was heard and the whole line turned to ride back in a retreat that became a panic as they were followed by a few hundred Sikh horsemen. In the headlong flight, the fugitives rode right through and over the British artillery, causing confusion and dismay far in the rear among the hospitals. Four guns fell into enemy hands and it was not until Lane's gunners had poured some rounds of grape into the pursuers, while a wing of the 9th Lancers once more confronted the enemy, that the Sikh horsemen moved back in a leisurely retreat.

The Sikhs now began to drift from the field, retiring into a strong position on the nearby Rassoul Heights. Gough had captured 40 enemy guns and lost 2,400 killed and wounded and, in deepening darkness, he fell back on Chillianwalla, taking his wounded with him. This technical victory aroused such feelings of alarm and indignation in England that Sir Charles Napier was dispatched at a few hours notice to supersede Lord Gough as Commander-in-Chief.

Late in January, Multan fell and on 19 February the besiegers reinforced Gough's army. Withdrawing from the front of the British force, the Sikhs were slowly followed by Gough who faced a strong Sikh encampment at Gujerat on 20 February 1849. The Sikh's crescent-shaped position lay in front of the town and included three or four fortified villages approached by a fair expanse of level country, green with young corn. Gough had under command some 23,000 men with 90 guns, including 18 heavy siege-pieces. Personally leading the right and right centre against the enemy centre, he marched his force forward 2 miles with the precision of the parade ground, then they halted, deployed and lay down in ordered lines; the skirmishers and artillery batteries went out in front and, together with the heavy pieces, began a two-hour cannonade which utterly crushed the fire of the Sikh guns, although not without some loss to the British. It was the first time in either of the wars against the Sikhs that Gough had an advantage in numbers and weight of artillery metal and he did not waste it.

The infantry began to advance in line, lying down more than once to avoid the hails of grape and roundshot which the Sikhs were still firing at them. Although under great pressure, the Sikhs themselves remained steady; their infantry held their position and their cavalry hovered on either flank waiting for the chance to pass round into the British rear; they were only held off by artillery fire and counter-charges by British cavalry. The three Sikh villages fell after a desperate and prolonged resistance and, in a long and majestic line, the British army swept on up the plain towards Gujerat, preceded by a strong line of skirmishers and light artillery. Campbell was ordered to storm a dried-up water course held in considerable strength by the Sikhs but he preferred to dislodge the enemy by enfilading artillery-fire and so he passed his division across this formidable defence without firing a musket-shot or losing a man. The Sikhs began to flee from the field and the British cavalry were thrown in to ride over and trample them down. Thus a retreat was transformed into a rout, and the British did not draw rein until they had ridden 15 miles beyond Gujerat. The Sikh army had lost its camp, its colours and 53 guns.

Next morning, the British continued the pursuit of the broken Sikh army who, with a certain dignity, laid down their arms. Within a few years the Sikhs showed themselves to be among the most loyal and brave of the Indian soldiers who marched and fought under the banner of the Empress Queen.

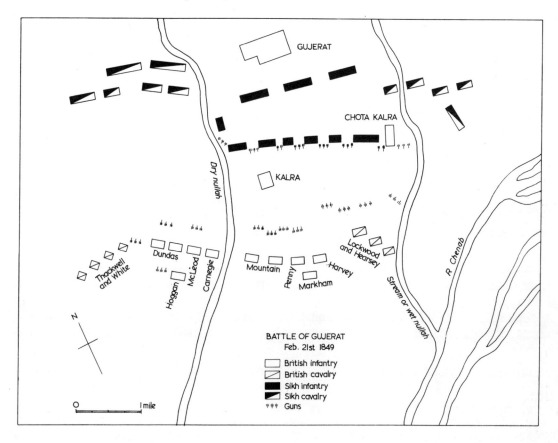

BATTLE OF GUJERAT
Feb. 21st 1849

British infantry
British cavalry
Sikh infantry
Sikh cavalry
Guns

15 North-West Frontier of India 1847-54

In 1847 began the frequent punitive expeditions of British and native troops to bring law and order to the North-West Frontier. The militant tribesmen of the Swat Valley on the North-West Frontier of India had long considered the plains of Peshawar to be open ground for cattle-stealing. Realising that only a show of force would alter these habits, in October 1847 Major Lawrence with Lumsden and troops of the newly formed Corps of Guides together with some Sikhs, fought a brisk action with the tribesmen before returning to British territory.

In December 1849 Lieutenant-Colonel Bradshaw led the 60th Rifles, 61st Foot, some artillery, cavalry and 200 men of the Guides under Lumsden to attack and destroy the insurgent village of Sanghao, which had refused to submit. The village was very strong, lying beneath a precipitous rock 200ft high, and protected on either side by two spurs with steep paths up which the tribesmen retreated when the force attacked. Later, about 10,000 tribesmen from many parts of the area congregated in and around the village. Holding them frontally with the artillery and infantry, the cavalry charged in from the flank in a completely successful attack that dispersed the tribesmen in all directions, leaving the village to be destroyed. British losses were 3 killed and 22 wounded.

(In January 1866, Brigadier-General Dunsford with 4,000 native infantry and cavalry with artillery again destroyed Sanghao and other insurgent villages and the villagers were directed to re-establish themselves on sites away from the hills, more readily accessible to law and order).

A punitive expedition went out in February 1850, after a large force of Afridis attacked and almost wiped out a party of sappers working on the Kohat Pass road. The Commander-in-Chief, General Sir Charles Napier, who was in Peshawar at the time, immediately ordered out a force under the command of Brigadier Sir Colin Campbell and accompanied it in person. Fourteen days' rations were taken and the troops were told that there were to be no reprisals and that any man found plundering would be hanged or flogged. In addition to native cavalry and infantry, the force included the 60th Rifles; the 61st Foot and the 98th Foot, with Horse Artillery, including 25½ inch mortars carried on elephants.

The village of Akhor in the Pass was defended by tribesmen on the heights around it. Ascending on the right, the 60th Rifles and the 1st Punjab Infantry, commanded by Captain J. Coke, and the Guides under Lieutenant H. Lumsden, advanced on the left. The enemy, behind stone breastworks, strongly opposed the advance, but the position was quickly carried by the 1st Punjabis, covered by two Horse Artillery guns. This village was destroyed, together with Zargun Khel further on, after being attacked by the

60th and 98th Regiments, assisted by the Horse Artillery. The troops were kept awake all night by desultory fire on the camp, but the march continued next day through the narrow and difficult Pass, commanded by tribesmen on the heights above, which had to be stormed by the 1st Punjab Infantry on the left, while a detachment of the 60th Rifles, supported by the 98th, took the heights on the right. Throughout the day, the rearguard was under constant attack by large bodies of tribesmen.

During the night, a picquet of the 23rd Native Infantry beat off an attack on the heights to the front of the camp, while those to the rear were firmly held throughout the night by two companies of the 31st Native Infantry under Captain Dunmore. The party of native infantry sent up next morning to relieve them took the wrong path so that Dunmore's force came down before the heights were occupied, allowing the watchful tribesmen to swarm in and badly cut-up the descending force, who had to be extricated by artillery.

On 13 February after burning villages and crops, the force turned back, fighting its way through the narrow defile with fierce Afridi opposition in front, on the flanks, and in the rear. 19 men were killed and 24 wounded in these operations.

On 11 March a force under Sir Colin Campbell marched into the Swat Valley to confront several thousand tribesmen in the area of Sam Ranizai. The tribesmen came to terms and without fighting offered to pay a fine, but they withheld payment so that further coercion was necessary, and on 15 May, Campbell led forward his force of 3,270 men including the 32nd Foot, the Guides and Punjab Cavalry and Infantry, Gurkhas and other native infantry together with horse artillery and two heavy howitzers drawn by elephants. Elephants were as useful in this difficult and mountainous country as they were in jungle terrain, but they required much bulk food and had to be suitably led — each elephant required a specially trained driver (*mahout*) capable of keeping up with the ordinary train: when guns or waggons stuck at narrow corners on steep mountain-roads the elephants could push from behind with their heads. But they were dangerous under fire because they panicked, and elephant batteries had bullock teams to take the guns in and out of action under enemy fire.

In considerable strength the tribesmen were holding a deep nullah near Shakot. Campbell planned to break the enemy's centre with artillery fire and then to attack on the left with the cavalry, while the infantry went forward in line of quarter columns, advancing in echelon of regiments from the right. The infantry charged home under heavy fire and the Gurkhas had a sharp hand-to-hand battle. The Horse Artillery galloped to the edge of the nullah and enfiladed the enemy whenever they could fire without hitting the British troops. During the course of this action the guns fired 2,613 rounds.

Suddenly the tribesmen broke and fled, chased by the cavalry and the Horse Artillery who repeatedly unlimbered to fire upon the fugitives so that the enemy suffered heavy losses before dispersing. The British casualties were 11 killed and 29 wounded. Shakot was destroyed and the expedition returned to British territory.

In December 1852, after the murder of officers of the Customs Department by the

Hassanzai tribe, a force of native troops including Guides together with a troop of Royal Artillery with four guns and a mountain battery under Lieutenant-Colonel F. Mackeson went out. Although they were encumbered with tents, camels and impedimenta for an ordinary march, the three columns successfully negotiated the snow-clad Black Mountains and destroyed the tribal villages at a cost of 15 killed and wounded.

In 1852 the Utman Khel, a tribe of Pathans who occupied the hills to the north of Peshawar, constantly made raids into the fertile valley below. On 11 May 1852 Colin Campbell with a force of artillery, cavalry and infantry, including the 32nd Foot, Gurkhas, Sappers and Miners, and Guides infantry, marched out and attacked the village of Pranghar on a hill flanked by spurs and heights. The musket fire from the village was considerable, but gradually diminished as shells from the guns bursting in clouds of dust among the huts and towers. Then Campbell sent in the infantry who carried the village at the run, driving the tribesmen before them; the abandoned village was destroyed. The official account said: 'Considering that ten pieces of artillery opened on their village, it must be owned that its inhabitants made a gallant defence.' trouble, raiding down into the Kohat and Peshawar districts, and on 29 November 1853 a force including the 22nd Regiment, the Gurkhas, the Guides and Mountain Artillery set out to reach them by an alternative route through the Sargasha Pass; this was so narrow, steep and winding that it was only possible to move through it in single file. Against some opposition, the villages were reached and Lieutenant Hodson led his Guides to capture the surrounding heights.

The 22nd Regiment and the Gurkhas, aided by artillery, drove the enemy before them and by noon heavy columns of flame and smoke were rising from every Bori village, while all the time the tribesmen poured down matchlock fire from the surrounding hills. Pressed at every step, the British now began a fighting retreat until they came to Taruni where they were concerned to find hundreds of Afridis of other tribes sitting on the hills watching the battle — they had promised their loyalty but the temptation to descend and cut off the harassed force must have been very great. Instead, they sent deputations to the Bori tribesmen warning them not to come any further and they actually brought water to the thirsty soldiers. Moving out on to the plain on an easy level road, the force reached camp at 11pm having been under arms for eighteen hours at a cost of 8 killed and 29 wounded from the force of 1,700. The Afridis had rather smaller losses.

In August 1854 a force under Colonel S. J. Cotton went out to destroy some border villages of the hostile Mohmands; it included the 22nd and 42nd Foot, together with native infantry, cavalry and guns. Shahmansur Khel, the first village, was defended both by matchlock-men in the houses and towers and by tribesmen on the surrounding heights. Mountain-guns drove the enemy off these heights and the infantry was able to clear and destroy the village; the houses were levelled by elephants and the grain stocks were carried away or burned. By the same methods two other villages were captured and destroyed at the cost of 1 killed and 16 wounded.

16 The Second Burmese War 1852

Because of repeated violation of the Treaty of 1824, the Indian government decided to send an expedition into Burma. It consisted of the 18th Regiment; the 35th Regiment; the 51st Light Infantry; the 80th Regiment; regiments of native infantry; and the Madras Artillery and Sappers. On 5 April 1852 a party of the 18th (the Royal Irish) stormed the brick walls and stockades of Martaban and the transports steamed further up the River Irrawaddy. On the evening of 9 April the force lay off Rangoon facing the Golden Pagoda; this was 350ft high on a small conical hill and its summit was formed of a succession of terraces defended by stockades mounting twenty-five guns (some were eighteen-pounders) and swivel-guns. The town rampart was 15ft high with a ditch running round it 20ft wide and 12ft deep.

On Sunday 11 April the steamers opened a fierce cannonade against the Rangoon defences on the right and those of Dalla on the left, destroying or setting on fire the stockades, and exploding charges and magazines until the air was filled with black smoke. The pagoda at Dalla was stormed by seamen and marines at great cost to the Burmese soldiers whose gilded hats made them easy targets. Just after 3 am next morning, covered by fire from the steamers, the troops were landed, each man carrying sixty rounds of ammunition and one day's cooked provisions. The right column consisted of the 18th Regiment; the 51st Light Infantry; the 40th Bengal Native Infantry, with the sappers and miners carrying the scaling-ladders; in the rear followed the artillery. The other storming column was formed by a wing of the 80th Regiment and the 35th Regiment with the 9th Madras Native Infantry. The Burmese artillery opened fire on them and skirmishers poured musketry from the jungle around the pagoda, but they were quietened by the four guns of the Bengal artillery which went to the front and opened fire.

On that day, the heat was taking as much toll of the little army as were the Burmese marksmen. Next morning, the 80th Regiment with four guns, preceded by skirmishers, moved through the dark jungles under heavy fire from Burmese cannon and musketry, driving the enemy before them. At 700 yards from the last stockade of the pagoda, a nine-pounder and a twenty-four-pounder howitzer, together with heavy eight-inch howitzers of the Naval Brigade, opened fire whilst a storming-party formed up to attack the eastern entrance of the Great Pagoda. The attackers had to cross a valley 800 yards wide before reaching the hill, which was divided into three terraces each defended by a 14ft high mud-and-brick wall, on which the mighty temple towered. In the face of heavy fire, the wildly cheering troops rushed forward till they reached the eastern gate and, bursting it open, dashed up the long flight of steps in the centre of the terrace to gain the last and upper terrace with the Burmese flying in all directions. In this action 3 officers were killed and 2 died of sunstroke; 17 men were killed and 132 were

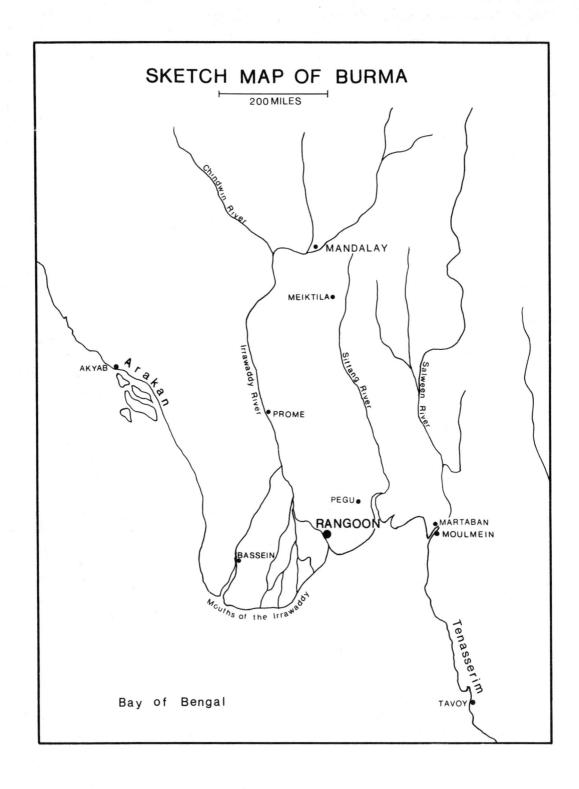

SKETCH MAP OF BURMA

200 MILES

Chindwin River

MANDALAY

MEIKTILA

Irrawaddy River

Sittang River

Salween River

Arakan

AKYAB

PROME

PEGU

RANGOON

MARTABAN

MOULMEIN

BASSEIN

Mouths of the Irrawaddy

Tenasserim

Bay of Bengal

TAVOY

wounded. The number of Burmese casualties is unknown but they left behind them 92 brass and iron guns and 82 iron swivel-guns.

On 17 May, General Godwin took 800 men packed into four small river-steamers 60 miles up an unknown river lined with stockades to attack the town of Bassein. Encountering no resistance on the journey, they met fierce opposition on arrival when the Burmese obstinately defended their strong mud fort. But in less than fifty minutes the 51st Regiment was in possession, and 800 Burmese were dead or dying.

On the morning of 26 May a sudden Burmese attack was made on Martaban, the natives positioning themselves around a small white pagoda. The steamer *Feroze*, 3½ miles from this pagoda, threw in shot and shell with such precision that the handsome building was knocked to pieces and the Burmese were forced to retire.

During this period, the people of Pegu had risen against their Burmese rulers, and a British expedition, consisting of three companies of British and native infantry with some seamen and marines packed on board the steamer *Phlegethon*, towing men in boats, was sent to aid them. Attacking in small boats, the naval landing-party saw some hot action when its beached boats were captured by the Burmese and then recaptured by the sailors. While the infantry rested in some huts near the river out of the blazing sun, intending to attack when it was cooler, the Burmese sent a force of about 1,500 men against them, led by 30 chiefs mounted on ponies, with men carrying gilt umbrellas over their heads. They were repulsed without loss by the small British force who followed them to capture their pagoda and destroy its granaries before carrying off the canon.

To attack a Burmese force at Prome on the left bank of the Irrawaddy, a small flotilla of river-steamers managed to get right up the river, arriving suddenly in front of the surprised Burmese defenders. Marines and sailors landed and captured the town with a single casualty.

With nine-tenths of the Burmese Empire conquered, a military road was built between Prome and Calcutta, and the whole of Arakan as far as the south-east coast of Asia was thus opened up.

17 The Eureka Stockade Australia 1854

The fight at the Eureka Stockade on Sunday, 3 December 1854 (the only battle that has taken place on Australian soil) may be regarded as a civil disturbance although it possibly averted a fairly serious situation. It arose from differences between the governing officials and the large numbers of adventurers who flooded into the colony of Victoria when gold was discovered in 1851.

In 1854 feeling was running very high in Ballarat, one of the principal gold-fields, where armed resistance was freely discussed and weapons secretly collected. With insurrection in the air, reinforcements of mounted and foot police were sent to Ballarat from other mining camps. On 28 November detachments of the 12th and 40th Regiments of British infantry were attacked by an excited mob of diggers while on the march to Ballarat; several soldiers were wounded and their baggage-waggons were rifled in search of weapons. Next day 12,000 diggers held a noisy and provocative meeting and the insurgent flag 'The Southern Cross' was raised: it was blue with the four principal stars of the great southern constellation worked on it in silver.

At an early hour the following day, all the police and military in the camp formed up and advanced upon the diggings; with the skirmishers out in front and cavalry on the flanks, there was all the appearance of a strong and hostile force. The diggers retired, pelting the troops with stones, and firing a few shots. After a few arrests some of the troops retired to their camp. Peter Lalor, the diggers' leader, now swore-in more than 500 men to ' . . . defend their rights and liberties for the Southern Cross'. Armed with guns, pistols, pikes and makeshift weapons, the men formed into squads and marched to the Eureka plateau where, on a plot of round about an acre in extent, a stockade had been hastily made of wooden slabs, ropes and overturned carts. Inside the stockade were a few mining claims, so that the area was dotted all over with shallow holes, later to be used as rifle-pits. It was a place of little defensive strength and later was said to have been formed rather as a site for the insurgents to drill in than as a fortification; it was positioned on the Eureka plateau because this commanded the Melbourne road, along which reinforcements of military were known to be advancing.

Lalor sent messengers round to other mining camps asking for assistance, but very little arrived and so he drilled his men and sent parties out to search for arms and ammunition. In the evening men went in and out of the stockade; many of them went into town in search of food and drink and did not return; possibly they deserted on hearing the rumour that troops and police were to attack the stockade at dawn on Sunday 3 December. Others despaired of the enterprise and withdrew to their own tents and huts.

The military force marching up from Melbourne was formed of 800 men of regular

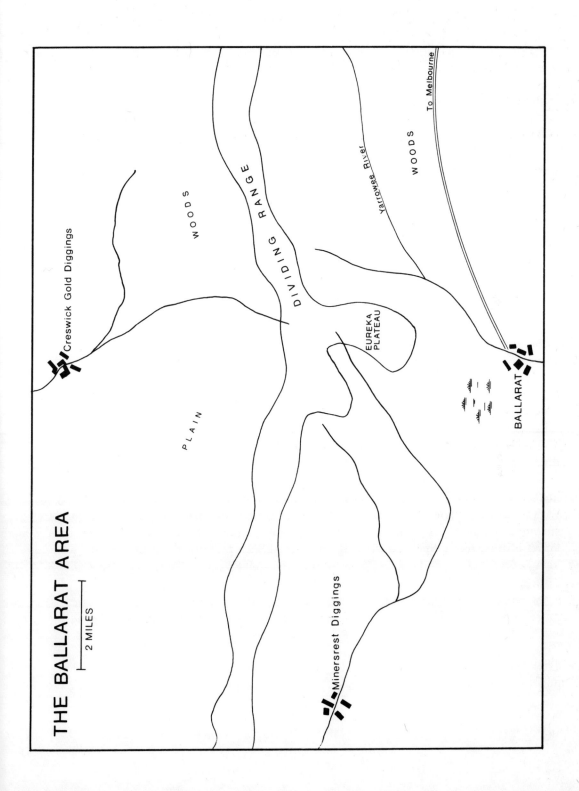

THE BALLARAT AREA

2 MILES

Creswick Gold Diggings

WOODS

DIVIDING RANGE

WOODS

Yarrowee River

To Melbourne

EUREKA PLATEAU

PLAIN

BALLARAT

Minersrest Diggings

line regiments and a large party of sailors from HMS *Electra*, there were four field-guns together with a strong force of cavalry, but the party that attacked the stockade consisted only of about 276 military and police.

Before daylight on the Sunday morning, the blast of a military trumpet roused the defenders, only about 200 in number. In confusion, the sleepy and surprised diggers rushed to the breastworks and began to fire scattered and ill-aimed shots at the line of red-coated men they could see approaching some 100 or 150 yards away in the dim early-morning light. The attacking force replied with a measured volley that killed or wounded 6 men, and soon bullets were flying in all directions. The diggers concentrated their fire on those who appeared to be officers, killing one and wounding another. Peter Lalor fell with a shattered arm and shoulder at the same time as his two subordinates were killed. The faint-hearted began to drift away from the eastward end of the stockade, but the majority of the diggers, many armed with pikes, stood and resolutely awaited the military attack. With a loud cheer the soldiers swarmed over or tore down the stockade and for a short time pike crossed bayonet, but almost at once insurgents were driven from their shallow holes, surrounded and made prisoner. Later the military and police were accused of bayoneting and shooting wounded men.

As soon as the assaulting force burst into the stockade, policemen climbed up the flagstaff and tore down the Southern Cross flag. After setting fire to the tents and the stockade, the military and the police formed themselves into a hollow square with their 125 prisoners in the middle, many of these were wounded but they were made to march by the soldiers' bayonets. It is thought that 30 were killed and another 50 or 60 were seriously wounded. The army lost 5 killed and a small number wounded.

The defenders of the Eureka Stockade had little chance of success. They were ill-disciplined, ill-armed and surprised by the sudden dawn attack. They lacked ammunition and some of their weapons picked up afterwards were found to be loaded with pebbles instead of bullets. The stockade was too large for the diggers to defend it effectively with their inadequate supply of arms and there were enough soldiers and policemen to surround the defences completely. However, the insurgents fought with great courage and it is quite likely that had the original 500 all been present, the attack might well have been repulsed, and diggers from other fields have been encouraged to join the insurgents and extend the rebellion to other towns.

Although the Eureka Stockade was only a very little 'battle' it had consequences more important than those following many a far larger and more furious struggle.

18 The War with Persia 1856-7

A secondary result of the Crimean War had been a breach in the friendly relations between Great Britain and Persia, resulting in the occupation of Herat by the Persians and their refusal to evacuate the town. Under General Stalker, an expedition of 7,000 men was despatched from Bombay and, early in December 1856, a landing was successfully effected near Bushire. The Persians only put up a weak resistance and as the town was defended only by a mud wall on which were mounted four pieces of cannon, the British flag was soon hoisted above the Persian lion. Six weeks later, General Outram, with General Havelock as second-in-command, arrived to take over command, bringing with him reinforcements which almost doubled the original force. He moved out to attack the enemy position at Khushab, to the east of Bushire, and the Persians were routed.

There was no further action until 24 March 1857, when the whole fleet, with troopships in tow, steamed up the river to occupy Mohammerah in the delta of the Tigris. Without interruption from the Persians, the convoy steamed up the river, coming to anchor below and in full view of the forts of Mohammerah.

The British attack began at daylight on 26 March when all the men-of-war, with their steam up, sailed out to silence the guns of the batteries. The remainder of the transports, a squadron of about fifty sailing ships and steamers, remained at anchorage. At 6.30 am *Victoria* and *Falkland* opened fire with their great guns, and at 7 am *Feroze* and *Assaye* steamed into a good position about 300 yards from the forts and opened fire with 18-inch shells. Fire was returned by the Persians. The boats of the fleet towed into position a mortar-raft which threw 5½-inch bombs into the enemy's works. Taking stations at 800 yards distance, *Ajdaha, Clive, Victoria* and *Falkland* opened fire with a great roar.

The day was calm and sunny and there was just enough breeze to blow clouds of smoke clear of the ships, allowing a good and steady aim to be taken so that very few shots were wasted. At 8 o'clock the commodore ran up the signal for a closer attack. *Victoria* took her station astern of *Assaye*, thus becoming the third ship in the line off the batteries. About 200 yards from the mouth of the creek the water suddenly shoaled and *Victoria* grounded; she was thus exposed to the concentrated fire of all the guns of the forts and she took a severe battering. Eighteen large round shots were later found buried in her hull and her rigging was cut to pieces. She remained in this exposed position until noon, when *Feroze* dropped down and drew some of the enemy's fire from her. *Ajdaha; Semiramis* and the two sloops-of-war came up at the same time and a very heavy fire fight took place between the ships and the shore. At 12.30, the magazine of the north fort blew up with a bellowing roar, sending up a dense column of smoke and dust. A deafening cheer rang from ship to ship and the intensity of fire was redoubled.

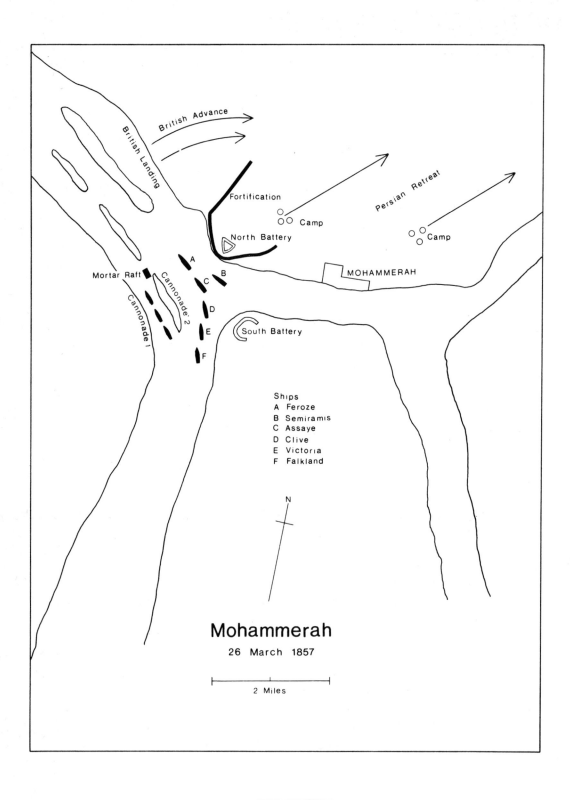

British Advance

British Landing

Fortification

Persian Retreat

Camp

North Battery

Camp

MOHAMMERAH

Mortar Raft

A

B

C

D

E

F

Cannonade 2

Cannonade 1

South Battery

Ships
A Feroze
B Semiramis
C Assaye
D Clive
E Victoria
F Falkland

N

Mohammerah

26 March 1857

2 Miles

Three other similar explosions quickly followed and the fire of the Persians began visibly to slacken and by 2 o'clock it had completely ceased. Then *Berenice*, the river steamers, and the steam transports moved on past the silent and shattered batteries with the soldiers and sailors loudly cheering. Under General Havelock, the troops of the expedition were landed, covered by the guns of the fleet. At the same time the northern forts were captured and the Union Jack was hoisted over them.

At 2.30 the enemy opened fire again, but only with jingals (light field guns) and musketry. For thirty minutes the fleet responded with grape and cannister until boats crews of *Falkland* landed and carried the place by storm. Havelock's force marched inland to take possession of the town of Mohammerah and the fortified camp of the Persian army without encountering any resistance. The river-steamers, with about 300 men, were despatched up the River Karun to destroy the enemy magazines at Ahwaz. They came up with the retreating Persian army and attacked and brilliantly defeated it.

Further operations were checked by the Shah suing for peace and agreeing to the evacuation of Herat. A treaty was signed in March 1857.

19 The Storming of the Taku Forts 1859-60

In June 1859 an English fleet under the command of Rear-Admiral Hope was sent to take the Taku Forts at the mouth of the River Pei-ho. The Chinese had blocked the river-mouth with cables and chains, floating booms and rafts and rows of iron stakes planted in the river-bed. The shallow water precluded the use of any ships larger than Hope's eleven small gun-boats bearing four or six guns and crewed by forty to fifty men. A landing-force of about 600 marines and sailors was to get through the barrier, silence the guns and occupy the forts.

The Chinese rapidly served the fort guns, firing so steadily and aiming so truly they almost appeared to be crewed by trained European artillerymen. The operations began at 1 pm and by early evening six of the eleven gun-boats were disabled or put out of action, whilst the others had taken a severe battering and suffered heavy losses among their crews. At 6.30 it was decided to bring in the landing-party (which had been sitting in their boats for hours under hot sun), in an effort to carry the South Fort by a bold rush. Accompanied by 60 French sailors, a party of marines, and a detachment of sappers with scaling-ladders, the party scrambled ashore on a mud bank 500 yards in front of the right bastion of the fort. It was not possible to get any nearer as the tide had fallen, and the column had to make its way across 500 yards of mud and weeds, cut up with ditches and pools so soft in places that the men sank to their waists. Struggling through the clogging mud and water, the sailors and marines came under very heavy fire from the fort as, regardless of the covering fire from gunboats, the Chinese crowded on to the ramparts and added their small-arms fire to that of the guns. Shot and grape, balls from muskets and swivel-guns, rockets, and even arrows fell among them in showers and soon dead and wounded lay on all sides, some sinking into the mud and being smothered. Less than 150 men reached the second of the three broad ditches in front of the fort, and only 50 crossed the third just below the ramparts. Unable to fire because their cartridges were wet, these survivors reared their only scaling-ladder against the rampart and ten men climbed up it; most of them were killed by a volley that crashed upon them. The ladder was thrown down and broken and the survivors were left with no alternative but to retire. Under the pitiless light of flares, rockets and fire-balls, and beset by heavy fire, they scrambled back, having lost 68 men killed and 300 wounded.

In August 1860 an allied force of British and French troops under General Sir Hope Grant and General de Montauban made a second attempt to capture the Taku Forts. With the allied fleets watching the entrance of the river, 11,000 British and Indian troops and between 6,000 and 7,000 French troops landed at Peh-tang, some eight miles north of Taku, where a wide expanse of marshes separated the force from the forts. By an inland march, these marshes were turned and the allies defeated the Chinese field-army

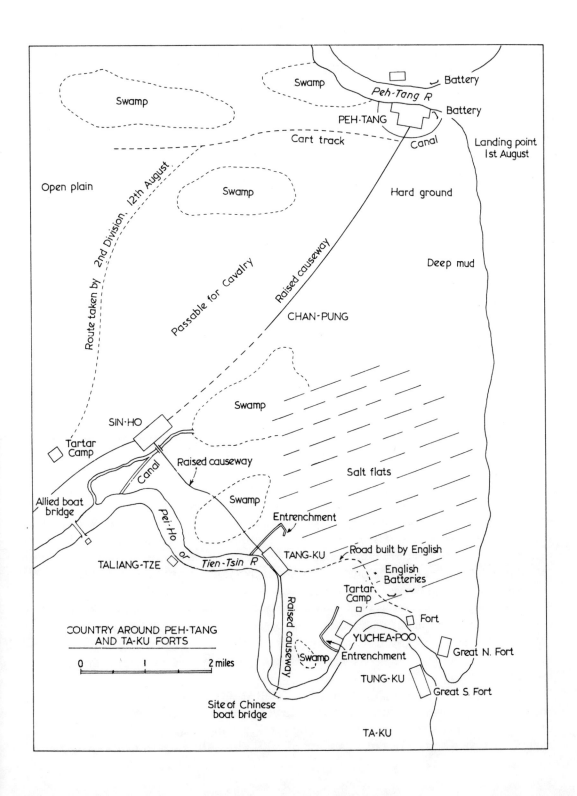

Swamp

Swamp

Peh-Tang R

Battery

PEH-TANG

Battery

Cart track

Canal

Landing point
1st August

Swamp

Open plain

Hard ground

Deep mud

Route taken by 2nd Division, 12th August

Passable for Cavalry

Raised causeway

CHAN-PUNG

Swamp

SIN-HO

Tartar
Camp

Raised causeway

Canal

Salt flats

Swamp

Pei-Ho or Tien-Tsin R

Allied boat
bridge

Entrenchment

TALIANG-TZE

TANG-KU

Road built by English

English
Batteries

Tartar
Camp

Raised causeway

Fort

COUNTRY AROUND PEH-TANG
AND TA-KU FORTS

0   1   2 miles

YUCHEA-POO

Swamp

Entrenchment

Great N. Fort

TUNG-KU

Great S. Fort

Site of Chinese
boat bridge

TA-KU

at Sin-ho on 12 August. They came down the north bank of the Pei-ho, and seized the walled town of Tang-ku, 3 miles above the forts.

In addition to the North and South Forts previously attacked by Admiral Hope, there were also the Small North Fort and the Small South Fort a little higher up the river on opposite banks; these were square mud structures surrounded by double ditches full of deep water and belts of sharpened bamboo stakes, and could best be assailed from the land side as their guns were mounted to protect the river-mouth. In the face of opposition from the French commander, Sir Hope Grant decided to attack the Small North Fort and on the evening of 20 August he placed a battery of forty-four guns and three 8-inch mortars before the fort. At 5 am on 21 August they began their bombardment and soon one of the magazines of the fort blew up with a deafening explosion and a dense cloud of smoke. At the mouth of the river, Admiral Hope's ships engaged the two outer forts so as to keep their garrisons occupied.

The ground in front of the Small North Fort was so narrowed by the swamps that the attacking force was limited to 2,500 English (mainly the 44th and 67th Regiments) and 400 French. The storming-parties began to advance soon after 6 o'clock, the British led by a party of marines carrying a pontoon-bridge for crossing the ditches; this had to be abandoned when most of the men fell from the first volley fired by the defenders of the fort. The French employed Chinese coolies to carry bamboo ladders which they laid across the ditches and, standing up to their necks in water, they supported them under heavy fire while the Frenchmen scrambled across. Soldiers swam and struggled through the muddy water or scrambled over the ladders; some ran across a drawbridge that had fallen when its ropes had been cut by Major Anson, who had crossed the ditch and hacked at them with his sword. The stormers found themselves crowded together between the inner ditch and the rampart and, although the Chinese could no longer reach them with their muskets, they were able to drop cannon-shot, rocks, explosive grenades, jars of lime, and stifling stink-pots down on to their heads. As fast as the scaling-ladders were placed against the ramparts the Chinese threw them down, spearing and shooting all who mounted them. A French infantryman who had reached the top of the wall, where the bombardment had broken it down, carried on a continuous fire by means of reloaded rifles handed to him by his comrades until he was shot down. Some British officers drove the points of their swords into the mud walls and, by holding up the hilts, made a series of stepping stones so that their comrades could mount. A French drummer got in through an opening, together with the standard-bearer of his regiment who rushed forward with the French tricolour but Lieutenant Chaplin, wounded in three places, managed first to plant the colours of the 67th on the high central battery of the fort.

Fierce hand-to-hand fighting wiped out almost the entire Chinese garrison; the few who tried to escape were either injured as they jumped from the high wall of the fort or else were impaled upon the sharp bamboo stakes planted along the deep ditch at its foot. They lost 400 men out of a garrison of 500, whilst the English had 21 killed and

184 wounded.

With the fall of the Small North Fort, the Small South Fort, only 400 yards away, was abandoned and white flags were hoisted on the two larger forts, but the Great North Fort refused to surrender and the guns of the captured forts were turned on it, together with other guns brought up from the English batteries. As storming-columns were forming up, the French general noticed that the ramparts opposite him were unmanned and he sent men into the fort where they opened the gate and allowed their comrades to enter. About 2,000 prisoners were taken without a shot being fired — they were disarmed and, much to their surprise, told to go home.

Later in the day Sir Robert Napier, at the head of the storming column, took possession of the other forts, finding no less than 600 guns of varying calibres mounted in them. On the same day, Admiral Hope's gunboats steamed up the river and cleared away the barricades where the fierce fighting of last year had raged. The way to Tientsin and Peking was open and a few weeks later the armies of England and France marched in triumph into the Imperial City.

20 The Maori Wars 1861-4

The war in New Zealand, which lasted more than four years, consisted of a series of engagements that spasmodically flared up whenever peace seemed to have been secured. It was an unpopular war with the troops, who admired the courage and dignity of the Maoris, respecting them as gallant and even chivalrous foes, whereas the settlers hated them for burning their homesteads and killing their friends. First-rate fighting men and military engineers, the Maoris were a skilful race of warriors whose mode of warfare was rapidly to construct a 'pah' (fort) more or less impervious to artillery fire, and to hold it only long enough to inflict delay and loss upon the enemy; they then evacuated it and built another work of the same kind further back. The British troops found it particularly exasperating that, after heavy losses, the bulk of the defenders had disappeared under cover of night to take up a fresh position. These 'pahs' often consisted of continuous lines of rifle-pits covered and concealed by flat roofs banked with earth and hidden by ferns; the timber supports of the flat roofs rested on the ground, leaving a space of four inches at ground level, from which the muzzles of the Maoris' double-barrelled guns protruded. Superior at short range, these weapons were more quickly loaded than the muzzle-loading Enfield rifle of the British soldier. At close quarters the Maoris fought desperately with a short, flat, sharp, double-edged stone club called the 'meri'.

To defend hereditary rights to land, the natives of Taranaki took up arms in 1861 and soon a skirmishing-type of insurrection was in full swing. Supported by artillery, a force landed and attacked the Maoris at Puketekaure, but it was driven from the field by a Maori force less than twice its number, who possessed no artillery and were armed only with common muskets, fowling-pieces and double-barrelled guns; but so closely did the Maoris press the British during their fighting retreat that their dead were left upon the field and a number of the wounded were abandoned.

Well led and possessing both energy and courage, the Maoris were a formidable enemy who kept the war ebbing and flowing until March 1861, when hostilities ceased. But by mid-1863, the province of Auckland was again aflame with insurrection, the Maoris concentrating their forces at Pokewa, 35 miles south of Auckland.

On 12 July 1863, British troops made contact with the Maoris at Koheroa, in an excellent defensive position on a narrow, fern-covered mountainous ridge about 5 miles long, with precipitous sides that allowed only direct attack. The 14th Regiment, supported by detachments of the 12th and 70th Regiments, went forward along the narrow fern-ridge under heavy fire from their unseen enemies, and chased the Maoris out of the first line of rifle-pits. Coming up to the second line, they were received with a rattling volley which checked them momentarily, but they went forward again when General

Cameron galloped up and led the charge that drove the enemy in confusion before them, some swimming and others crossing the near-by river in canoes.

Both sides had about 500 men in the fight, which lasted more than two hours and covered an area of 5 miles. The British force had 12 killed and a number wounded; the Maoris lost 40 warriors and many wounded. Although the Maoris had every advantage in their knowledge of the ground, as well as the skilful construction of their three lines of rifle-pits, throughout the war they were never on any occasion able to bring more than 600 men into the field. Their excellent use of the bush, however, and their

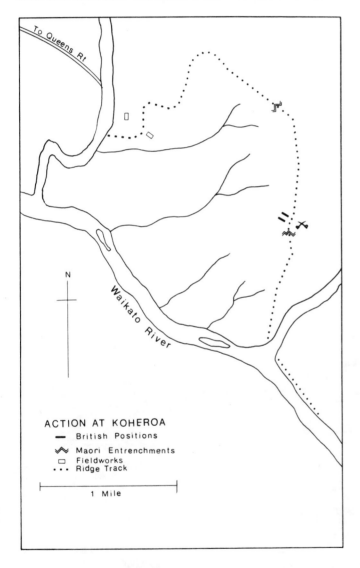

ACTION AT KOHEROA
- British Positions
⌒ Maori Entrenchments
▢ Fieldworks
••• Ridge Track

1 Mile

knowledge of the countryside made them a formidable enemy although, before hostilities ceased, the British strength had risen to 25,000 men.

The Maoris spent the next few months in constructing a strong line of entrenchments at Rangariri, the narrow isthmus dividing the Waikato River from the lake Waikare. Completely blocking the road up to the right bank of the river, the works consisted of a line of high parapets and a double ditch with the customary Maori palisading, its ends sunk in the ground and bound together with tough vines; the centre was strengthened by square redoubts of very formidable construction and a ditch 12ft wide and 18ft deep

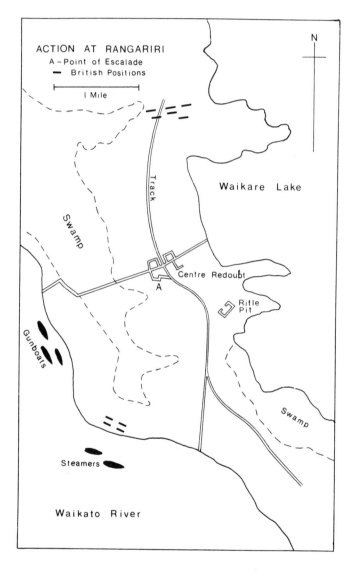

ACTION AT RANGARIRI
A – Point of Escalade
— British Positions
1 Mile

to the top of the parapet. In the rear were two strong lines of rifle-pits, the last of which was on the summit of a high ridge.

On 30 November 1863, 300 men of the 40th Regiment embarked in steamers to land south of the position, while a force of 860 under General Cameron himself marched from the north by the right bank of the river. The artillery on land and the gun-boats on the lake were to open fire at the same time as the 40th Regiment landed to the south. But wind and current made the gun-boats almost unmanageable and when the signal was given, only one of them was ready to fire while the steamers carrying the 40th Regiment were far from the selected landing-place. After shelling for an hour and a half, General Cameron gave the order for the frontal assault.

On the right, 200 men of the 65th Regiment carried scaling-ladders and planks to cross the ditch; a detachment of the 12th Regiment formed the centre; the 14th Regiment prolonged the line of skirmishers and supports to the left. Detachments of the 40th and 65th were in reserve. At the entrenchments the skirmishers of the 65th used their ladders to mount the parapet and force the first line. Wheeling to the left, they charged up the hill and carried the second line of rifle-pits, driving the enemy before them until the advance was checked by the deadly fire from the centre redoubt. The remainder of the troops, finding it impossible to penetrate the position on the left, joined the attack of the 65th. Meanwhile, the 40th had landed and, without waiting for companies to form, the first men ashore carried the ridge, honeycombed with rifle-pits, in the rear of the enemy's position.

The centre redoubt, where the Maoris were fighting desperately, could not be taken because the ladders were too short to reach the top of the palisade. His guns having little effect upon the strong fortifications, Captain Mercer RA led his men, armed only with short swords and revolvers, through a narrow opening in the rear of the work, just wide enough to allow one man at a time to squeeze through. But Mercer and every man who attempted to pass through the opening was shot down. A second assault was made by seamen with cutlasses and revolvers but it failed; the blue-jackets preceded a third assault by throwing hand-grenades, which fell short and rolled back into the ditch, wounding some of their own men.

The British force held the ground they had gained until daylight, when the Maoris put up a white flag and surrendered unconditionally, 183 natives giving up their arms. The British lost 41 killed and 91 wounded; the Maoris must have lost heavily; 41 bodies were found in the works but a great many more men were shot or drowned in the swamps. Many of their wounded were removed during the night, and none were found among the prisoners. It was with relief that the British soldier heard, soon after their defeat at Rangariri, the Maoris had sued for peace and laid down their arms.

When hostilities began again in the spring of 1864, the British force included the 68th Regiment; the 43rd Regiment; detachments of the 14th and 70th Regiments and a small force of the Royal Artillery, in all about 1,700 men, together with a naval brigade. From one of the ships was landed an Armstrong 110-pounder gun, probably the heaviest gun ever used on shore against tribesmen.

The Maoris had built their Gate Pah on a narrow strip of land with swamps extending on both sides, so that it was almost impossible for the position to be taken otherwise than frontally. The pah was a series of inter-communicating trenches, with three tiers of rifle-pits, garrisoned by about 400 natives, it was a work that would have been a credit to European military engineers. When the sun rose, thirteen guns and mortars blazed away and the big Armstrong gun fired no less than a hundred shells before it ran out of ammunition. Later it was discovered that the Maoris, crouching in their hollowed-out shelters, suffered very few casualties and were greatly encouraged by the realisation that, even though the shells made a terrible noise they killed or wounded very few men. At 4 o'clock a 600-strong storming-column, consisting of the 43rd Regiment and the naval brigade, rushed forward to the breach made at the left angle of the pah. Encountering very little opposition. they streamed in through the wide gap in the stockade. Except for some dead or wounded Maoris lying around, the area seemed deserted; the men broke ranks and even laid down their weapons as they began to search for plunder. Suddenly, under their very feet, the Maoris manned their trenches and poured point-blank fire at the stormers; from all points, dusky figures sprang up as if from trap-doors, yelling and firing, flourishing spears and axes. The storming-party thought that it had been led into an ambush; it panicked, and a struggling mass of soldiers and sailors streamed back out of the breach in wild confusion, rushing from the pah in disorder. They spent an anxious night wondering about the wounded and dying who had been left behind in the pah, but it is pleasant to record that both sides acted with chivalrous respect and the Maoris even made efforts to relieve the suffering of the British wounded.

During the night, the men set to work to throw up a line of advanced entrenchments within 100 yards of the stockade, so as to maintain possession of all the ground that had been won. Completely untroubled by fire from the pah, just before midnight an officer penetrated the breach and returned to report that the position had been abandoned. Mindful of yesterday's reverse, the officers did not lead their men into the fort until dawn.

The British lost 9 officers and 23 men killed and 5 officers and 75 men wounded; the Maoris lost very few killed and wounded — 20 dead and 6 wounded men were found in the pah and 10 more dead were picked up in the swamp.

During a further encounter at Te Ranga a few weeks later, the 43rd Regiment made amends for their behaviour at the Gate Pah.

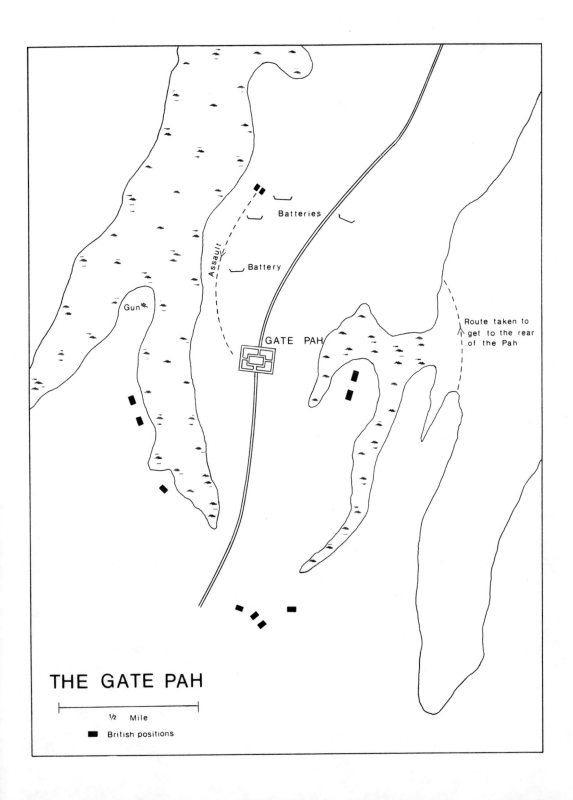

Batteries

Assault

Battery

Gun

GATE PAH

Route taken to
get to the rear
of the Pah

THE GATE PAH

½   Mile

■■   British positions

21 Operations in Sikkim 1861

Lying south of the Himalayan Range, west of Nepal and north-east of Tibet, Sikkim was the objective of an expedition under Lieutenant-Colonel Gawler; it was made up of about 12,000 men including the 6th Regiment, native infantry and four guns. On 1 February 1861 the expedition marched out, and in the operations that followed the infantry stormed stockades with trifling losses but bad roads and poor supplies made it an arduous operation.

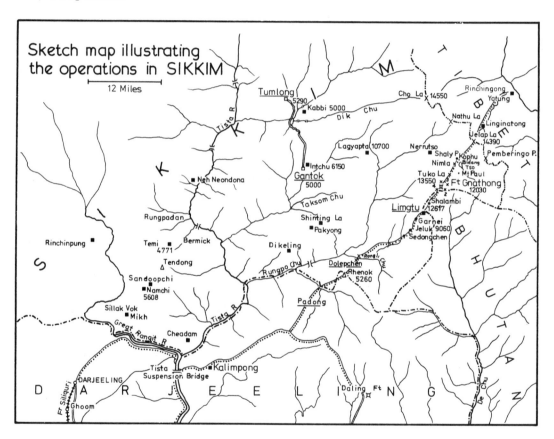

Sketch map illustrating the operations in SIKKIM

12 Miles

22 Expeditions on the North-West Frontier 1858-67

In April 1858 Major-General Sir Sydney J. Cotton led an expedition of 4,877 men with six guns, including the 31st and the 98th Foot, in operations against the Khudu Khels. Operating in three columns, the force destroyed forts, villages and crops, driving the enemy from his position by bayonet charges, after highly effective fire from the Enfield rifles that were being used for the first time on the Frontier. The enemy closely harried the force on the return journey from an operation costing 6 killed and 29 wounded.

On 2 January 1864 some 6,000 Mohmand tribesmen threatened Fort Shab Kadar, garrisoned by about 1,800 men with three guns commanded by Colonel A. Macdonell and including 150 sabres of the 7th Hussars and the 3rd Battalion Rifle Brigade. Shouting and screaming, the tribesmen advanced in an irregular formation, to be attacked by the 7th Hussars who gradually folded the enemy's right on his centre whilst the artillery raked his retiring wing, causing many casualties. Charging three times, the Hussars continued the turning movement until the tribesmen were driven away by the Rifle Brigade, advancing in skirmishing order. British losses were 2 killed and 17 wounded.

In 1867 disturbances with the Black Mountain tribes made it necessary to mount a punitive expedition which, to avoid weakening the border posts, was supplied from stations in the Punjab and the North-West Provinces. To reach the scene of operations, many regiments marched long distances during the hot season — the 38th Foot covered 250 miles in ten days; the 20th Punjab native infantry marched 422 miles and the Sappers and Miners 600 miles in twenty-nine days of forced-marches. During their march the 6th Foot lost 38 men from heat apoplexy. Under the command of Brigadier-General A. T. Wilde, the force, including the 6th, 19th and 38th Foot, together with Guides Cavalry, Gurkhas, Sikhs, Punjabi Infantry and Bengal Cavalry with artillery, numbered 9,500 men. Lasting three weeks, the arduous operations in mountainous country, constantly hampered by lack of water, saw strong defensive positions stormed and rebellious tribesmen completely defeated at a loss of 5 men killed and 29 wounded.

23 The Ambela Expedition 1863

In autumn 1863, in the face of objections from Sir Hugh Rose the Commander-in-Chief, it was proposed to send a punitive force about 5,000 strong through the Chamla Valley to drive out into the plains beyond a fanatical group of Pathans who had been raiding from their village at Malka. No trouble was expected from the other tribes in the territories bordering the Chamla Valley; they had no sympathy for the fanatics and held different religious opinions. Sir Neville Chamberlain, a soldier of great experience and reputation, commanded the force which included the 71st Regiment; the 101st Regiment; native infantry regiments; Guides; Cavalry; infantry and mountain artillery.

The force left on 18 October, intending to move northwards through the Ambela Pass during the first day's march, so as to be about 16 miles down the Chamla Valley on the second day; the third day's march of 6 miles was to bring it to Malka. In the event, it found great difficulty in traversing the Ambela Pass and after three days the elephants and baggage animals had blocked the Pass and the whole expedition came to a dead stop. The Bunerwal tribesmen who lived near the Pass were afraid that the British operations were merely a cloak to annex their territory, and so they closely watched operations. The enforced three-day halt in the Pass appeared to confirm their fears and in alarm they attacked the column, wrecking in a single stroke the original British plan: with a strong and warlike tribe flanking the line of march for 17 miles an advance up the Chamla Valley was out of the question.

With one man in ten of his force sick, Chamberlain found himself in serious trouble as other tribes flocked to join the Bunerwals. Although his camp had stone-walled forts on either flank, broken ground made it easy for the enemy to creep up to the defences and on 25 October their attack was only repulsed after several hours of hard fighting, costing the British force 124 men killed and wounded.

Unable to advance into the valley that lay before him because of his inability to keep the Pass open behind him, Chamberlain could not move from his present position into open ground, for that would mean giving up the Pass and retaking it at serious cost every time he wished to send out a convoy. He had no choice but to sit and wait for the reinforcements marching long distances to reach him.

The key to his defences was the Crag, a high rocky hill commanding all the lower defences but small enough to be defended by only 12 men. On 30 October it was captured by tribesmen who were driven out by the bayonet in a day of constant attack and counter-attack costing 55 casualties. On 6 December a party working on the road into the Chamla Valley was cut off by tribesmen and lost 3 British officers and 78 other ranks while fighting its way back to the main force. On 11 November, in a night attack on the Crag, which lasted for six hours, 2,000 tribesmen attacking in waves were

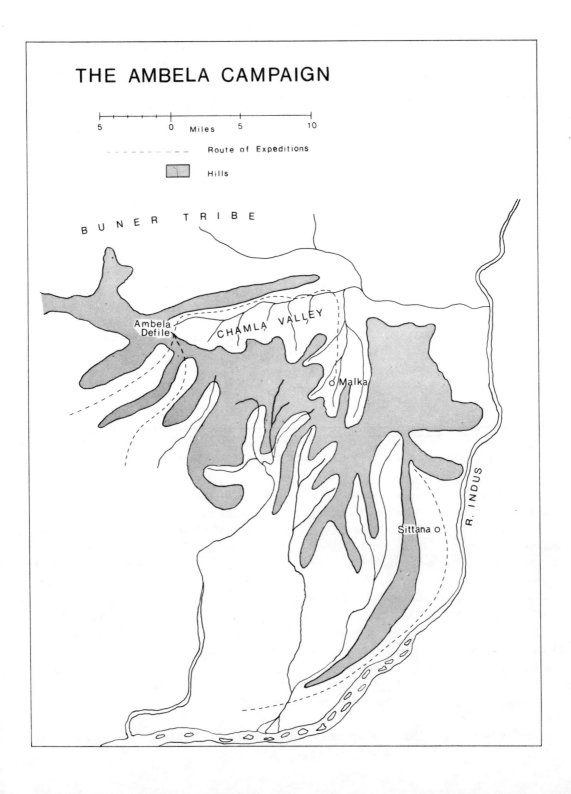

THE AMBELA CAMPAIGN

5   0   Miles   5   10

- - - - - -   Route of Expeditions

Hills

B U N E R   T R I B E

Ambela
Defile

CHAMLA VALLEY

○ Malka

R. INDUS

Sittana ○

beaten back by bayonets, rocks, and stones. It was forty-eight hours before the small garrison, its muskets so foul that they could scarcely be loaded, could be withdrawn and replaced by a fresh party. On 13 November, distracted by a flanking fire and then shaken by a surprise attack, the small garrison panicked and rushed down the slope. Straightaway, the 101st Regiment retook the position at a cost of 158 men.

On 18 November the British lost another 118 men in fighting that lasted from morning until dark. Two days later, the garrison was again thrown out, but Chamberlain turned his guns upon the position in order to prevent the enemy from occupying it, and then led in person the 71st Regiment and the 5th Gurkhas in a counter-attack. The Crag was recaptured, but Chamberlain himself was severely wounded, and 137 men were killed or wounded.

The morale of the British force was low after a month on the defensive against a wiry and dangerous enemy. The weather was growing colder and there were more than 450 sick and wounded who could only be sent to the rear with strong escorts; this seriously weakened the defensive strength of the force. As a repetition of the 1841 disaster at Kabul was feared, it was decided that the force should be withdrawn, but Chamberlain refused, and so Sir Hugh Rose dispatched Colonel John Adye and Major Frederick Roberts VC to the Ambela Pass to report on the actual state of affairs. At the same time he directed substantial reinforcements to force-march to the area. Adye and Roberts supported Chamberlain's optimism, and formed the opinion that the attack on 20 November had seriously weakened the tribesmen; they advised Sir Hugh Rose that operations should be prosecuted to the bitter end and so on 30 November Major-General Garvock took over from the wounded Chamberlain, to command a force strengthened up to about 9,000 men, including the 93rd Highlanders. The force pushed forward and in two days' hard fighting lost 24 men killed and 157 wounded. The tribesmen then dispersed to their homes.

For reasons of prestige, it was imperative that the village of Malka, the original objective of the expedition, should be destroyed, but in the time that it would take to organise an expedition large enough to do this, the enemy would be able to reorganise, and so, in the hope that the tribesmen had no stomach left for fighting, it was decided to send some British officers with a small escort to destroy Malka. It was a gamble that might have cost the lives of every officer and man of the party, but on 19 December Colonel Reynell Taylor, Major Roberts and four other officers with an escort of 200 Guides, set out from Ambela and burned Malka three days later. They returned slowly, surrounded by thousands of threatening tribesmen who repeatedly halted the small column whilst they argued whether it should be slaughtered or allowed to proceed. The accidental firing of a single shot would have precipitated a massacre, but the tribesmen allowed the force to near Ambela and then drew off and went back to their territory.

Originally intended to be a three-week military promenade, the Ambela Expedition had lasted three months at a cost of nearly 1,000 casualties, half the total losses sustained between 1849 and 1890 in forty-two expeditions on the North-West Frontier. It was thus the largest operation of that period.

24 Japan 1864

Emerging from a medieval era, Japan was in such a disturbed state in 1863 that the British government considered it necessary to protect British interests in Yokohama. The force that was sent included Royal Marines, the 20th Regiment, two companies of the 67th Regiment and detachments of Royal Engineers, Royal Artillery and Indian Infantry, and by late December they were encamped on high ground overlooking Yokohama harbour.

In September 1864 an allied expedition of English, French, Dutch and American warships anchored in the Straits near the town of Simonoseki and began to bombard several batteries of heavy guns mounted in redoubts on the shore. The Japanese put up a surprising resistance but were gradually overwhelmed by the weight of the firing from the allied warships, and on the morning of the following day, on 6 September, a landing-force of two battalions of the Royal Marines and a naval brigade with a battalion of Dutch sailors and marines landed to destroy the batteries. The Dutch re-embarked and later, marching back to the shore in the evening, the British marines and sailors were fired upon by a Japanese force concealed in the thick bush. Deploying, they chased the Japanese back through the bushes until they came upon a large well built stockade defended by guns. As *Perseus* had grounded and was stuck fast within range of the guns of this stockade, it was necessary for the latter to be captured before nightfall, and in the face of hot fire, the marines pushed on up one side of the valley, with the naval brigade on the other. Pressing strongly forward, the marines and sailors crossed the ditch, and helped each other to climb the 8 ft-high wooden palisade. The stockade was abandoned by its defenders and the marines, having lost 7 killed and 26 wounded, set fire to the buildings and blew up the magazine.

For the next four days, working-parties with covering escorts landed, spiked the guns in the batteries, and blew up the magazines. The Royal Marine battalion and the other British troops remained at Yokohama until September 1865.

25 Bhutan 1865

In December 1864 long-standing frontier disorders forced the British to send a small force to Bhutan, a mountainous territory on the borders of Tibet in the north-eastern quarter of India. Under the command of Brigadier-Generals Mulcaster and Dunsford, the expedition was formed of native infantry and cavalry, together with the Royal Artillery with mortars and Armstrong guns, while three companies of Her Majesty's 48th and 80th Regiments and some native infantry were held in reserve at Darjeeling. Advancing in four columns with the guns drawn by elephants and bullocks, the force encountered sporadic but determined resistance from Bhutanese, who opposed it with matchlocks, bows and arrows, stones thrown from slings, and other similar primitive weapons. In each case their stockades and defences were soon demolished by the Armstrong guns and the mortars, and the defenders were put to flight.

Towards the end of December, the British occupied Dewangiri, leaving a garrison under Colonel Campbell. Hearing that the main Bhutanese force was massing at a hill-fort at Bishensing, General Mulcaster set out on a 50-mile march with a column of 2,000 men and a transport-train including 150 elephants. When he reached Bishensing he found that the 'fort' consisted of a single stone house occupied by an aged lhama!

At the end of January, Colonel Campbell was attacked by a force of Bhutanese with slingers hurling stones and archers firing arrows, whilst matchlock-men belched leaden balls out of bell-mouthed matchlocks. The fighting continued throughout the night and, as soon as day broke, Colonel Campbell, who was suffering from fever, led a charge against the Bhutanese, who fought with obstinacy from behind rocks and other natural cover. In the end they broke and fled, leaving behind about 60 dead and wounded, whilst the native infantry lost 4 men killed and 31 wounded. For three days the Bhutanese hovered in the vicinity of the small camp, cutting off the water supply and placing themselves across the direct line of communication with the plains of Assam. Colonel Campbell sent for reinforcements, to be told that the general thought the force at Dewangiri was sufficient for the defence of the place.

On the night of 4-5 February, Colonel Campbell began to evacuate the post, dividing his force so that 250 native infantry carried and escorted the sick and wounded; 50 carried the guns (two twelve-pounder howitzers), the remaining 200 men forming the advance and rear guards. Covered by picquets who kept up a fire to divert the enemy, the force marched out over rocky and mountainous country covered with heavy undergrowth in which it was easy to get lost in the dark, and it was not long before the native infantry began to panic. The retreat became a rout, the wounded were left behind, and, when their porters refused to carry them any further, the guns were abandoned and thrown down a ravine. After considerable difficulty, Campbell

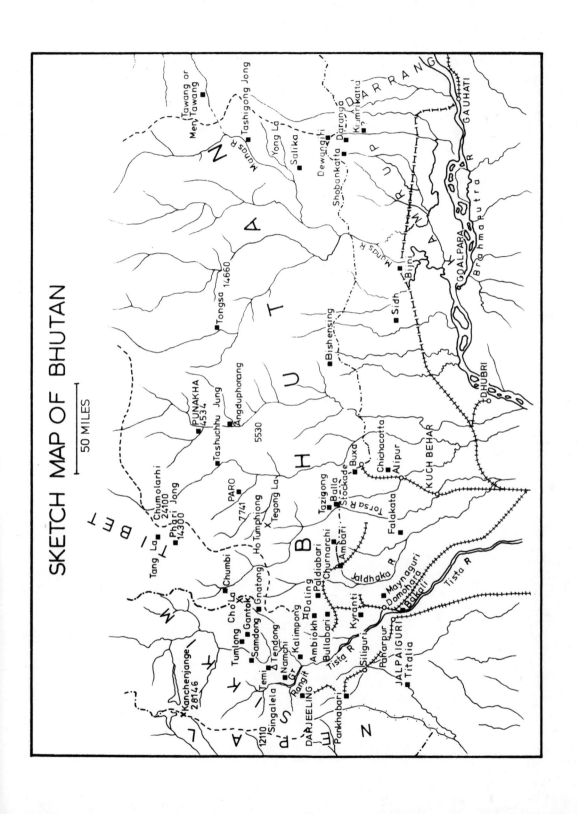

SKETCH MAP OF BHUTAN

50 MILES

TIBET

Tang La
Chumolarhi 24100
Phari Jong 14300
Chumbi
Cho La
Gnatong
Tumlong
Gantok
Samdong
Tendong
Namchi Gr
Temi
Rangit R
Singalela 12110
Kanchenjange 28146
DARJEELING
Pankhabari

Manas R
Tongsa 14660
PUNAKHA 4534
Tashuchhu Jung
Anduphorang
5530
PARO 7741
Ho Tumphiong
Tegong La
Kalimpong
Ambiokh
Bullabari
Paldiabari
Daling
Chunarchi
Ambari
Tazigong
Balla Stockade
Buxa
Kyranti
Siliguri
Tista R

Tawang or Men Tawang
Tashigong Jong
Yong La
Salika
Dewangiri
Shobankata Diarangu
Darranga
Kumrikata
DARRANG
GAUHATI
M A N A S R
Mangs R
Bishensing
Sidh
Bijni
Chichacotta
Alipur
KUCH BEHAR
Torsa R
Falakata
Jaldhaka R
Maynaguri
Domohata
Bakali
Tista R
Pararpur
Paharpur
JALPAIGURI
Titalia

GOALPARA
Brahmaputra R
DHUBRI

BHUTAN

and most of his men reached safety, having lost everything except the clothes they stood up in. The wounded were treated kindly by the enemy who fed them and returned them to the British.

Elsewhere, the occupying forces suffered some petty defeats, largely through lack of numbers. This, coupled with the news of Campbell's retreat, disturbed the authorities in Calcutta, who decided to form the Bhutan Field Force under the command of Brigadier-General Tombs. The force included five batteries of artillery; the 55th Regiment from Lucknow; the 80th Regiment from Dumdum, and at least four regiments of native infantry, encumbered by an over-large supply train — the reserve ammunition of the 80th Regiment alone amounted to 500,000 rounds of Enfield ball-cartridge.

During March 1865 a number of quite fierce actions were fought out, but by the end of that month, with the rains at hand, it was essential that operations be concluded. On 1 April an advance guard 1,000 strong attacked a central stockade flanked by two others at Dewangiri. Sikh and Pathan infantry poured over the palisade of the central stockade, unopposed by the disorganised defenders. Joined by the stormers repulsed from the stockade on the right, the native troops began an indiscriminate slaughter of the Bhutanese, and killed 120 of them before British officers and the men of the 55th Regiment gave the wounded water and helped them to escape.

Dewangiri was considered untenable during the rainy season. Its buildings were destroyed and the European force retired from the area. In the following year, it was again necessary to send a force 7,000 strong to Bhutan to suppress a further rising.

26 The British Expedition to Abyssinia 1868

In order to release British prisoners held by King Theodore of Abyssinia, it was decided in 1867 to send an expedition on a march of more than 400 miles over unknown country under tropical conditions. It was a tremendous effort for that time, for all transport had to be brought from either India or Europe: mules were bought up by the thousand in Spain, Italy and Asia Minor; camels were purchased in Egypt and Arabia; transport-trains, including elephants to carry the artillery, were organised in India. Under General Sir Robert Napier, the force of 10,000 men was formed of the 4th, 26th, 33rd and 45th Regiments; the 3rd Dragoon Guards; Indian infantry and cavalry; Mountain Artillery and a naval brigade with rocket-troughs. Sailing from India, the expedition landed at Annesley Bay, where a camp was built and, early in December 1867, the advance guard left the coast and moved up on to the plateau 7,000ft above the sea. The remainder of the expedition followed during January. It was short of baggage-animals, for many of the mules had died from neglect and lack of water almost as soon as they were put ashore.

By the time the force reached the plateau of Dalanta, some eight miles from Magdala, Theodore's capital, on 7 April, it was only about 4,000 strong, as it had left detachments en route to cover the line of communications. It was formed of the 4th and 33rd Regiments together with native infantry and cavalry; the Naval Brigade; and some mountain guns. There were 460 cavalry, including two squadrons of the 3rd Dragoon Guards. The area to be advanced over on the following day, probably against strong enemy opposition, was an impressive one. Descending some 4,000 feet to the Bachelo River, the ground rose beyond it in a succession of billows one behind the other, with the steep crags of Magdala rising above a saddle formed between two steep peaks. To the right was Fala with a flat top; to the left, a few hundred feet higher, was Selassi. The only ascent seemed to be by a zig-zag road cut in the face of Fala. Native encampments and gun positions could be seen through field-glasses. From the Bachelo River a steep ravine ran up through the hills almost directly towards Magdala, carrying a road made by Theodore for the transport of his cannon.

At daybreak on 10 April the advance guard (under General Sir Charles Stavely) began to descend the road into the ravine, preceded by Colonel Phayre and 800 Sappers and Miners. It was very hot, and the men filled their water-bottles from the thick and muddy water of the river before the advance force, consisting of the 4th Regiment, Royal Engineers, and native infantry, struck off to the right over the hills that would lead them on to the Arogi plateau opposite Fala, where the enemy had positioned some guns. It was an extremely difficult climb and the mounted officers could only begin to scramble their horses up the slopes after the Pioneers had cut a rough track for them.

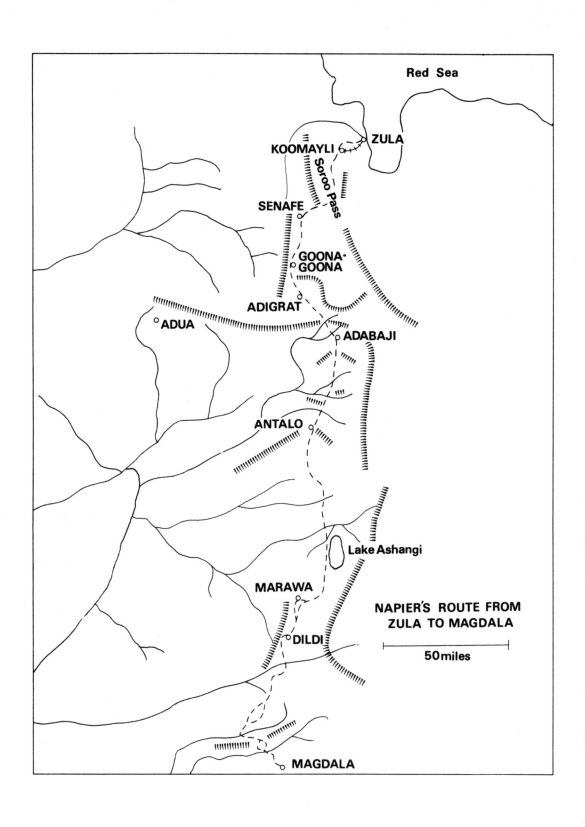

Red Sea

KOOMAYLI

ZULA

Soroo Pass

SENAFE

GOONA-GOONA

ADIGRAT

ADUA

ADABAJI

ANTALO

Lake Ashangi

MARAWA

NAPIER'S ROUTE FROM
ZULA TO MAGDALA

DILDI

50 miles

MAGDALA

Misunderstanding a message sent back by Colonel Phayre that his Sappers and Miners held the head of the valley and that the road was quite practicable, the baggage train and guns, protected only by a guard of 100 men of the 4th Regiment, was left to proceed alone up the ravine in full view of the enemy. Realising how vulnerable this was, General Staveley, leading the advance-guard, ordered the men of the 4th Regiment (who were lying exhausted on the ground after climbing the first hill) to press forward with all speed to protect the baggage-train. Spurred on by the sudden crash of an Abyssinian gun and an explosion as the shell struck the ground, the tired men rose to their feet and began climbing. By now large bodies of white-clad infantry and cavalry were pouring down the road, the scarlet robes of their leaders and their multi-coloured flags making colourful patches.

The 4th Regiment was scrambling up a steep slope that led to the crest of a low hill; a small ravine lay to its front and, 100 feet below, there was a plateau extending to the foot of Fala and Selassi. The little ravine widened out to the left until it fell into the main valley, half a mile away — the Punjab Pioneers were immediately despatched to this point. They were joined by the naval rocket brigade at the point where the side valley ran into the main valley. With well drilled speed, the sailors unloaded the rocket projectors from the mules and, in less than a minute after they had arrived from the crest, a rocket whizzed out over the plain, followed by a stream of erratic missiles whistling and hissing in rapid succession.

The Abyssinians momentarily halted but, urged on by their chiefs, came plunging rapidly forward again until they were only about 100 yards from the edge of the slope up which the 4th Regiment was laboriously toiling. In the nick of time the line of skirmishers breasted the slope and set foot on the plateau, to open a rapid fire with their Snider rifles. It was the first time that these breechloaders had been in action and their rapid fire had a devastating effect upon the Abyssinians, who recoiled and retreated slowly and reluctantly. Followed by other infantry, the 4th Regiment advanced rapidly, driving the enemy away off the plateau to the right into a ravine where the rockets again drove them further away from Magdala.

Large numbers of Abyssinians were rushing forward away to the left upon the few Punjab Pioneers who were defending the head of the road. Before they were actually among the Indian troops, Colonel Penn's steel guns had arrived at the top of the road and unlimbered by the side of the Punjabis, to fire on the natives over open sights. Those Abyssinians directly attacking the baggage-train were halted by the massed fire of the breech-loading rifles of that part of the 4th Regiment acting as escort to the baggage. Then, scattered by the artillery fire and disorganised by the unexpectedly rapid fire of the the infantry, the Abyssinians were dispersed by a series of bayonet-charges. In a few minutes the remnants of the force that had poured confidently down into the valley fled up the opposite side of the ravine under heavy fire from the infantry and rockets on their flanks. Throughout the action, the Abyssinian guns from Fala maintained a constant but very erratic fire, so that most of their shells passed high over

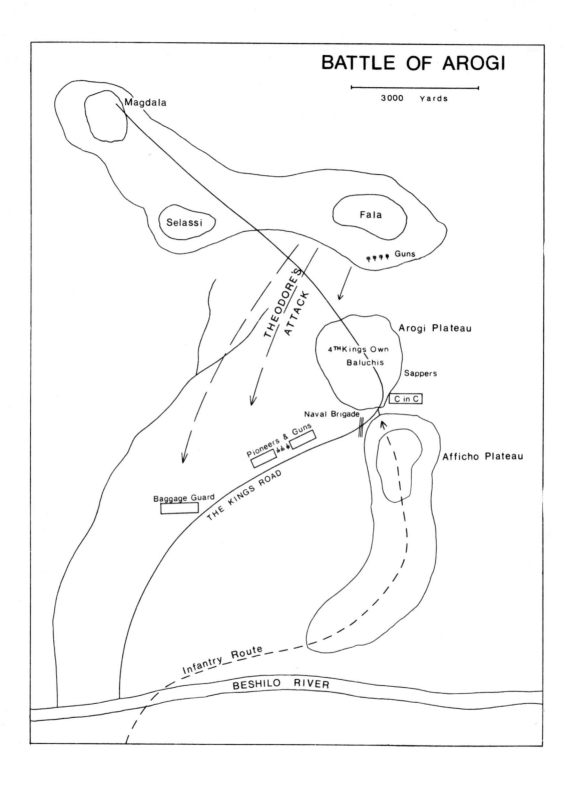

BATTLE OF AROGI

3000 Yards

Magdala

Selassi

Fala

Guns

THEODORE'S ATTACK

Arogi Plateau

4TH Kings Own
Baluchis

Sappers

C in C

Naval Brigade

Pioneers & Guns

Afficho Plateau

Baggage Guard

THE KINGS ROAD

Infantry Route

BESHILO RIVER

the heads of the troops and burst behind them.

Theodore's army had suffered a crushing defeat — only about 600 of the 5,000 who had sallied out remained. The courage of the poorly-armed Abyssinians had impressed the British soldiers who saw that they had not thrown away their weapons as they retreated, nor had they gone back in rout. Not a single man was killed on the British side and only 30 were slightly wounded. During the next two days, Abyssinian chiefs came in, promising to surrender their arms and disperse their men. In the hope of securing better terms, Theodore released some of his captives but then changed his mind and, backed by a few loyal followers, prepared to hold Magdala itself.

The British planned their attack, inflamed with the discovery that 350 prisoners had been slaughtered on the previous day and their corpses thrown over the precipice to lie, a pile of gashed and mutilated naked bodies, on the plateau 100 feet below the British camp. With the guns and rockets firing over their heads to cover the advance, the 33rd Regiment moved forward, followed by the 45th with a party of engineers who had the job of blowing in the main gate. When they reached the path leading up to the gate, the infantry formed line and opened fire, while the engineers and the leading company advanced forward; then the troops stopped firing and the storming-party dashed up, under fire from a high wall that extended a few yards on either side of the gateway. Maintaining their covering fire, the attackers awaited the explosion that would send them forward through the shattered gateway: then back came the astounding news that the engineers had forgotten to take the powder-bags to blow in the gate! Providentially, some men of the 33rd discovered a spot halfway up the road where the wall was broken sufficiently to allow them to scramble into the town, and, running through the narrow streets, they burst upon the defenders of the gate, scattering them in all directions; they then opened the gate for the rest of their party. Progressing through the city in the face of very little resistance, the British infantry found the body of King Theodore, who had shot himself.

All resistance ceased. The town was taken over and at least 100 chained prisoners were released. Napier rested for three days and then put Magdala to the torch while the army began its long march back to the coast to crown one of the most remarkable expeditions of the nineteenth century.

27 Canada:The Red River Expedition 1870

The tough and fiercely independent fur-trappers of the Red River area were greatly disturbed when, in 1869, they heard of the Act of Confederation of Canada. Their hot tempers fanned into open flames by Louis Riel, a half-breed of considerable energy and shrewdness, they decided to rebel in an attempt to hold the lonely territory that had been virtually their own since, two centuries before, Charles II had conferred it on the Hudson Bay Company. Declaring it independent of their own provincial government, the rebels took Fort Garry and formed themselves into an army 400 or 500 strong. Riel tried, without success, to stampede on to the warpath the numerous Indian tribes in the area. This attempt, coupled with the brutal murder of a hostage, persuaded the Canadian government that an expedition should be sent to restore law and order in the Red River area.

Under command of Colonel Garnet Wolseley, Deputy Quartermaster-General in Canada, the force consisted of 1,200 men, including 350 men of the 60th Royal Rifles and small detachments of the Royal Engineers, the Royal Artillery, the Army Service Corps and the Army Hospital Corps. Two-thirds of the force were volunteers from the militia of the twin provinces of Ontario and Quebec, formed into two battalions. With the force went four seven-pounder brass mountain-guns.

The first half of the 1,200 miles journey was by steamer through the great lakes of Huron and Superior to Thunder Bay, reached on 25 May 1870. From the landing-place (now Port Arthur) a corduroy road was laid — built of logs some 12ft wide, roughly trimmed and rolled into position crossways along the track; it made a jolting, racking way for the wagons. As they built this strip through the green forest that stretched for hundreds of miles from the landing, the soldiers laid aside their arms and worked with spade and axe. Their horses, worked by teamsters who became discontented and difficult to handle, were soon exhausted and it became evident that the guns, weighing 200lbs apiece, as well as the 250 boats specially built to navigate the miles of lakes and rivers that lay ahead, could never be transported on wagon-wheels along this road. Manned by experienced watermen hired by Wolseley and piloted by local Indians, the flotilla of heavy boats was sent up the Kaministiquia River, turbulent and full of rapids. This meant that they had frequently to be taken from the river and manhandled across rough country to avoid unnavigable stretches. Day after day, waist deep in water, the men hauled at ropes and pushed the boats until they were worn out. Meanwhile, the heavy wagons laboured along the primitive highway, their crews tormented by black flies and mosquitos until their hands and faces were raw and swollen. Forests, rivers, floods, fires and flies were the enemies of the little force. At Lake Shebandowan, still more than 500 miles from Fort Garry, the entire expedition took to lakes and rivers that had known nothing more than the paddles of Indian canoes, and finally they reached the mouth of the Red River, after a journey of three months — six weeks with oars and poles, and forty-seven laborious portages from lake to lake.

Scouting-canoes were sent out, and the troops disembarked to march along the bank of the river, keeping level with the seven-pounder guns mounted in boats. Camp was pitched some 6 miles below Fort Garry, and at Point Douglas on 24 August the whole party disembarked and, formed up in battle order, advanced through deep mud to seek out the enemy. Riel and his rebels had never believed in the existence of the expedition and, as it approached, they took to their heels and fled. A bloodless victory had been gained without loss of a single man — the only shots fired were a victorious volley as the troops occupied the fort.

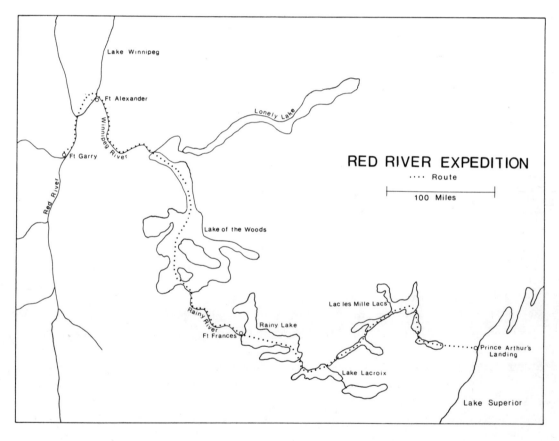

28 The Ashanti War 1874

In 1873 naval landing-parties, the 2nd West India Regiment and two native regiments repelled a large-scale invasion of Cape Coast by Ashanti tribesmen, but their strength was insufficient for the expedition that was considered necessary to punish the Ashantis for their temerity. In January 1874 Sir Garnet Wolseley led out a force composed of a battalion of the Rifle Brigade; the 23rd Regiment; the 42nd Regiment; the 1st and 2nd West India Regiment; some native infantry; a small party of Royal Engineers; a battery of mountain-guns crewed by native artillerymen; and a landing party of sailors and marines. On 31 January the force reached Amoafu where the Ashanti army had positioned itself in dense jungle; here progress could only be made in single file along tracks worn into ditches through long use. The ground underfoot was undulating, interspersed with clearings that were soft and swampy depressions. The force moved forward in a hollow-square formation, the 42nd in the lead, extending to right and left of the path in a skirmishing line wherever the bush allowed. Two of the little mountain-guns moved along the path with them. On either flank, the naval brigade with their rocket-tubes and the native infantry hacked a path parallel to the main track.

The jungle trees amplified the noises of battle; the roar of the native muskets combined with the hiss of bullets and the swish of rockets to form such a noise-filled pall of smoke that each column was uncertain of the whereabouts of its comrades. The Ashantis were invisible in the dense bush so that the only target for the Snider rifles of the attackers was given by the puffs of smoke that spurted from the bushes. After an hour, two companies of the 23rd advanced along the main path to help the 42nd, while two companies of the Rifle Brigade went up the left-hand road to cover the rear of the naval brigade.

Unable to move forward because of a swamp to their front and the heavy fire sweeping the only path forward, the 42nd lay down and replied to the enemy fire. Then one of the little mountain-guns was pushed boldly forward to fire round after round of grape into the enemy until his fire slackened and the 42nd was able to advance. Step by step the men moved slowly forward through bush so thick that all movement had to be on a narrow path. Suddenly the 42nd drove out from the upper end of the path and with a cheer sprang into the open space before the village of Amoafu, which was stormed and taken. The 42nd had 104 casualties out of 450 men in this action.

The British right column had been holding its own, although hard pressed, but suddenly a roar of firing in the rear of the column showed that it had been turned by the Ashantis. First the attack was held and then repelled when Wolseley advanced his troops, sweeping round from the rear so as to drive the enemy northward before them.

The British force sustained 250 casualties. The natives fought with great courage and resolution and it was calculated that they lost about 2,000 men. Their old and worn-out muskets, firing three or four rough lead slugs, compared badly with the breech-loading rifles, the guns and the rocket-tubes of the British force. On the other hand, they greatly outnumbered Wolseley's men and their position was admirably suited for their peculiar method of fighting.

The British force was involved in more jungle fighting as it moved forward to capture Kumasi, the Ashanti capital. The Ashantis resisted stoutly throughout and at times they attacked in such masses that the whole bush swayed and moved as they pushed forward. Advance was only possible because the troops used the deep-set paths as trenches to hold off the enemy, while the rest of the force filed along behind them. All the time there was a continual din of musketry backed by the lugubrious roar of the great war-horns and the wild war-cries of the natives. Kumasi was captured with the 42nd playing a prominent part, and the blood-stained village, which had seen many sacrifices and atrocities, was burned to the ground. Wolseley led his force back through the jungle with very little resistance from the well-beaten natives.

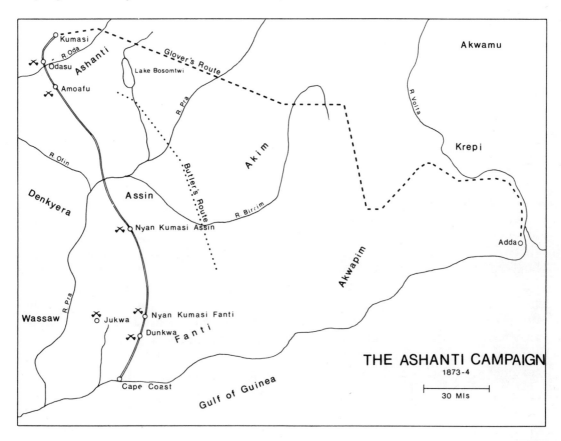

THE ASHANTI CAMPAIGN
1873-4

30 MIs

29 The Expedition to Perak 1875-6

In November 1875 Ismail, the deposed ruler of Perak, led his followers in an attack on the British Residency, and murdered the Resident. In an attempt at punishment Captain Innes of the Royal Engineers was killed while leading 170 men in an abortive attack on a strong enemy position, and so an expeditionary force of 2,000 men, including the 3rd Regiment and the Gurkhas, was sent from India to link up with landing-parties from the *Thistle* and *Fly*. In native boats the force moved up-river and disembarked in the deep mud bordering the green steamy jungle and the dense mangrove trees. As it came up to the stockade and village held by the rebels, the force came under heavy fire, but the small guns were landed from the boats and the stockade and houses were battered and set on fire; then the advance-guard of 450 men (including 300 Gurkhas) charged in and carried the village with a rush. Ismail and a number of his followers got away and took up up fresh positions in the jungle. A mixed infantry and naval force fought its way through the dense forest, storming and capturing artfully concealed stockades and pushing the enemy before it. On 4 January 1876 Brigadier-General Ross led his force to attack and storm Kotah Lama, the stronghold of the most turbulent of the rebellious natives.

When it was learned that Ismail and his band were lurking in the mountains over-looking the Perak River, a surprise attack, guided by friendly natives, was successfully launched on 19 January 1876. Ismail's force was completely routed with great loss so that he fled, leaving behind him seventeen elephants and all his baggage. On 21 January, the village of Rathalma was attacked with rockets and artillery; the Malays were driven out and put to flight, without the attackers sustaining a single casualty. Ex-Sultan Ismail was captured on 22 March.

This was a conflict about which little was known in England, although at least three naval brigades and considerable numbers of troops were employed. For days, under a fierce and burning sun, the sailors and soldiers worked untiringly, poling heavily-laden boats against strong currents. In addition to their own arms and equipment, they carried guns, rockets and ammunition through the dense and dark jungle over paths that were so nearly impassable that only 3 or 4 miles could be covered in a day. Often drenched by torrents of tropical rain and marching through waist-deep muddy water, they had to toil through jungle so dense and dark that not a vestige of sun or sky could be seen overhead. For at least a month they were without vegetables or bread, eating no other food than tinned meat and the flesh of an occasional wild buffalo.

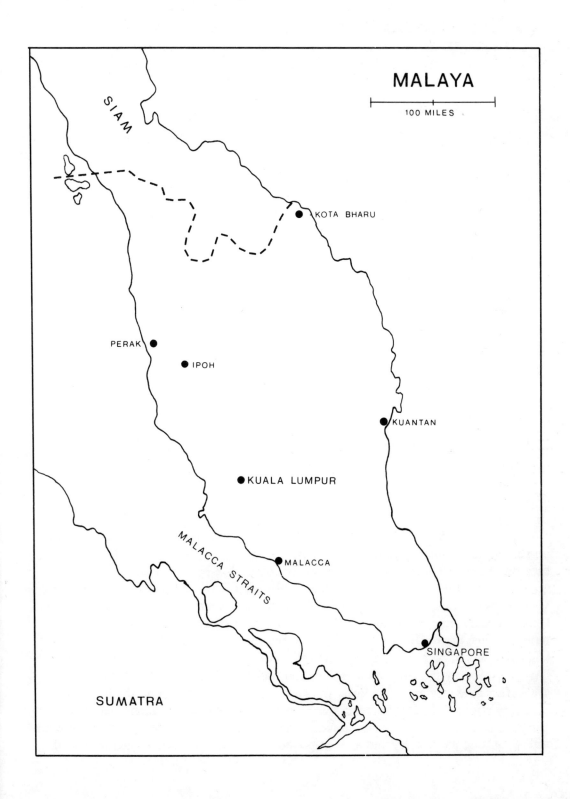

MALAYA

100 MILES

SIAM

KOTA BHARU

PERAK
IPOH

KUANTAN

KUALA LUMPUR

MALACCA STRAITS

MALACCA

SINGAPORE

SUMATRA

30 The Kaffir War 1877

During the last months of 1877 chief Kreli led his Galekas, a Kaffir tribe, in an unsuccessful attack on a police post. Detachments of the 24th and 88th Regiments, together with Frontier Armed Police and some 5,000 Fingoes (a friendly Kaffir tribe), attacked Kreli's kraal and took the Galekas completely by surprise. A sharp fire of shrapnel-shell on the flimsy huts, together with independent rifle fire at 200 yards range, set the village on fire and completely destroyed it. The Galekas fled on all sides with 1,550 casualties, while the European force had 9 men wounded.

Shortly after this a sharp combat took place at Umtsinzani, when the desperate Galekas, leaving their women and children and cattle hidden in a safe place, charged courageously forward, but were mowed down by case-shot at 60 yards range until they were driven to seek shelter behind boulders and ant-heaps. Under a bright African moon, they again advanced and for an hour and a half there was an incessant rattle of musketry and the booming of guns until they were beaten off and retired in disorder.

Sir Arthur Cunnynghame, Lieutenant-Governor and Commander-in-Chief for the forces in South Africa, ordered every available man to the area of operations. A detachment of the 84th Regiment was turned into mounted infantry and even the band of the 24th Regiment laid aside its instruments, to be instructed in the use of the seven-pounder gun. The naval brigade furnished by HMS *Active*, with two guns and two twenty-four pound rocket-tubes, accompanied the European force that began to cross the Kei River early in December. A reward of 500 head of cattle or 1,000 pounds was offered for the capture of Chief Kreli, but no man could be found to betray his chief, although it was known that the Galekas were starving and actually eating the bark of trees.

Early in 1878 the Galekas, now allied to the Gaikas under Sandilli, concentrated on an undulating plain with deep and heavily wooded ravines on either flank, fronted by ground covered with rough foliage and boulders. The Kaffirs attacked along the ravines against the 24th, the 88th, and a naval rocket party and, as they were moving forward, the police and the Fingoes doubled round to overlap their right flank. Driven back into the ravine by the galling fire from the rifles of the British infantry and the naval rockets, the Kaffirs were heavily attacked by the police and the Fingoes, losing large numbers of men. Throughout the action the ravines and wooded areas were heavily shelled by the two-pounder guns and rockets, and after an hour and a quarter the Kaffirs gave way and were hotly pursued, leaving 54 dead behind them.

A very strong defensive post had been erected at Quintana and garrisoned by three companies of the 84th Regiment, a naval brigade with a twenty-four pound rocket-tube, and some Irregular Cavalry and a seven-pounder gun. At 6 o'clock in the morning the

Irregular Horse and one company of the 24th went out to draw the enemy and, pretending to fall back, were hotly pursued by Kreli and his Galekas from the south and Sandilli with his Gaikas from the north-west. The natives, about 4,000 strong, rushed furiously towards Quintana across the open ground until they were within 500 yards, when the troops rose and opened heavy fire on them. The rockets hissed into them and the case-shot fired by the field-pieces mowed them down; nevertheless the Kaffirs stood for about twenty minutes and returned fire until a heavy mist suddenly came up and, by obscuring them, saved them from heavier losses. But in about thirty minutes, when it lifted, the Kaffirs had moved to within 150 yards of the trenches. More rounds of case-shot and file-firing from the Martini-Henry's routed them, however, and the Irregular Horse went out in pursuit. When the action ended, 300 enemy dead lay around the camp, together with many wounded, whilst the European force lost 9 Fingoes and 2 Irregular Horse wounded.

The Gaikas and Galekas never recovered from this reverse and soon Kreli surrendered and was permitted to settle in his old kraal, whilst Sandilli of the Gaikas continued operations for some months. He was later killed.

During these operations British soldiers for the first time used the Martini-Henry rifle, and a musketry sergeant-instructor killed a Kaffir at 1,800 yards range.

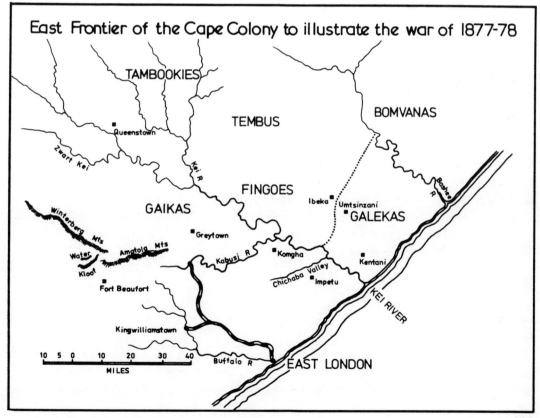

East Frontier of the Cape Colony to illustrate the war of 1877-78

31 North-West Frontier 1878-9

Operations against the Khyber Pass Afridis, 1878
From the moment when the British army advanced into Afghanistan in November 1878, the Afridis of the Khyber Pass began to give trouble. Against them Brigadier-General G. A. Tytler VC, led a force of about 2,500 infantry and cavalry with five guns, including the 1/5th Fusiliers and the 51st King's Own Light Infantry, together with Sikhs, Gurkhas, Punjabis and Bengal Lancers. After marching through the deserted Bazar Valley, on the night of 21 December the force encamped and during the night became aware that the tribesmen were all around them. Next morning they marched up the steep, winding road to a pass that ascended 1,000 feet in 1½ miles; immediately they began their march they came under fire, and eventually had to charge the enemy at the head of the pass before the column of men, horses, baggage and guns could get on. Throughout, the rearguard had to fight fiercely and only kept the enemy back with considerable difficulty.

Near the top of the Pass the road narrowed to a rocky defile only 5 feet wide; about 200 yards from its outlet was a sheltered position occupied by about 100 tribesmen who had crept unobserved through a narrow gorge. As the head of the column emerged, its ranks broken, it was met with a hail of fire. The tribesmen were dislodged by rifle and bayonet, and the column was able to move on to open ground 4 miles from the top of the pass where the tribesmen ceased to oppose them. Astonishingly only 1 man was killed and 7 wounded. The expedition carried out its tasks and returned to British territory.

Operations against the Jawaki Afridis, November 1877-January 1878
In October 1877 a punitive expedition against the Afridis was mounted. Under Brigadier-General Keyes, it consisted of 2,000 troops of the Punjab Frontier Force; the 5th Gurkhas; a small number of cavalry and six guns, working with a force from Peshawar under Brigadier-General Ross which included the 51st Foot, the 9th Foot, the 4th Battalion Rifle Brigade and the Royal Horse Artillery, with native infantry.

Advancing steadily under fire through narrow passes and defiles, the force destroyed villages and crops and blew up some fortified towers. At 3 am on 1 December the troops, with mule batteries, clambered over a succession of ridges to take the Jawakis' principal stronghold of Jummu completely by surprise, so that the Jawakis fled to the hills. The British lost 9 men.

Towards the end of January 1878 the Jawaki headmen sought peace. They found the British conditions unacceptable but, after 250 British cavalry had attacked and completely defeated them on 15 February, they came in and submitted. Throughout the campaign British losses were 11 killed and 51 wounded.

Expedition against the Utman Khels, 1878
Typical of the skirmishes and small affrays that flickered constantly on the wild North-West Frontier of India was that against the Utman Khels; the two officers concerned figure prominently in later events. In February 1878 a small force of Guides, cavalry, and infantry mounted on ponies, under the command of Captain W. Battye with Captain P. L. N. Cavagnari, made a night ride of 32 miles, dismounted and marched a further 2 miles over heavy ground and then 4 miles along a river bank; they then climbed for a mile up a steep, narrow path to reach the village of Sapir at daylight. Before the sleeping tribesmen knew what was happening, the troops rushed in and took the village.

In March 1878 the same two leaders led another small expedition to Shakot in the Swat Valley using the same tactics as before; the village was surrounded after a night march and the villagers surrendered without resistance. The force then marched back to Mardan, covering 50 miles in twenty-four hours.

The Thal-Chotiali Field Force, 1879
In March 1879 troops moving back to India from Kandahar were used to open up a direct route from the Punjab to Quetta and Pishin so as to avoid the length and heat of the Sind-Bolan route. The force included the 15th Hussars, the 70th Regiment, Gurkhas, native cavalry and infantry with mountain-guns, making a total of about 8,700 men.

Only slight opposition from tribesmen was encountered and repelled. There were 200 enemy casualties after accurate shelling by the mountain-guns followed by a charge. British losses were 3 killed and 7 wounded.

Operations against the Mohmands, 1879
In April 1879 a small detachment of 130 native troops under Captain Creagh was besieged in the village graveyard of Kam Dakka by tribesmen who were encouraged by the fact that the force had no artillery. From early morning until mid-afternoon several assaults were only repelled by bayonet charges and, towards the end of the day, with ammunition running low, the enemy was within 60 to 100 yards.

In the late afternoon three companies of British Infantry, two guns of a mountain battery and two companies of Gurkhas, together with a troop of Bengal Lancers arrived from Dakka. Withdrawal without heavy loss was impossible until the enemy could be dislodged from strong positions within 100 yards of the graveyard. The Bengal Lancers managed to advance under cover to a point within 200 yards of the enemy; then they charged and dispersed the natives down a steep bank into the river. The besieged left the graveyard, carrying their dead and wounded and, as soon as the tribesmen flooded into the enclosure, the mountain-guns shelled it with common-shell and percussion fuses. The withdrawal was led by cavalry and infantry with baggage and wounded following; then came the mountain-guns with detachments of infantry and cavalry in the rear. Throughout, the enemy pressed the rearguard closely and kept up a heavy fire upon the column. Next morning the hard-pressed column was met by a force that marched out from Dakka and the tribesmen were dispersed, having lost about 200 killed and wounded. The British casualties were 6 killed and 18 wounded. Captain Creagh was awarded the Victoria Cross.

Expedition against Zakha Khel Afridis of the Bazar Valley, 1879

As the Afridis failed to tender their submission, in January 1879 a force was assembled to destroy their villages in the Bazar Valley. Lieutenant-General Maude commanded a force of about 3,500 infantry and cavalry with 8 guns (2 of them on elephants). In three columns, the force included the 5th Fusiliers; the 25th Foot; the 51st Foot; the 1st/17th Foot; the 4th Battalion Rifle Brigade; and the Royal Artillery, besides Gurkhas, Guides and other native troops. The columns marched for some days over difficult country and frequent skirmishes occurred while they were sniped at incessantly by day and night. Feeling that a further advance might well spark off a frontier war, General Maude halted in a strong defensive position and sent back for instructions. Although the force was given permission to advance, it returned to British territory, having lost 5 killed and 13 wounded.

Expedition against the Zaimukhts, 1879

This tribe of Pathans began to give trouble during the war in Afghanistan and on 8 December 1879, Major-General Tytler VC moved out with the 2nd/8th Regiment, the 85th Foot, and the Royal Artillery together with native cavalry and infantry. Marching on the stronghold of Zawo, the force advanced by a ravine and, greatly helped by the screw-guns, the right column got on to high ground and hotly engaged the enemy, while the main body of men pushed on up the rough bed of the narrow defile until it arrived at a village about 3½ miles from its objective. The two guns of the mountain battery worked round to the left of the ravine and opened fire at 700 yards range, while the 29th and 85th, in two columns attacked the village and captured it.

Attacking again at 7.30 am, they dispersed the tribesmen from new positions and then, pushing on up the defile, fought off attacks from both sides with the guns covering the infantry who advanced under heavy fire and showers of boulders from the heights. Zawo was captured and burned, together with two other villages and fortified towers. The The British force lost 2 men killed and 2 wounded, while 40 tribesmen were killed and 100 wounded.

32 The Second Afghan War 1878

In the summer of 1878, in order to counter the large Russian mission which arrived in Kabul, a similar mission headed by General Sir Neville Chamberlain was ordered to proceed to Afghanistan. It was, however, turned back at the fort of Ali Musjid, just within the Afghan frontier at the entrance to the Khyber Pass. The governor-general of India demanded an apology from the Amir of Afghanistan for the insult and asked that a British Resident should be allowed in Kabul. No answer to this request came within the prescribed time and so war was declared on 21 November 1878, when a force under General Sir Samuel Browne advanced on Ali Musjid. A massive Indian fort mounting fifteen guns, it stood in a commanding position 500 feet above the deep gorge of the Khyber Pass; another line of fortifications constructed across the Pass was manned by Afghan soldiers. The British force included the 10th Hussars; the 17th Regiment; the 51st Regiment; the 81st Regiment; the Rifle Brigade; native infantry and cavalry; and artillery, including a mountain battery.

A battery of nine-pounders jingled into position 1¾ miles from the fort and went noisily into action; the mule-batteries and elephants, dragging heavy forty-pounder guns, moved forward. The 81st Regiment and the 14th Sikhs threw forward a line of skirmishers to clear the villages and cover the mountain spur, and soon the guns of the fort were silenced and in the fast-waning light of evening the Sikhs and the 27th Punjabis made a furious rush over the broken ground against the strongly held Afghan sangars. Darkness won the race and, after suffering heavy casualties, the Sikhs and Punjabis reluctantly fell back, leaving Ali Musjid with guns silenced and walls shattered and gaping.

Just before dawn an Indian merchant cautiously entered the camp; he had been a prisoner in the fort for the past four days, and had escaped when the Afghans abandoned the position. General Tytler's brigade (17th Foot, Sikh Infantry, and Guides) was sent round to come in from the north and cut off the garrison's retreat and, further up the pass, the Afghan commander and his force blundered into Tytler in the darkness and were all taken prisoner.

Even before war had been proclaimed, General Roberts and the Kurram Field Force had been concentrating on the frontier. Its total strength was 14,269 and included the 8th Regiment; the 72nd Regiment; the 10th Hussars with native infantry and cavalry, together with troops of Horse and Royal Artillery and two mountain batteries. After hostilities began, the force was joined by another battery of Royal Artillery, a squadron of the 9th Lancers, the 67th and 92nd Regiments, and native infantry and cavalry. On 20 November 1878 the force moved out, slowly pushing forward in three columns, frequently having to build roads for the artillery while hawk-nosed, dark-eyed Afridis sat watching, like vultures, on the hilltops. On 26 November the force reached the

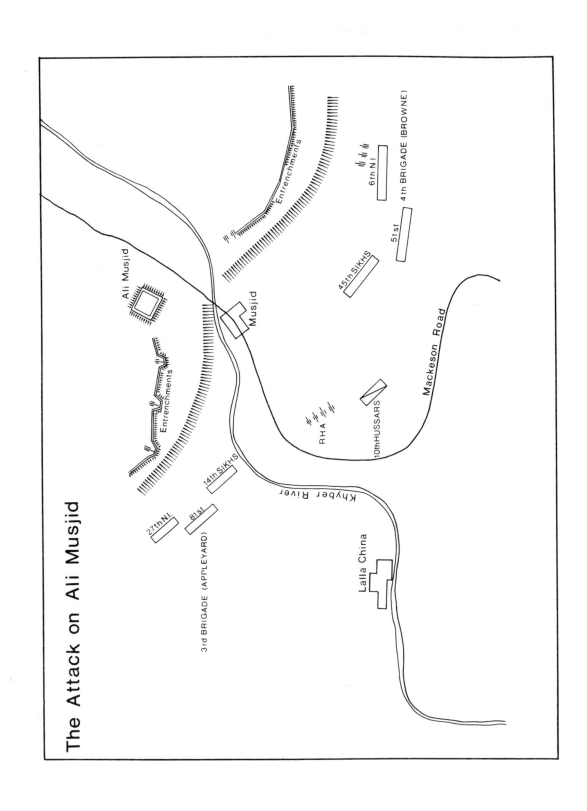

The Attack on Ali Musjid

Ali Musjid

Entrenchments

Entrenchments

Musjid

6th NI

4th BRIGADE (BROWNE)

51st

45th SIKHS

Mackeson Road

RHA

10th HUSSARS

14th SIKHS

Khyber River

27th NI

81st

3rd BRIGADE (APPLEYARD)

Lalla China

Kurram fort where Roberts left his sick with a small garrison, and marched out two days later to force the Peiwar Kotal, about twelve miles away. It was intensely cold and snow was falling. During the next three days reconnaissance revealed the position to be a strong one, with batteries of field-guns positioned to rake the whole pass. A feint attack was to be made on the Peiwar Kotal whilst a strong flanking force went up the Spin Gawi (White Cow Pass) leading to a ridge along which a force could work its way to turn the enemy's position at the Peiwar Kotal. General Roberts accompanied the turning force, which included the 72nd Regiment, the Gurkhas and other native infantry, a mountain battery, and a four-gun elephant battery. The remainder of the force under Brigadier Cobbe was to make a direct attack.

On a bitterly cold night under a pale moon, the turning-force toiled up the rough and boulder-strewn Spin Gawi nullah conscious that unless the Pass was in British hands before daybreak many lives would be lost in the attack on the Kotal. In spite of two shots being fired by mutinous native infantry to warn the Afghans, the force succeeded in nearing the summit of the Pass while it was still dark, without being detected. At 6 o'clock in the morning, the leading troops found themselves confronted by an eight foot high abattis of felled trees from which an Afghan picquet opened fire. This barrier with another 80 yards further on, was carried by the Gurkhas and the 72nd, the little hillmen and the Highlanders dashing forward amid dark pinewoods in the half-light of early morning, driving the enemy before them up the slopes. The tribesmen resisted

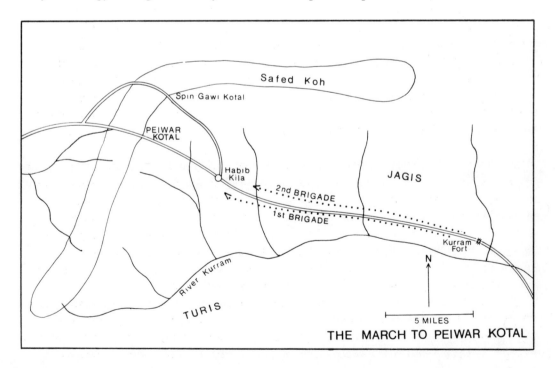

THE MARCH TO PEIWAR KOTAL

fiercely and actually disabled one of the four field-guns that had been so laboriously dragged up the steep ascent, before, in the light of the gradually dawning day, the disheartened enemy streamed away across the plateau of the Spin Gawi Pass towards the Peiwar Kotal, with the mountain-guns hastening their retreat. At 7.30 General Roberts heliographed to Brigadier Cobbe that the whole of the column was on the summit.

Five guns were quietly pushed forward in the darkness to engage the batteries at the head of the Pass and at 6 o'clock in the morning the 8th Foot and 5th Punjab Infantry began the direct attack. Within three hours they were within effective range of their Snider and Martini-Henry rifles and, working slowly through the depths of a dense pine forest, drove the enemy before them until the first ridge was cleared. Brigadier Cobbe was severely wounded in the attack on a second ridge, and enemy resistance was so fierce that the guns kept up a sustained fire until 2.30 in the afternoon; they had to be cooled at intervals when they became dangerously hot. The Afghans turned their fire on the slowly advancing infantry now reduced to the 8th Foot and some 40 or 50 men separated from other regiments. They had to surmount a deep chasm and a mile and a half of rocky track, all under cannon and musketry fire, with the enemy showing no signs of wavering, but struggling to within 800 yards of the Afghan guns, they set up a withering fire that led to their abandonment.

From the flanking column, General Roberts ordered his men to advance immediately if the enemy showed signs of wavering and, although there were in fact no such signs, the 8th Regiment charged down the road, bayonets fixed, and the Kotal fell before their rush. The Afghans fled in such haste that they abandoned their tents and their guns; apart from their dead, there was no sign of the enemy troops: they had vanished among the forests or along the Kabul Road. A body of 4,000 men in a strong position with a number of guns had been dislodged at a cost to the British of 4 officers and 90 other ranks killed or wounded. The 8th Regiment with some guns, under the command of General Thelwall was left to garrison the Kotal whilst the rest of the troops marched on.

Under General Sir Donald Stewart, a force was operating in the vicinity of Kandahar and, on 16 January, the column passed through the Shikapur Gate of Kandahar and so captured this important city, the key to the whole country, without firing a shot — it had been deserted that morning by the Afghan troops who had fled to Kabul. A squadron of the 15th Hussars about 100 strong with a force of Afghan cavalry about twice its number blundered into each other during a dust storm at Siafoodeen on 4 January 1879 and, in the resulting mêlée, the Hussars had 2 men wounded as they put the native horsemen to rout with 24 dead and 9 taken prisoner.

British convoys were constantly being menaced in the Khost Valley and so General Roberts formed the Khost Valley Expedition composed of a squadron of the 10th Hussars, a wing of the 72nd Highlanders, with native infantry and cavalry and a mountain gun battery. On 6 January the force came up to the Fort of Matun where they were

120

met by a local chieftain and large numbers of well-armed tribesmen. The British camp was pitched with great care outside the fort; rifle pits were dug; picquets patrolled outside the camp area and every man stood-to. During the evening fires began to blaze on every hill, and it became evident that tribesmen were hovering all round; at daylight, the camp was surrounded by masses of Mangals, Wazaris and Kostwals massing for an attack.

The squadron of the 10th Hussars went out in a north-easterly direction and skirmished with the enemy, doing some excellent shooting with their short Martini-Henry carbines. The tribesmen moved rapidly into a rocky area so that the cavalry could get no nearer than 60 yards as they drew further and further from the camp. Suddenly musket-fire burst out on every side of the valley and crowds of tribesmen rushed across the plain towards the camp: the enemy had been gathering overnight in the villages to the British right rear and had attempted to lure away the cavalry before attacking. The mountain-guns created havoc amongst the closely packed ranks, driving the tribesmen back until the only serious attack seemed to be that against the right front, where thousands of natives were massing. Turning on them, the artillery fired repeatedly until they began to stream off towards their villages in their rear. Then Roberts sent out his infantry in skirmishing order with cavalry on the flanks; they took each village in turn, ferreting out with the bayonet those tribesmen who had hidden in the houses. Over their heads shells from the mountain-guns burst amongst the fleeing enemy. The native cavalry then took up the pursuit and soon the whole area was cleared of tribesmen. The villages were destroyed and the force returned to camp at Matun, with 2 men killed and 4 wounded. The enemy lost at least 100 killed and twice that number wounded.

On 26 January General Roberts, leaving the wounded in the fort at Matun with a garrison of about 300, marched his column to Sabbri, about twelve miles away. The column had hardly got there when a message arrived that the Mangals were gathering in force to storm the camp at Matun, and so Roberts turned his column round and made a forced-march back, reaching the Matun area, where the valley was black with about 6,000 Mangal tribesmen preparing to storm the British camp. The sudden appearance of Roberts and his column took them by surprise and, as they did not immediately attack, Roberts decided to destroy the fort with gun-powder. Then, covered by the cavalry, the force began to retreat with tribesmen all around them, frequently skirmishing until they were driven off by the cavalry carbines at about 600 yards range. When the infantry and artillery had put 3½ miles between themselves and the enemy, the cavalry retired to join the column and the Mangals abandoned the chase.

During this period Brigadier Thelwall, commanding the force left at the Peiwar Kotal, had strongly fortified the position in expectation of an attack by the Mangals but, as at Matun, they held back and finally dispersed to their mountain strongholds.

On 21 February 1879, the Amir of Afghanistan died and was succeeded by his son, Yakoub Khan, who celebrated his accession by stirring up the frontier tribes to rebel against the British so that expeditions had to be sent to deal with them. On 2 April

Brigadier Gough marched out of Jellalabad with a force of about 400 men of the 17th Regiment, 300 of the 27th Regiment, 300 native infantry, two squadrons each of the 10th Hussars with Guide cavalry and four Royal Horse Artillery guns. Near the small town of Futtehabad, Gough found large numbers of tribesmen entrenched behind stone walls and breastworks in a position that could only be attacked from the front, and so, covered by cavalry, the guns went forward and opened fire at 1,400 yards, gradually withdrawing whilst continuing to fire; the enemy was drawn from his position and came swarming out in pursuit, even attempting a flanking movement by scrambling down a ravine and coming up within 250 yards of the guns. All the tribesmen were now out in the open and their great length of front nearly turned the left flank of Gough's small force but, coming up quickly, his infantry effectively checked them by briskly file-firing and by using bayonets at close quarters. In spite of the Horse Artillery sending shell after shell screaming and exploding among the enemy the tribesmen pushed on to within 400 yards of the guns.

Now that the enemy was well into the open, the Hussars and Guides charged, led by Major Wigram Battye, whose reputation on the frontier was already tremendous. While the cavalry cut and re-cut its way through the wild crowds of shrieking tribesmen, Battye was killed, and this so enraged the Guides that they went berserk. Although vastly superior in numbers, the tribesmen began to fall back, then faltered and fled, pursued by the cavalry for 5 miles and leaving more than 400 killed on the field. British casualties were 40 killed and wounded, the Guides suffering most heavily. Gough blew up the towers and some of the villages before returning.

General Tytler's division was sent to teach the Mohmands, the Shinwarris and the Afridis that a rising in the British rear was unwise. In a very successful expedition which cost the enemy more than 250 killed, the Afridis were dispersed, five villages were destroyed and some sharp fighting took place.

During the advance of the united columns on Kabul the young Amir Yakoub Khan asked for a peace conference at Gundamuk and on 26 May a treaty was signed which placed the affairs of Afghanistan under British control; guaranteed that country against foreign (ie Russian) aggression; and provided for a British Resident at Kabul and for the British to have complete command over the Khyber Pass.

33 The Third Afghan War 1879

In September 1879, after the murder of Sir Louis Cavagnari, the British Envoy in Kabul, and the surrender to the British of the Amir Yakoub Khan who had been dethroned by his own mutinous troops, General Roberts hastened back to the country and began to advance on Kabul. On 6 October forward cavalry patrols discovered large numbers of Afghans occupying a defile and range of hills between the towns of Charasiah and Kabul. The horsemen dismounted and engaged the enemy with carbine fire until the arrival of 3 Royal Artillery guns and a wing of the Gordon Highlanders with 100 native infantry and a squadron of native cavalry, all under Major White. At the same time General Baker's Infantry Brigade (67th Regiment, 72nd Regiment, and 92nd Regiment) was sent to carry the heights and push on towards the hills. In a spirited duel at 1,500 yards range, White's three guns engaged four rifled-guns of the enemy while the 92nd Regiment scaled the steep and rocky hillside. The Horse Artillery guns dispersed the enemy whenever he could be seen mustering for an attack, until his guns were silenced. Then the Highlanders routed the Afghans in an attack where Major White himself went on ahead and shot dead the Afghan leader. Four guns were captured in a defile and in

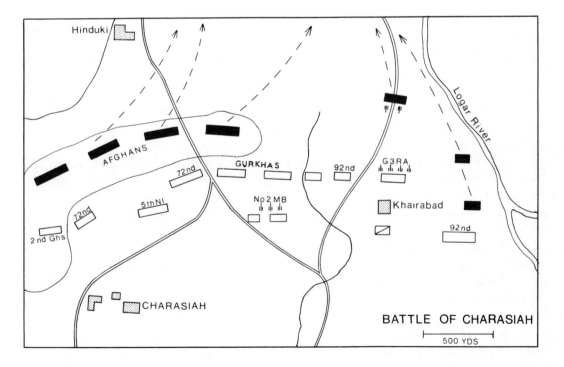

BATTLE OF CHARASIAH

500 YDS

their attack the Highlanders lost only 3 men killed and 6 wounded.

Major Baker's force had pushed forward over very precipitous ground through a range of hills defended by at least 4,000 of the enemy. Backed by the mountain-battery and some Gatling guns, the 72nd Highlanders led the attack, supported by native infantry, and for two hours the battle swayed to and fro, with the Gatlings jammed and the mountain-guns for once of little use. At last the hill was taken in the rear by a turning movement made to the right by the 92nd who, with pipes playing and colours flying, came rushing up the slope. The enemy gave way and the leading brigade crowned the heights. Before dark the Afghans were completely routed and fleeing towards Kabul with 400 killed and many wounded. 20 guns were abandoned. British losses were 83 killed and wounded. In this battle of Charasiah less than half of Robert's force had routed the entire army of Kabul and captured almost all its artillery.

In early December an attempt was made by two columns to trap the enemy, but the force of 500 men led by General Massy came into action unsupported and was defeated by 4,000 Afghans. The guns were lost, but the Gurkhas later recaptured them.

Welded into a strong and dangerous force by Mahomed Jan, a competent and audacious leader, the Afghans now made some partially successful attempts to capture the heights from which an attack could be made on Kabul. Knowing the enemy to be about 45,000 strong, General Roberts reluctantly abandoned his plans for offensive operations and withdrew his troops from all isolated positions in order to concentrate his whole force within the protection of the Sherpur cantonment, a mile outside Kabul; this gave a strong defensive position large enough to hold all the troops, the horses of the cavalry and the transport animals together with supplies and stores. The defences were strengthened, abattis were built on all sides, while the Engineers closed the gap between the western face of the Behmaru Heights and the western walls of Sherpur. Besides their twenty-three guns, the defence also utilised eighteen guns captured from the Afghans. A war beacon blazed on a ridge just above the city before daylight on 23 December and the dull roar of many thousand voices rose on the wind as the Afghans made a feint attack on the south-west angle of the defences (held by the 72nd Highlanders); then from the north-east, close to the village of Behmaru, they put in an attack in great force. Taking cover behind every ridge and rock, the enemy worked his way towards the defences of Behmaru to gain possession of a small village from which he was able to pour in a very heavy musketry fire. Mountain-guns failed to dislodge the tribesmen from this village but their steadily increasing numbers were turned back on a number of occasions as they rushed at the defences. At the same time, a very brisk fire was maintained against the south-west front and large bodies of men were seen massing as though to attack from the south and west.

Kept informed by telegraph and heliograph, General Roberts ordered four guns of the Horse Artillery to advance through the gorge towards the plain north of the village of Behmaru so as to bring cross-fire to bear on the village from which the Afghans were firing. The Punjab Cavalry dismounted and moved through the gorge to cover the advance of the guns, whose fire soon drove the enemy out of the village. This reverse, together with their losses in attacking the defences, discouraged the Afghans so that they began to stream out of all the villages they occupied, and at once Roberts ordered every sabre in pursuit. Out went the cavalry to circle well round to the north-east of Sherpur, cutting off the fugitives before they could reach the shelter of the hills, and later it was estimated that the enemy's losses were not less than 3,000 killed and wounded while the British had 5 killed and 33 wounded.

The garrison remained undisturbed in Kabul until Spring 1880, supplied by a continuous train of camels, oxen, mules, ponies and men in columns, laboriously traversing the deep and dark defiles that led from Peshawar to Kabul. The route was littered by the bones of baggage-animals: the Kurram column alone lost 9,496 camels, and by March 1880 it was estimated that 80,000 animals had perished.

Commanding a well-balanced force of 7,000 infantry, cavalry and artillery, Sir Donald Stewart left Kandahar early in April with orders to occupy Ghazni. On the morning of Monday 19 April the force came upon about 15,000 enemy horse and foot well positioned on an undulating ridge near Ahmed Kheyl, 23 miles south of Ghazni. Seeing Stewart's column, the enemy left his position and advanced rapidly, to come under artillery fire at 1,200 yards range. So fast did he advance that the range soon had to be reduced to 400 yards and then, as the tribesmen drew near, case-shot was used and finally the guns were loaded with shrapnel with heads towards the charge, to explode

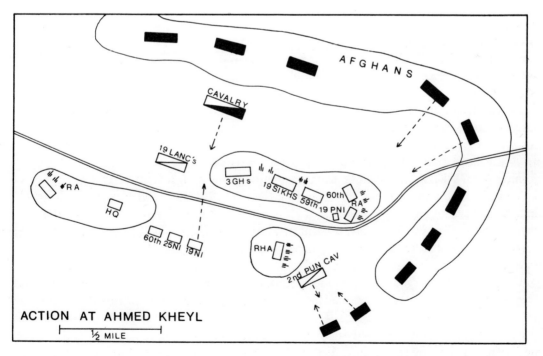

ACTION AT AHMED KHEYL
½ MILE

at the muzzle so that heaps of dead and dying littered the ground. At the same time, concealed by grassy ridges, the enemy cavalry was pouring down two ravines to turn Stewart's left flank, covered by the Bengal Lancers. Struck before it could charge, the Indian cavalry was sent reeling back in disorder right into the centre of Stewart's position, so that his force was now in a semicircle, with a gap in the centre.

In the face of heavy musketry and artillery fire, the Afghans displayed great courage, making a fierce attack upon the British flanks and front and pouring through the gap between a regiment and the guns. In spite of the infantry standing firm and the artillery pouring in shot at point-blank range whilst the cavalry charged repeatedly, the situation was very bad, for the British right flank had been badly shaken by the desperate on-slaught of the enemy, and fierce attacks by enemy horsemen on the left flank had rolled the cavalry back. The 3rd Gurkhas, who were formed in company squares with open spaces between, had a surging mass of men and horses forced down upon them but they opened fire at point-blank range on the enemy cavalry as it swept through. The Afghan horsemen were finally halted and then, relieved from the pressure on their rear, the British cavalry fell upon the shattered column with lance and sword and hurled it back.

The Afghans began to retreat to the cover of villages and orchard walls from which they kept up a parting fire as they gradually left the field. Their departure became a rout as they were pursued by the native cavalry. The British force had 17 killed and 115 wounded, whilst the enemy lost 1,000 dead and more than 2,000 wounded.

Stewart sent his cavalry forward to capture Ghazni; this was done without a shot being fired and then the men marched from Ghazni to Kabul, where, on 25 April, Stewart had a fierce encounter with 6,000 tribesmen, losing 2 killed and 11 wounded. On 2 May Sir Donald Stewart entered Kabul and took control of political affairs, but early in June he was ordered to evacuate the city as part of a British policy of with-drawing troops from Afghanistan.

Ayoub Khan, brother of Yakoub Khan and claimant to the throne, was meanwhile rallying considerable numbers to his standard and was marching from Herat with a large force of regular infantry and cavalry, thirty-six guns, and numbers of tribesmen from the most fierce and warlike of the western tribes. To prevent local tribes from joining Ayoub Khan, the Wali of Kandahar moved out with his native troops supported by Brigadier General Burrows commanding the 66th Regiment, with native infantry and cavalry, totalling 2,300 men and 6 guns. On 14 July, Wali's troops mutinied and were dispersed by Burrows' cavalry and artillery, leaving the small British force to face Ayoub Khan at the head of an army now swollen to more than 12,000 infantry and cavalry, including Russian artillery officers.

On 27 July the Afghan army made a flank march screened by hills to the north, and worked its way, undetected, along the northern slopes of a range of hills that bounded the plain on which stood the British camp. Believing the enemy to be at Maiwand, only 3 miles away, Burrows ordered an advance; cavalry skirmishing took place as the forces deployed into battle formation. Ayoub Khan deployed seven regiments of infantry in his centre with a number of guns; on his right were 400 cavalry and on his left 2,000 Ghazis, while the Afghan cavalry made a feigned attack and retreat on Burrows' right front. The British commander depleted his already weak force by dispatching two guns and a squadron of cavalry after the retreating enemy and then ordered his line to advance in support. He thus left an advantageous position and exchanged the shelter of a ruined fort and village for a position with undulating ground to his front that gave the enemy cover from his fire, and with heights from which the enemy's guns were able to play upon his front and flank troops. Although few in number, Burrows' rifled nine-pounders were superior in range and accuracy to the Afghan's smooth-bore artillery, but the advantage was lost when the range decreased to less than 1,000 yards.

Burrows had the 66th Regiment in the centre with Jacob's Rifles and the Bombay Grenadiers on the left and right; his guns were placed at intervals along the front. A charge of Afghan regular cavalry on the British left at the same time as the fanatical Ghazis hit the front and right caused the Bombay Grenadiers and Jacob's Rifles to fall back step-by-step. Two British guns were captured, to be recaptured by the bayonet but in the end one of them remained in possession of the enemy and was turned to fire upon the retreating British troops. The British position became a two-sided triangle with the Berkshire Regiment forming its apex, the native regiments at the sides being badly cut up by the Afghan artillery on the flanking heights. To counter this, Burrows sent out parties to skirmish up the hills which he should have occupied and held before

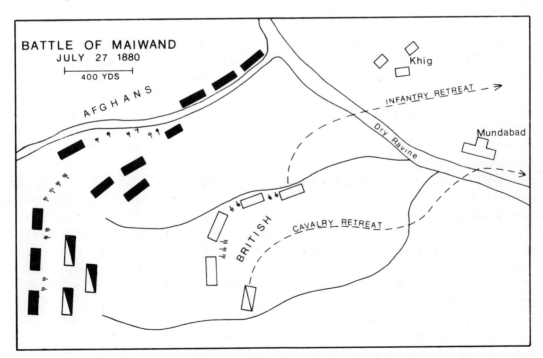

BATTLE OF MAIWAND
JULY 27 1880
400 YDS

AFGHANS

Khig

INFANTRY RETREAT

Dry Ravine

Mundabad

BRITISH

CAVALRY RETREAT

the battle began, but the men were beaten back. Then the Ghazis worked their way round to attack the rearguard and the baggage and stores were saved only at the cost of 100 killed and wounded. By 1 o'clock in the afternoon the 400 or so remaining men of the 66th Regiment, under fire from more than 4,000 rifles and 30 guns, fell back in good order by alternate wings, twice forming square when attacked by cavalry. In their attempt to cover the left wing, Jacob's Rifles were thrown back in hopeless disorder by hordes of yelling Ghazis and fled to the rear of the 66th, carrying that regiment's band with them. Stragglers from the 66th, Jacob's Rifles, the Bombay Grenadiers, and some artillerymen separated from their guns put up a dogged resistance from a small enclosure until ammunition ran out; then desperate hand-to-hand fighting took place. During this part of the action a British gun that had escaped the enemy fired so quickly and with such deadly effect that it became too hot to be serviceable and was captured.

Burrows succeeded in extricating the remains of his infantry and attempted to retreat along the Kandahar Road, but the troops were badly disorganised by thousands of terrified camp-followers. Meanwhile the cavalry was still making sporadic charges, and the artillerymen stuck bravely to the last remaining gun until they were cut down. From that moment the flight was confused and disastrous, with about 100 officers and men of the 66th Regiment making a determined stand in a garden surrounded by almost the whole Afghan army and fighting on until only 11 men were left with the regimental pet, a little white dog, scampering among them. Their ammunition gone, the small party charged out of the garden and stood in the open, back-to-back, until the last man had been shot down.

Throughout the battle, Burrows, who had two horses shot from under him, had set a most spirited example and now he led the few survivors of his force in a fighting retreat for 16 miles towards Kandahar. The few cavalry who remained made repeated charges to beat off pursuers until, 7 miles west of Kandahar, they were met by a small force who covered their disorderly retreat. The force lost 1,302 officers and men together with their guns. Two Victoria Crosses were awarded; two senior officers were court-martialled and honourably acquitted; and General Burrows was removed from the Brigade staff.

General Primrose, in command of Kandahar, withdrew his 3,000 men into the citadel and prepared for the expected assault. On 11 August, Ayoub Khan threw up siege works in front of Kandahar, deployed his 10,000 men around the citadel and opened fire on the city with his own guns and those he had captured at Maiwand. In an attempt to halt firing from a village near the citadel, an ill-conceived sortie was made on 16 August, to be completely repulsed with 200 casualties including most of the senior officers. On 26 August, Ayoub Khan moved his army from the immediate vicinity of Kandahar, although he still threatened the city.

On 8 August, Sir Frederick Roberts set off from Kabul to march 318 miles to Kandahar through mountainous country peopled by fierce and warlike tribes who might well seek to bar his way. The force consisted of the 9th Lancers; the 2nd

Battalion 60th Rifles; the 72nd Highlanders; native cavalry and infantry; two Royal Artillery batteries and one mountain battery — nearly 10,000 men with more than that number of horses, mules and other baggage animals, and thousands of native camp-followers. Extending fully 6 miles on the road, the column marched 16 miles a day under conditions of the strictest march discipline. After travelling 240 miles in seventeen marches, Roberts relieved the garrison of Khelat-i-Ghilzie and on 31 August, after some rearguard skirmishing with tribesmen, he was close enough to Kandahar to send out a reconnaissance in strength. Mountain-guns and cavalry moved along the Herat Road,

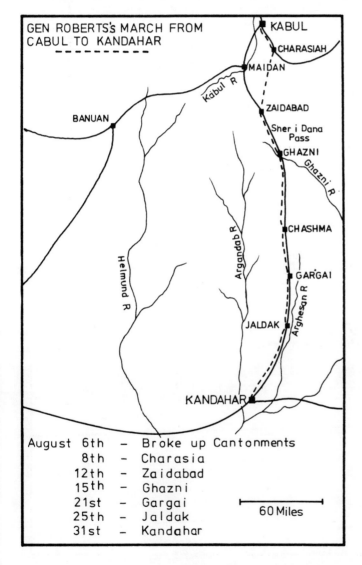

GEN ROBERTS's MARCH FROM
CABUL TO KANDAHAR
- - - - - - - - - -

KABUL
CHARASIAH
MAIDAN
Kabul R
ZAIDABAD
BANUAN
Sher i Dana
Pass
GHAZNI
Ghazni R
Argandab R
CHASHMA
Helmund R
GARGAI
Arghesan R
JALDAK
KANDAHAR

August 6th — Broke up Cantonments
        8th — Charasia
       12th — Zaidabad
       15th — Ghazni
       21st — Gargai
       25th — Jaldak
       31st — Kandahar

60 Miles

while Highlanders and native infantry went forward in skirmishing order opposed by large bodies of the enemy who were allowed to come within 200 yards and then were mowed down by heavy file-firing which drove them into cover. On the right flank, the cavalry and two mountain-guns were holding 5,000 Afghans at bay, dashing in and scattering them after they had been shaken by the artillery fire. So heavy were the Afghan attacks on the Gurkhas and Highlanders that they were forced to form in company squares whose independent file-firing shattered the attackers, who gave way and were pursued by Gurkhas and Lancers.

Roberts planned to attack Ayoub Khan's army, which was strongly entrenched on a precipitous mountain ridge, by a frontal attack which would clear the village of Gundi-Mulla; a movement left was then to turn the Paimal Hill and finally to take the Baba Wali in reverse and come up to Ayoub's camp at Mazra on its right flank. At 9.30 in the morning of 1 September, the Gurkhas and the 92nd Highlanders carried the village of Gundi-Mulla, and then the 72nd Highlanders and the Sikhs steadily advanced, under a hot fire from garden-walls and houses, to clear the way to the low spur of hills near Paimal. Fighting among the loopholed walled enclosures was desperate as the Ghazis hurled themselves upon the British and native infantry, dashing their shields against the bayonets and grappling with the men as they strove to wrench away their muskets. After most severe fighting the infantry emerged at the point of the hill and pressed on, sweeping the enemy through the closely wooded gardens and orchards to take the

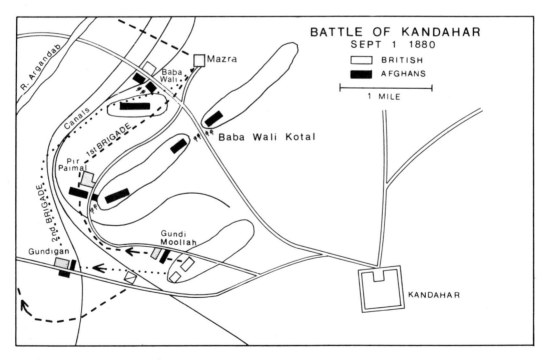

130

village of Paimal soon after noon.

Now the British encountered the regular soldiers of those regiments that had revolted in Kandahar; they were fighting from an entrenched camp westward of the Baba Wali Kotal, commanding an open space of ground. Guns on the Baba Wali were wheeled round so as to increase the heavy artillery fire poured upon the advancing troops, while the screw-guns of the mountain battery replied. The Highlanders and Gurkhas stormed forward to drive the enemy out of his entrenchments and then took the ridge that over-looked Ayoub's camp in the entrenched village of Mazra. Quite defeated, the Afghan force fled in all directions, leaving thirty-two guns behind. British casualties were 40 killed and 228 wounded, while the enemy lost about 1,200 men. The pursuit, taken up by the cavalry, was greatly hampered by broken ground. The Battle of Kandahar was the last action of the Afghan War and in September the Kandahar Field Force was broken up and General Roberts returned to India.

34 The Zulu War 1879

Sir Bartle Frere, the High Commissioner, was convinced that the Zulu nation should be restrained. He therefore demanded unacceptable conditions from Cetewayo, the Zulu Chief. When these were not answered in early 1879, Great Britain declared war on the Zulu nation. Before this, preparations for the forthcoming war had been taking place in the Colony of Natal and a large force was gathered together under the command of Lieutenant-General Lord Chelmsford. It consisted of 7 regiments of British regular infantry; 2 squadrons of mounted infantry; 1 naval brigade; 2 companies of Royal Engineers; 800 Colonial volunteers and police; 300 native horsemen, and a native infantry contingent about 9,000 strong, totalling 6,639 imperial and colonial troops; there were 9,035 natives with 802 conductors and drivers in charge of the 700 wagons that formed the transport train.

The force was to enter Zululand in five columns at different points, concentrating on Ulundi, the capital. Lord Chelmsford attached himself and his staff to the strongest and most important third column, made up of the 1st and 2nd Battalions 24th Regiment; 1 squadron of mounted infantry; about 200 Natal volunteers; 150 Natal Police;

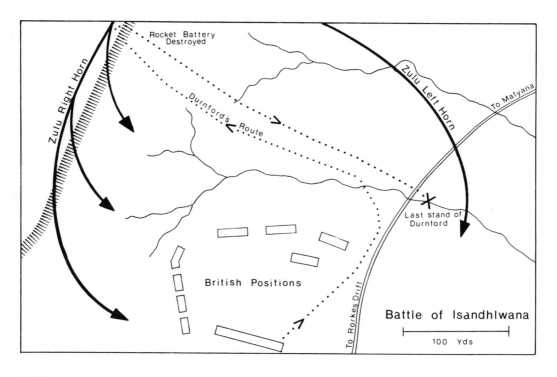

Battle of Isandhlwana

2 Battalions of the native contingent; some native Pioneers and 6 Royal Artillery guns. Crossing the Buffalo River on 11 January, the column moved slowly forward, constructing roads for the guns and transport over swamps and heavy ground. It was not until 20 January that camp was pitched at the foot of the Isandhlwana Hill; the tents and long lines of picketed horses were in regular order, but the wagons that should have been ranged end-to-end around the camp to form a laager were drawn up uselessly in line in the rear.

Receiving information that large numbers of the enemy were on a range of hills about twelve miles away, Chelmsford marched out at daylight on 22 January with the 2nd Battalion 24th Regiment, the mounted infantry and four guns. Lieutenant-Colonel Pulleine was left in command of the camp with 6 companies of the 24th, 2 guns of the Royal Artillery, and about 80 mounted men and 4 companies of the native contingent reinforced during the morning when Colonel Durnford rode in with some of the second column and the rocket-battery. Reports began to come in of large numbers of the enemy approaching from all directions, and so Durnford took to the front of the position two troops of Natal native horse and the rocket-battery, escorted by a company of the native contingent. Coming upon large bodies of rapidly moving Zulus about five miles from the camp, he extended his men and opened a steady fire but was forced into a steady retreat by overwhelming numbers, while the rocket-battery, deserted by its escort, was overrun and slain to a man. Sorely pressed, Durnford's men disputed every inch of ground until they made a desperate last stand in a dried-up river bed near the camp.

The Zulus attacked the camp in a half-circle, with another force pushing round the English left to cut the wagon road and line of retreat to Rorke's Drift. The defenders were firing steadily and to good effect while the guns, which had been firing shell, now poured in case-shot at close quarters. At this the Zulus wavered and the wide-swept horns of their army worked their way round the flanks to show themselves in the rear of the English position just at the moment when the native contingent broke and fled in disorder, laying open the right and rear of the 24th. The firing began to slacken, because reserve ammunition-boxes were screwed down and could not be opened. The Zulus poured through the fatal gap in the line and the English soldiers were lost in the middle of a fierce hand-to-hand conflict as horse and foot, English and Zulu, struggled slowly in confused groups through the camp towards the road to Rorke's Drift. Surrounded by bodies, the 24th stood their ground and fought to the last man, while fleet-footed Zulus chased fugitives trying to reach the river. More than 1,300 Europeans and natives were lost in this action, but at least 2,000 Zulus were killed and hundreds wounded.

Shortly after 3 pm on 22 January, mounted fugitives from Isandhlwana galloped into Rorke's Drift, to tell the story of the disaster and to report that a large force of Zulus was now advancing on the post. A mission station of two stone buildings with thatched roofs at a crossing point of the Buffalo River, Rorke's Drift was in direct line of communication with Natal. It was garrisoned by a company of the 2nd Battalion 24th Regiment under Lieutenant Bromhead and Lieutenant Chard of the Royal Engineers. In the small hospital were some sick and wounded men.

Chard hastily ordered the place to be put in a state of defence; the walls were to be loop-holed and barricaded, and parapets were to be built up from bags of mealies around overturned ox-wagons. A company of native infantry, part of the garrison of the Drift, fled on hearing of the approach of the Zulus, so that the strength of the force was 139, of whom 35 were sick or wounded men in hospital. About 4,000 Zulus appeared at 4.30 in the afternoon and from then until after midnight the post was continuously attacked. During the course of the conflict, repeated attacks drove back the desperately fighting defenders until they were confined to one building and an enclosure with a redoubt of mealie bags. The hospital, defended to the last by its patients, was set on fire and provided the light by which the fighting took place until the small hours of the morning, when the Zulus retired at the approach of an English column, carrying away their wounded and leaving about 400 dead around the post. The garrison lost 17 killed and 12 wounded. Lieutenants Chard and Bromhead, together with nine other soldiers, received the Victoria Cross for their gallantry.

Alarmed by the sound of firing, Chelmsford's force had returned to Isandhlwana to spend an anxious night amid the ruins of the camp. Next morning the men marched towards Rorke's Drift, expecting to find the post burned to the ground and its garrison

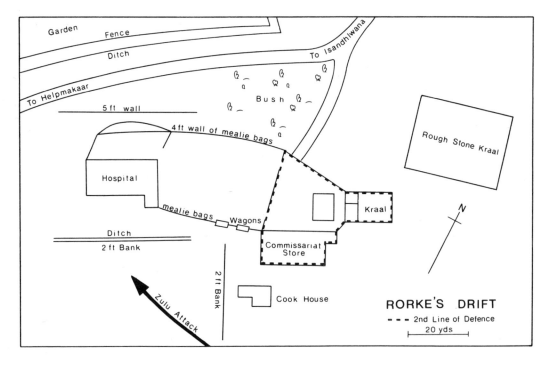

slain, but they discovered that its defence had secured the Colony of Natal from invasion. Chelmsford's despatches reached London in February and accelerated the sending of powerful reinforcements. In South Africa, colonial troops undertook duties at Capetown and set free the regular garrison; the warship *Shah* embarked the St Helena garrison and sailed for Durban, providing an immediate force of 650 men including 300 bluejackets, while the movement orders of the 57th Regiment were cancelled and the troops were sent to Napal.

At the end of January three fortified posts guarded the frontier of Natal: Colonel Wood had a well entrenched camp at Kambula Hill and the remains of the third column held Rorke's Drift, now heavily fortified, while Colonel Pearson, at Etshowe with about 1,200 European soldiers, was right in the middle of occupied territory and had either to be reinforced or relieved. Deciding on the latter, on 27 March Chelmsford sent out a column formed of the 57th and 91st Regiments; 6 companies of the 60th; 5 companies of the 99th and 2 companies of the 3rd Regiment; a naval brigade; a squadron of mounted infantry; 2 field-guns; 4 rocket tubes and 2 Gatling guns, making 3,390 Europeans and 2,280 natives, with 122 wagons. Over a comparatively open route, the column marched cautiously in the closest possible order, surrounded by a screen of mounted troops and bivouacking at night in a laager of wagons. On the third day, 31 March, large bodies of Zulus were seen and an attack was anticipated at the Ghingilovo stream where the British laagered for the night. At daybreak, two dense columns of

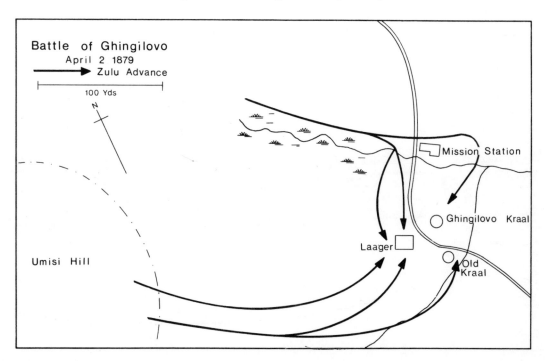

Battle of Ghingilovo
April 2 1879
Zulu Advance
100 Yds
N
Mission Station
Ghingilovo Kraal
Laager
Old Kraal
Umisi Hill

Zulus came rapidly in sight on the further side of the river crossing at different points and deploying into a wide and loose order, while at the same time another force came in to attack the southern and western faces of the defences. The Gatling guns opened fire at 1,000 yards and, although frequently jamming, knocked over numbers of Zulus but failed to stop their advance. When the leading lines of Zulus got within 300 yards, a sudden sheet of flame burst from the English position and lines of natives fell as though swept down by a scythe. From the cover afforded by the long grass, the Zulus kept up a heavy but erratic rifle fire with the weapons they had captured at Isandhlwana; attack after attack was made with despairing courage. None got to close quarters; the Zulus were blasted by withering and steady volleys until they were scattered in confusion all over the plain. Chelmsford now launched the cavalry at the Zulu flank and the little band of horsemen put the enemy groups to hasty and disordered flight. British losses were 11 killed and 52 wounded in this action, which made it possible for Pearson's garrison at Etshowe to be relieved and withdrawn to Tugela.

Colonel Evelyn Wood at Kambula made a diversion in the north in order to draw away forces who might have opposed the march to Etshowe, planning an audacious operation calculated to draw a large Zulu force in reprisal. He attacked the Hlobane mountain some twenty miles from Kambula; this was a table-top eminence about three miles long with precipitous sides, with the only access to the summit a few difficult paths winding through rocks; it was commanded at every point by strong positions of

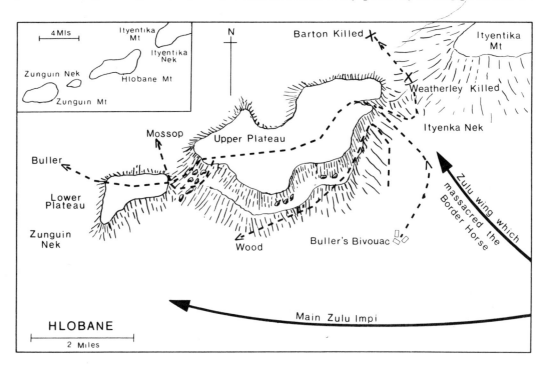

defence in caves and overhanging heights. It was occupied by a powerful Zulu tribe whose kraals were perched on an almost inaccessible terrace. The attack was entrusted to the mounted troops, divided into two parties: 400 white men and 277 natives under Lieutenant-Colonel Redvers Buller went against the eastern end and formed the main attacking force, while 200 white men and 440 natives under Lieutenant-Colonel Russell created a diversion at the other end of the mountain.

The two forces left Kambula and on 28 March, under cover of a morning mist Buller's party made a successful surprise assault up a narrow and very steep path, and the Zulus were routed in disorder on all sides, but just as Buller was about to withdraw from the heights a Zulu army was seen moving swiftly towards the Kambula camp. Colonel Wood ordered Russell's force to a point where it could cover Buller's retreat, but it went to the wrong place and took no further part in the operations. On the upper plateau, the heartened natives began to press very heavily upon the small party, leaving them as their only line of retreat a precipitous path at the western end of the plateau, down which many of the horses, although African bred and therefore surefooted, fell headlong from top to bottom. Buller was encumbered with wounded men and many of his horses had been killed, but he conducted the retreat with steadiness and heroism. With his Frontier Light Horse and a Boer contingent, he led the rearguard that held the enemy in check until the party reached level ground and were able to make their way back to Kambula.

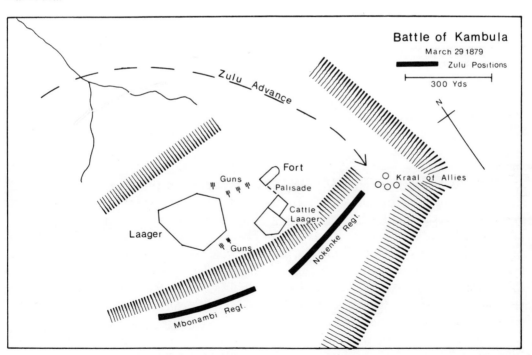

On 29 March, the Zulu army attacked the Kambula position defended by just over 2,000 men of all arms, including natives and sick. It consisted of a large wagon laager surrounding a hospital and stores, with a strong redoubt holding three companies of the men on a small knoll about 150 yards to the west. The Zulu army attacked with its right wing circling round the camp to the north and centre; the left wing kept to the south, out of artillery range. To prevent the whole Zulu army from delivering a simultaneous combined attack, Wood sent Buller and Russell out with the mounted men to tempt the Zulu right wing to a premature engagement. Pursued by the fleet-footed Zulus, the small party retreated to the camp until they drew the enemy within range, when the artillery opened fire. Committed to the attack, the Zulus pressed on and, in spite of inflicting heavy losses, did not get closer than 200 yards to the laager and redoubt. The Zulu centre and left assaulted the west and south of the camp, taking advantage of the broken ground that sheltered them from rifle fire, but Wood threw in a counter-attack of two companies of the 80th Regiment, whose massed musketry forced the Zulus back. Throughout the day they made attack after attack, each being beaten back by sheer weight of fire until late afternoon they began to retire, hotly pursued by Buller and his mounted men who kept pace with the running Zulus whilst maintaining a ceaseless and galling fire from the saddle in a pursuit that lasted more than 7 miles. The British force lost 28 killed and 55 wounded in this operation.

By the end of June, Lord Chelmsford had been strongly reinforced by four generals, two regiments of cavalry, two batteries of artillery, five battalions of infantry, and strong detachments of the Engineers and the Service Corps. Slowly and in the face of little opposition the force marched towards the Zulu king's kraal at Ulundi. On 3 July, Chelmsford crossed the Umvolosi River into open country with his force of 4,166 Europeans and 958 natives with twelve guns and two Gatlings, marching in a hollow square with the native contingent, ammunition and tool-carts in the centre; the force was screened by the cavalry, scouting wide on either side. When they were within a mile and a half of Ulundi, the Zulus began to mass and move towards the huge square which halted with every man facing outwards, the cavalry falling back and entering its protection.

Erratically firing their captured rifles, the Zulus advanced in a great converging circle. The artillery opened fire and shells were soon exploding with great effect amongst the masses of Zulus advancing over the open ground. When the natives came within rifle-range, steady and well-aimed infantry volleys began to take their toll and the Gatlings, though impeded by frequent jamming, rattled out showers of bullets. Prevented from making contact by sheer weight of fire, the Zulus began to waver and fall back. Chelmsford sent out the 17th Lancers to sweep down upon the now fleeing Zulus in a well-timed charge that turned the defeat into a hopeless rout. Buller and his mounted riflemen followed and the small knots of Zulus were scattered and overthrown. It was estimated that more than 20,000 Zulus were in the field at Ulundi and that their losses exceeded 1,500. The English lost 13 men killed and 78 wounded.

Sir Garnet Wolseley had been sent out to supersede Lord Chelmsford, but to all intents and purposes the war was over when he arrived, although Cetewayo was not captured until 29 August.

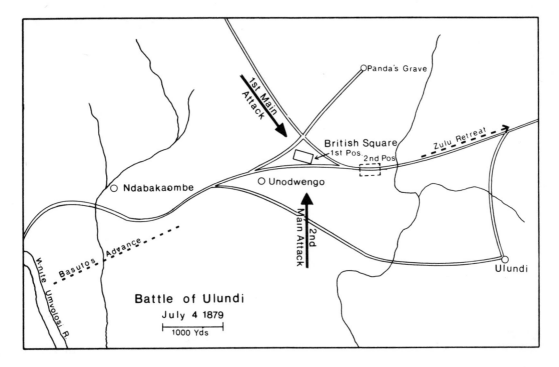

Battle of Ulundi
July 4 1879
1000 Yds

35 Operations on the North-West Frontier 1880-4

Expedition against the Mohmands, 1880

While the British army was occupied in Afghanistan, the Mohmands rebelled and on 11 January 1880 crossed the river into British territory. On 14 January a column was sent out from Dakka to make a frontal attack upon the Mohmand position, while another column from Landi Kotal attacked in flank and rear: with the river in their rear and under attack from all sides, the enemy was almost certain to be destroyed. The Dakka column consisted of 94 sabres of the 6th Dragoon Guards, 110 men of the 1st/25th King's Own Scottish Borderers; Bengal cavalry and 600 native infantry with four guns; and Horse Artillery, under the command of Colonel Boisragon. On the morning of 15 January the force was drawn up facing the Gara heights where the Mohmands had constructed strong breastworks and entrenchments. After an hour and a half's shelling by the artillery, the tribesmen were driven from their entrenchments and were dispersing when the infantry, covered by the fire of the guns, was sent in to advance steadily up the rugged precipitous hillside. By midday, the tribesmen were fleeing, completely routed, down the reverse slopes.

The Landi Kotal column, consisting of the 5th Fusiliers and the 25th King's Own Scottish Borderers with native cavalry and infantry and guns, had to make their way in single file along a very narrow path, so precipitous that some mountain-battery mules went tumbling over the edge. It was repeatedly necessary to send forward skirmishing parties to occupy heights commanding the route, and at one stage a 1,000ft hill had to be cleared by a storming-party of infantry. It was not until 5 o'clock in the afternoon that troops arrived within range of the river bank along which the enemy were fleeing, and although the mountain-guns opened up at 1,000 yards the enemy made good his escape and crossed the river.

Because of the late arrival of this column the combined movement was a failure, but the Mohmands had suffered a severe defeat, losing 70 killed and 140 wounded. The British losses were 2 killed and 3 wounded. The Horse Artillery fired 200 shells and the infantry used up 14,000 round of small arms and ammunition in this operation.

Expedition against the Malik Shahi Wazir Settlements, 1880

A force under Brigadier-General J. J. H. Gordon, consisting of 250 men of the 85th Regiment (Kings Shropshire Light Infantry) with 250 native cavalry and the same number of native infantry with two Royal Artillery guns, went out to extract fines levied against this tribe for cattle-stealing. Knowing that the expedition had to traverse the whole of the Kabul Khel settlements to reach those of the Malik Shahis the tribe felt that they would have sufficient warning to enable them to escape to the western hill country. To avoid this, on the night of 27 October 1880 the British force marched from Thal, making a wide detour so that they arrived at their intended positions by daybreak. The villagers awoke to find themselves surrounded. 2,000 head of cattle and 109 prisoners were taken and returned with the force to Thal. On 30 October the tribal chiefs came in and made their submissions and paid their fines. The prisoners were then released.

Expedition against the Mahsud Wazirs, 1881

With the end of the Afghan campaign, troops were available to deal with the Mahsud Wazirs who had been concerned in several serious outrages on the Thal-Kurram Road. Two columns were assembled and moved out in April 1881. From Tank, the first column was under Brigadier-General T. J. Kennedy and consisted of 4,000 native infantry cavalry and artillery of the Punjab Frontier Force. The second Column under Brigadier-General J. J. H. Gordon was formed at Bannu and included the 4th Battalion Rifle Brigade, native infantry, cavalry and mountain artillery with Royal Artillery guns. The two columns were accompanied by nearly 9,000 camp-followers, more than 4,000 mules, 1,500 ponies and 6,500 camels.

Keeping in touch by heliograph, the two columns advanced through Wazir country, meeting very little resistance, for most of the inhabitants of the area had never seen a European and their attitude was naively friendly. The expedition broke up on 22 May; it had sustained 32 casualties and proved to the Mahsuds that the natural difficulties of their country could not protect them from punishment.

In November and December 1881 the Bozdar Field Force, which included the Manchester Regiment, marched back to India from Kandahar and, striking off north-east through unknown country, opened up a new route.

The Zhob Valley Expedition, 1884

The depredations of the aggressive tribesmen of this region made a settled frontier impossible and allowed only sporadic work to be done on roads and railways. To warn off the tribesmen, an expedition was ordered into the Zhob Valley in October 1884. Under Brigadier-General Sir O. V. Tanner, it included the 1st Battalion Worcestershire Regiment; the 2nd Battalion North Staffordshires; and the 1st Battalion North Lancashires; native infantry and cavalry made up the remainder of the force, which totalled 4,220 infantry, 561 cavalry and 10 guns. Only scattered resistance and sniping were encountered and, after marching 700 miles, the force was withdrawn on 22 November. There were no casualties but considerable sickness amongst the troops because of the general unhealthiness of the area during this period of the year.

36 The First Boer War 1881

The Transvaal was formally annexed to Great Britain in April 1877, but three years later, on 16 December, the Boers proclaimed a Republic. On 20 December a detachment of the 94th Regiment marching from Lydenburg to Pretoria was intercepted by a strong party of mounted Boers who, when the column-commander refused to turn back, opened fire with deadly effect. In ten minutes 155 officers and men out of a total of 259 became casualties before the wounded British commander surrendered. Losing only 2 men killed and 5 wounded, the Boers were friendly towards their captives and helped to treat the wounded.

Sir George Pomeroy Colley, High Commissioner for South-Eastern Africa, hurried forward towards the frontier with a few companies of infantry stationed in Natal, a naval brigade, a squadron of Dragoons and mounted infantry, together with the Natal Mounted Police. Colley despised the Boers and was eager to distinguish himself before he was superseded by an officer of higher rank. Leading a relief column to raise the siege of the Transvaal towns, on 28 January 1881 he moved out to attack the Boers on Laing's Nek, a ridge about 23 miles north of Newcastle. The British force totalled about 1,160 men and consisted of five companies of the 58th, five companies of the 3rd Battalion of the 60th Regiment, 75 men of the Naval Brigade, 150 mounted men under Major Brownlow, and 4 guns. At 9 am the British force formed up with the mounted squadron on the left. After the guns had shelled parts of the enemy's position and the naval brigade had sent rockets into the Boer reserves in the rear of the Nek, the 58th advanced, covered by the mounted squadron on their right. In the face of heavy fire from a strong Boer force holding the hilltop, the mounted men swept up the hill, although the ground was completely unsuitable for cavalry and the horsemen should have been used as mounted infantry. The leading troop took heavy casualties and soon all their commanders were down. Fatigued and broken by the efforts of their uphill charge and unable to make any headway, the whole squadron gave way and retreated down the hill. Meanwhile the 58th was slowly progressing through the long entangling grass of the steep ascent in the face of a deadly accurate fire from the invisible Boers on the ridge above. When the cavalry was repulsed, the Boers moved down and opened fire on the now-exposed right flank and rear of the 58th. Soon every mounted officer was down and, with men falling fast on all sides, the order to retire was given. As befitted the last occasion on which the colours were carried into action by a British battalion, the men fell back without haste or confusion ' . . . in good order and with an erect and soldierly bearing . . . ' to re-form at the foot of the slope.

In spite of considerable British bravery, the battle of Laing's Nek was an unquestionable and severe defeat with 198 casualties — the 58th had to bury 75 officers and men

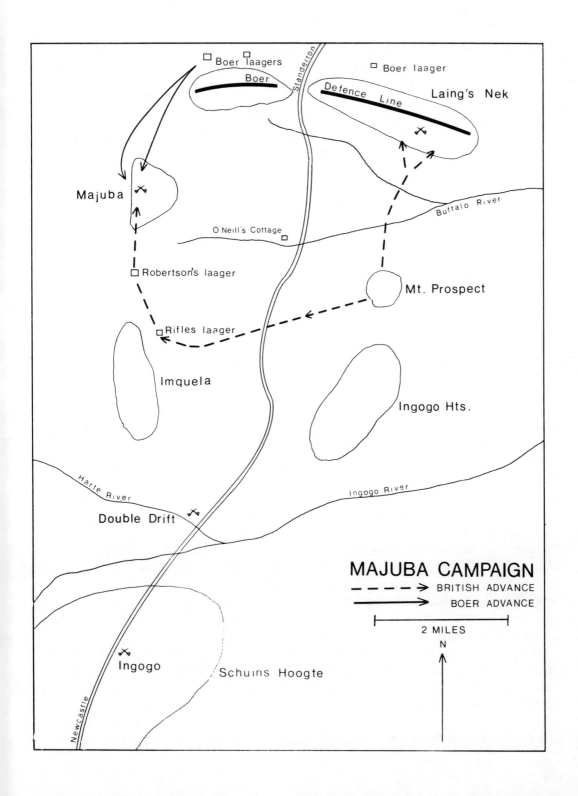

Boer Taagers

Boer

Standerton

Boer laager

Defence Line

Laing's Nek

Majuba

Buffalo River

O'Neill's Cottage

Robertson's laager

Mt. Prospect

Rifles laager

Imquela

Ingogo Hts.

Harte River

Ingogo River

Double Drift

MAJUBA CAMPAIGN

– – – → BRITISH ADVANCE

———→ BOER ADVANCE

2 MILES

N

Ingogo

Schuins Hoogte

Newcastle

out of a total strength of 494. The Boers lost 14 killed and 27 wounded. At the cease-fire, they behaved with great humanity, and freely allowed the wounded lying in front of their position to be cared for, bringing water to them and helping to bandage their wounds.

The confident Boers now began to intercept the British line of communications and to cut off convoys, so that the British camp was isolated. Determined to clear the Boers from the road, Colley marched out on the morning of 8 February with five companies of the 60th Rifles, two field- and two mountain-guns and a small detachment of mounted men. Leaving the mountain-guns and a company of infantry on a commanding crest north of the River Ingogo, about five miles south of his camp, he crossed with the main body and formed up on the south bank, where a gentle slope rose to the foot of a flat-topped ridge strewn with rocks and boulders and irregularly cut by rocky depressions. As the troops ascended the rise to the ridge, the Boers galloped forward and, taking advantage of the cover afforded by the intersecting valleys, directed a heavy and active fire on the guns and the skirmishers. The mountain-guns came into action and the engagement became heavy, until at noon companies of the 60th were pushed forward in the face of a deadly fire from behind cover.

The guns were in action with case shot at a range of less than 500 yards and the gunners who were freely exposed suffered heavily until the withdrawal of the guns, which fired only occasionally for the rest of the action. A company of the 60th who had advanced to cover the guns in the face of close-range Boer fire had many casualties. Realising that the enemy was being reinforced, Colley sent back to the camp for three companies of the 58th, who were ordered to move out and occupy the ridges north of the river and to cross it in support of the troops already deeply engaged and reduced by heavy losses. Convinced that the enemy intended to attack him next morning in overwhelming strength, Colley decided to withdraw under cover of darkness. It was a very cold, black night with the rain falling in torrents and, after the wounded had been searched for in the darkness and the horses from the abandoned ammunition waggons had been hitched to the guns, the force moved back in hollow square with the guns in the centre and the infantry in skirmishing order on four sides. The swollen and rapidly running river had to be crossed by the detachment in a body with locked arms, but even so many men were swept away. At 4 o'clock in the morning the force reached Colley's camp, although companies of the 58th Regiment spent the night on the northern ridges and were not withdrawn until the following day. The British losses amounted to 139 officers and men against the Boers' 8 killed and 6 wounded.

On 17 February Brigadier-General Sir Evelyn Wood VC arrived in Newcastle with the reinforcements from India – the 15th Hussars, the 2nd Battalion 60th Rifles and the 92nd Highlanders. Wood told Colley to attempt no further advance until he was stronger, and then he himself returned to Pietermaritzburg while Colley marched the new arrivals to his old camp. Sir George Colley was rated one of the most brilliant officers ever to have passed through the Staff College, although his experience of actual warfare was

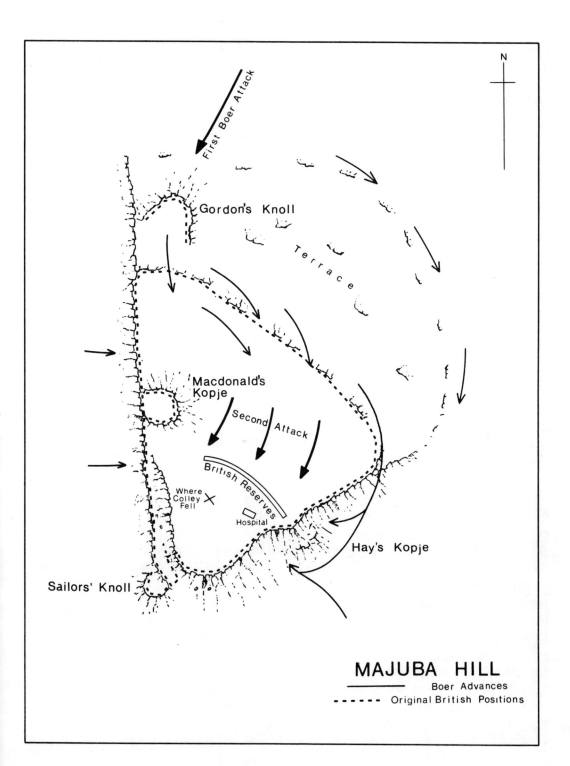

N

First Boer Attack

Gordon's Knoll

Terrace

Macdonald's
Kopje

Second Attack

British Reserves

Where
Colley
Fell ✕

Hospital

Hay's Kopje

Sailors' Knoll

MAJUBA HILL

Boer Advances

- - - - - Original British Positions

slender and he was unfamiliar with the character and temperament of the Boers. Thoroughly incensed by his two bloody defeats and regardless of his instructions not to advance further, he decided on a reconnaissance-in-force to the summit of the Majuba mountain, east of Laing's Nek — the highest point in the area. Knowing that a Boer force occasionally held the hilltop in daytime, Colley resolved to climb it by night, and at 10 pm on 26 February he marched out with a force of 22 officers and 627 men, formed of two companies of the 58th Regiment, the Naval Brigade, and three companies of the 92nd Regiment, while two companies of the 2nd Battalion 60th Regiment later moved out to a position at the foot of Inquela Hill and, further on, Captain Robertson's company of the 92nd dropped off as a link upon the narrow Nek between the Inquela and the Majuba, with orders to entrench themselves.

In single file, guided by friendly natives, the troops climbed the steep and rugged sides of Majuba, some 6,200 feet above sea level and more than 2,000 feet above the Boer position. It was a strenuous ascent for the heavily burdened men who had to negotiate great boulders, deep clefts, sharp crags and treacherous loose stones, sometimes having to climb on hands and knees, and it was not until 5 o'clock in the morning that the exhausted force, hopelessly confused during their upward scramble, gained the summit. Now only about 400 strong, the weary soldiers dropped where they stood to wait for daybreak. No entrenching tools had been brought, and some of the men tried to obtain cover by throwing up barriers of turf and stones. At dawn the Boers in the lower camp saw the British occupation of the mountain and considered a withdrawal but, seeing the troops on the summit to be in no great strength and without artillery, they began to climb the mountain-side under cover of boulders and shrubs. The older men, who were picked shots, supported the storming-party, firing at every soldier who exposed himself over the edge of the plateau.

As the morning passed, the attacking Boers hemmed in the British position on the north, the east and the south-west, climbing slowly and steadily upwards and moving quickly from cover to cover, protected by the steady and accurate fire of their comrades. As they were not in sufficient strength to hold the whole edge of the plateau, the defenders had to move from point to point in order to repulse the enemy advance. At noon the Boers reached the crest and opened a deadly, short-range fire. Unnerved by the accurate shooting, the morale of the British soldiers began to waver and the reserve, lying in the centre dip of the plateau out of reach of the enemy fire so that they had not suffered any losses, huddled for cover behind rocks and, when ordered up in support of the firing line, refused to move in spite of the threats and pleas of their officers. Sir George Colley was shot through the head and killed just before the remaining British soldiers suddenly decided that they had had enough and fled. Standing on the edge of the plateau, the Boers directed an accurate and persistent fire on the fugitives, picking the men off as if they were shooting game. Only the entrenchment made by the company of the 92nd prevented the slaughter from being much greater, although heavy fire soon made even this untenable and the survivors retreated under a murderous fire from the Boers, who then occupied the position. The surviving fugitives from the Majuba and the entrenchment reached camp under cover of artillery fire without any Boer attempts at pursuit.

The Boer leaders allowed the wounded to be carried in and a temporary hospital was established at a farmhouse near the foot of the mountain. Sir George Colley's body was brought into camp and buried with full military honours. Of the 650 officers and men in action on this disastrous day, 90 were killed, 330 wounded, 58 were prisoners and 2 were missing. The 92nd had 125 casualties; the 58th 93 and the naval brigade 36 men, more than half their strength. The Boers had 1 man killed and 5 wounded.

On 23 March peace terms were signed by Sir Evelyn Wood and the Boer leaders, giving the Transvaal people the right to complete self-government subject to the suzerainty of the Queen.

The total British force in South Africa or on the way there at the close of hostilities was made up of 13 infantry regiments, 5 cavalry regiments, 22 guns and 3 naval brigades — a total of nearly 20,000 men, exclusive of the British garrisons besieged in the Transvaal. If every Boer capable of bearing arms had been in the field, their forces would not have totalled more than 8,000 men. Throughout the short war the Boers lost 43 killed and 58 wounded whilst the British had more than 800 casualties.

37 The Bombardment of Alexandria 1882

The Battles of Kassassin and Tel el Kebir, 1882

In June 1882 Britain declared her support for the Khedive of Egypt against Arabi Pasha, his own Minister of War, who had set himself up as virtual dictator of Egypt. The Mediterranean fleet, under the command of Admiral Sir Beauchamp Seymour, lay off Alexandria for some weeks, unable to intervene to stop the rioting and massacre of Christians taking place in the town. During this period Arabi grew bolder, whilst his trained engineers frantically worked to strengthen the forts and to throw up new earth-works as they mounted heavy guns. On the morning of 10 July, the British demanded the surrender of the forts: if the demand was not met, they would be bombarded. Arabi rejected the ultimatum and so the British ships cleared for action. The fleet consisted of 8 battleships mounting sixty- and eighty-ton guns, with 11 small gunboats armed with sixty-four-pounders and seven-inch rifled-guns. The forts mounted mainly eighteen-ton and twelve-ton guns and large numbers of smaller calibre weapons.

At 7 am on 11 July the fleet opened fire and soon clouds of smoke and dust began to veil the forts. Under the dashing command of Lord Charles Beresford, little gunboats

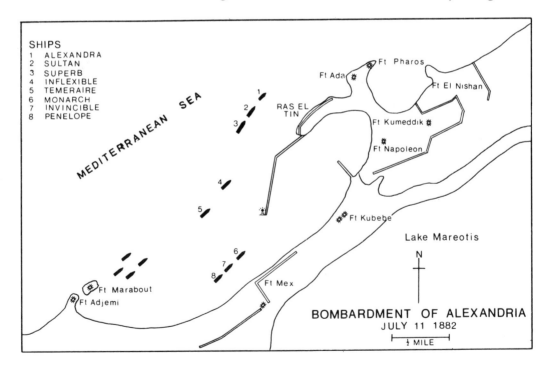

SHIPS
1 ALEXANDRA
2 SULTAN
3 SUPERB
4 INFLEXIBLE
5 TEMERAIRE
6 MONARCH
7 INVINCIBLE
8 PENELOPE

MEDITERRANEAN SEA

Ft Pharos
Ft Ada
Ft El Nishan
RAS EL TIN
Ft Kumeddik
Ft Napoleon
Ft Kubebe
Lake Mareotis
Ft Marabout
Ft Adjemi
Ft Mex

BOMBARDMENT OF ALEXANDRIA
JULY 11 1882
½ MILE

darted bravely inshore until they were under the very guns of the forts; their Gatlings and small-calibre guns sent fire rattling through the embrasures of the gun positions, causing heavy casualties amongst the gunners. The fleet bombarded the position through-out the morning, battering the earthworks and fortifications and occasionally setting off a magazine with a shattering roar. By one o'clock the return fire of the Egyptian guns ceased and a force was landed to occupy the forts. There was no sound or movement within the battered position and without any resistance the landing-party spiked the guns or burst the barrels of those that had not been put out of action by the bombardment.

Although one ship had received twenty-three hits and another fourteen, the fleet had only 10 men killed and 27 wounded after facing the fire of more than 100 guns for six hours; three of the ships did not have a single casualty and not one man was even wounded on any of the little gun-boats that fought so close in to the enemy guns. Arabi had lost almost every engineer and gunner in his service, as well as all his artillery. The fleet lay off-shore for two days while rioting, incendiarism and murder ran unchecked in the city, until at last landing-parties were ordered ashore and the sailors and marines fought a house-to-house battle with the looters until peace was restored.

Far from breaking the power of Arabi, the defeat spurred him to further resistance and a British army under Sir Garnet Wolseley was formed to land in Egypt, seek out Arabi Pasha and destroy his army. By mid-August an army of about 40,000 men from India, England and the Mediterranean garrisons of Malta, Cyprus and Gibraltar was aboard transports lying in Alexandria Bay. Arabi had about 60,000 fighting men disposed at the likeliest places all over the Delta — some in the neighbourhood of Alexandria, some at Cairo and some at Tel el Kebir, a commanding point on the railway between Ismailia on the Suez Canal and the capital. Wolseley intended Arabi to think that he was going to land the bulk of the British force in Alexandria and challenge him to battle at the Egyptian lines of Kafr Dowar; so, landing a force in that area as a feint, the convoy sailed eastwards towards the mouth of the Suez Canal. The British army began to disembark at Ismailia on 20 August.

Wolseley sent an advance-force under General Graham to Kassassin 20 miles into the very heart of the desert, to secure the precious water of the Freshwater Canal. Brushing aside enemy resistance at Mahuta, Graham reached Kassassin and entrenched himself, prepared to hold the position against all comers. His force, less than 2,000 strong, included a company of Royal Marine Artillery, the Duke of Cornwall's Regiment and the York and Lancasters, with some mounted infantry and a few guns. Stationed some miles to the rear at Mehsameh was Drury Lowe's Cavalry Brigade — the 7th Dragoon Guards and three squadrons of Household Cavalry, made up of the 1st and 2nd Life Guards and the Blues. The Egyptians made a number of attempts to drive the British from their position and on 28 August, aware that the enemy was preparing to attack him from the circle of sand-hills surrounding the area, Graham heliographed to the cavalry brigade asking them to come up and cover his right flank. By the time they arrived, the Egyptians had retired behind the sand-hills and so the cavalry went back to Mehsameh and off-saddled. In the cool of the evening the Egyptians again began to push forward from their sand-hills to threaten the British position; a messenger was therefore sent to call back the cavalry.

After holding his position for two hours, Graham ordered a counter-attack and general advance of his line. The cavalry moved forward, guided by gun flashes, and suddenly came upon the extreme left of the Egyptians who turned heavy gunfire upon them. Clattering and jingling to the front, the guns of the Horse Artillery rushed forward and unlimbered to clear their front; then Drury Lowe gave the Household Cavalry the order to charge. The three ponderous squadrons , cheering wildly, rode straight through the Egyptian battalions, trampling and sabring them into disorganised retreat. Another attack on Kassassin was beaten off on 9 September when the Bengal Lancers especially distinguished themselves.

The Egyptians now withdrew behind the entrenched lines of Tel el Kebir, 4 miles long on a ridge of rising ground — formidable lines that had been constructed according to the most advanced principles of military engineering and manned by about 22,000 men with many guns. Wolseley planned to carry out a night march with his force of 17,000 men with 67 guns and to attack the enemy position at first light. The night of the attack — 12/13 September — was more than usually dark, and the storming columns, moving at a speed of a mile an hour, fumbled their way forward, guided by the stars.

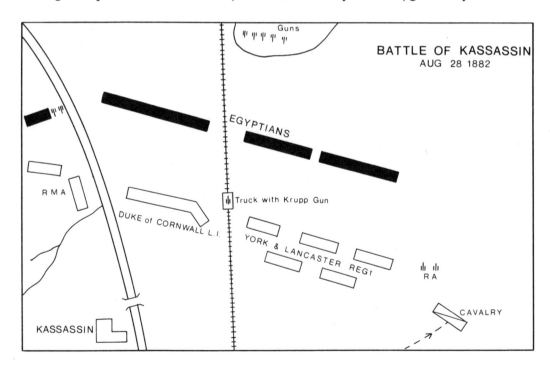

On the right marched the 1st Division commanded by General Willis, with the leading brigade, under Graham, consisting of the Royal Irish, the Royal Marines, the York and Lancasters and the Royal Irish Fusiliers. The Brigade of Guards – the Grenadiers, Scots and Coldstreams – under the Duke of Connaught, Queen Victoria's son, marched 1,000 yards behind them. The left of the attacking line was occupied by the 2nd Division led by General Hamley, the front position of honour and of danger being accorded to the Highland Brigade (commanded by one-armed Sir Archibald Alison), made up of the Black Watch, the Gordon Highlanders, the Cameron Highlanders and the Highland Light Infantry. In reserve, behind the Scots battalions, marched Ashburnam's Brigade of the King's Royal Rifles and the Duke of Cornwall's Infantry. In the interval between the divisions, forty-two guns were positioned. On the extreme right rear flank of the assaulting force rode Drury Lowe's cavalry, spoiling for another charge. On the other side of the Freshwater Canal, on the extreme left of the British line, marched the Indian contingent of General Macpherson, consisting of the Seaforth Highlanders, three battalions of native infantry, Bengal Cavalry and some mountain-guns. Their task was to turn Arabi's right flank which rested on the Canal.

The march began at 1.30 am with 5½ miles to cover; after hours of silent plodding through the cloying sand, the men knew that they must be approaching the enemy position. A faint paling of the sky showed dawn to be near; a few scattered shots were fired in front of the force and a single bugle sounded within the enemy lines; then the

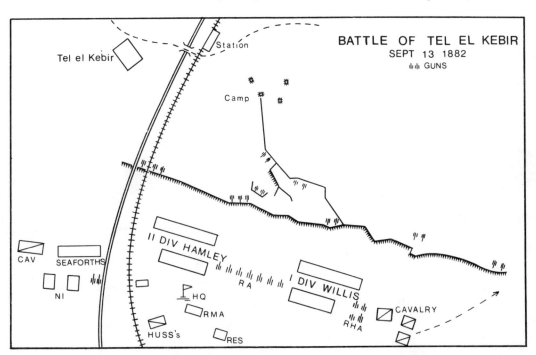

151

darkness was shattered by a torrent of firing from all along the Egyptian line of entrenchments. Bugles sounded the charge and the relieved men filled the air with lusty cheers
as they hurried forward. Bayonets had been fixed and not a single shot was fired by the
British, who only had to cover about 150 yards of open ground before reaching the
Egyptian lines; nevertheless nearly 200 men went down before reaching the 6ft wide,
4ft deep ditch in front of the enemy's 10ft high parapets. In the darkness, the Highland
Brigade on the left of the attack went forward faster than the rest and was the first to
break into the enemy's entrenchments. The bagpipes could be heard above the tumult
as Highlanders fought grimly with the bayonet and the rifle butt. On the extreme right
the Irish Regiments screamed wildly as they carried the position with the bayonet. On
the other side of the Canal the Indian contingent met with little opposition and turned
Arabi's right flank to complete the rout of his broken men. So quickly and successfully
had the works been stormed that the Guards in the second line did not fire a shot. Arabi
lost his camp, stores and guns and suffered casualties. The British force lost 339 officers
and men, 243 of them belonging to the Highland Brigade. Made frantic by the heat, the
British soldiers quenched their thirst in the nearby Canal, putrid with corpses of men
and the carcasses of animals, while the artillery and cavalry, with a naval landing party,
carried on the pursuit of the routed enemy. On the night of the following day the
British cavalry, after a forced march of about forty miles under a blazing sun, entered
Cairo just in time to save the city from destruction and to capture Arabi himself.

38 The Expedition to the Sudan 1884-5

After Wolseley's successful campaign, the virtual occupation of Egypt involved Britain in the Sudan, where control had been slipping from the Egyptian government's hands into those of the Moslem prophet, the Mahdi. Following the British government's refusal in 1882 to intervene in the Sudan, the Egyptian government engaged Colonel W. Hicks, a retired officer of the Indian army, who marched into the Kordofan desert in September 1883 at the head of some 10,000 disorganised Egyptian troops re-enlisted from the defeated army of Arabi. In November the force was utterly destroyed near El Obeid by a greatly superior force of Sudanese tribesmen, leaving Khartoum and all the country to its south at the Mahdi's mercy.

Leading a large force of tribesmen, Osman Digna besieged Sinkat about sixty miles from Suakin, cutting to pieces an Egyptian relief force on 6 November and another force near Tamai on 2 December. The Egyptian government now appointed Major-General Valentine Baker, head of the Egyptian police, to march to Suakin with a force of 4,000 men, a rabble of policemen and peasants. Near El Teb the force was attacked by Osman Digna and about 1,200 Sudanese tribesmen, who displayed the most reckless

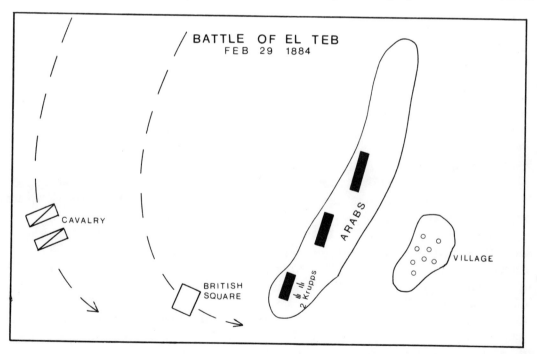

BATTLE OF EL TEB
FEB 29 1884

CAVALRY

ARABS

BRITISH SQUARE

2 Krupps

VILLAGE

bravery while the Egyptians showed the most craven cowardice. In indescribable confusion, with cavalry, infantry, mules, camels, baggage and casualties crushed into a struggling and surging mass, the Egyptian soldiers allowed themselves to be slaughtered by natives inferior to them in numbers and armed only with spears and swords. Unable to rally the Egyptian soldiers and realising that the position was hopeless, Baker and some of his staff hewed their way out of the struggling mass, leaving behind 112 officers and 2,250 men killed and wounded and losing their machine-guns, field-guns and 3,000 rifles. Four days later the besieged force at Sinkat were destroyed as they attempted to fight their way out.

Feeling itself in honour bound to save the garrison of Khartoum whilst evacuating the Sudan, the British government sent General Charles Gordon, a former Governor-General of the Sudan, to Khartoum. At the same time, Major-General Sir Gerald Graham VC was given command of an expedition against Osman Digna; he had two brigades of British infantry (under Major-General Sir Redvers Buller VC and Major-General Davis), some cavalry including the 10th Hussars, eight seven-pounder guns and six Gatling guns — a total of about 4,000 men.

On 29 February 1884 the force marched out from Trinkitat in a square formation with guns and Gatlings at the corners, and cavalry and mounted infantry thrown out to front and flanks and guarding the rear. The transport animals, carrying ammunition and medical supplies, were in the centre of the formation. The huge square plodded over the barren sandy soil to come upon the enemy positioned near El Teb, not far from the decomposing heaps of mutilated bodies of Baker's annihilated army. The Sudanese tribesmen were positioned in front of the village and wells of El Teb in shallow earthworks, rifle-pits, and a fortified building. The bugles sounded the advance and the bagpipes struck up as Graham marched his square to the right in an attempt to turn the enemy's left. The guns captured from Baker Pasha poured out a storm of shrapnel shells — they were served by impressed artillery men from the garrison of Tokar, recently taken by the Dervishes. The formation slowly plodded forward for about a thousand yards, with shells bursting over it and bullets bringing down men on all sides, before halting so that the men could lie down whilst casualties were treated.

It was noon and very hot as Graham brought his guns into action at 900 yards range and with the rattling Gatlings, they soon silenced the two Krupp guns. Then the square rose to its feet and moved forward without losing cohesion in a shoulder-to-shoulder wheeling movement towards the enemy's left flank; this brought the Black Watch to the front from their original position at the rear face. As the British infantry neared the defences, vast numbers of tribesmen threw aside their rifles and, flourishing broad-bladed spears and cross-hilted swords, flung themselves like a swarm of furious bees upon the levelled bayonets of the square, to be cut down in dozens by the fire of the Martini rifles and the Gatling guns. To stop the fierce onrush of the natives, some of the British soldiers had sliced off the heads of their bullets but even the huge wounds caused by these expanding 'dum-dum' missiles did not halt the courageous tribesmen.

Colonel Fred Burnaby of the Blues (out in the desert on sick leave) picked them off like driven hares with a double-barrelled twelve-bore loaded with pig-shot which brought down 13 natives for an expenditure of twenty-three cartridges. The few Sudanese who reached the square engaged in a sharp hand-to-hand fight until repelled. As they ran back they were swept by fire. The square continued to move forward and carried the entrenchments, turning the captured guns of one Arab battery on to those of the second; then it halted, re-formed itself and advanced slowly but steadily on the second Arab line of trenches and rifle-pits. As they had done before, the Sudanese came out of their holes and flung themselves upon the British who were in two long lines as Graham deployed his flanks. The fortified building was carried by a brilliant charge of the naval landing party. Every inch of ground was contested by the Sudanese who seemed to spring out of the ground like rabbits.

While the infantry fight had been going on, Stewart's cavalry had swept round the enemy's right flank, dashing after him in three lines while the tribesmen split into two large bodies to right and left so that the Hussars had to gallop 3 miles before catching them. The tribesmen flung themselves on the ground as the cavalry passed, attempting to hamstring the horses and throwing boomerangs of mimosa wood at their legs. On one occasion, thirty Arab horsemen, riding bare-backed and armed with two-edged swords, charged a whole squadron but after causing some casualties they were wiped out. The Hussars found it almost impossible to reach the crouching or lying Arabs with their sabres and later General Stewart adapted Arab spears as lances by weighting their heads with a roll of iron.

By 2 pm the position was taken and the Sudanese were streaming away towards Tokar, having lost over 2,000 killed alone in a convincing demonstration of the superiority of discipline backed by Martini rifles and machine-guns over numbers and fanatical courage. The British had 34 killed and 155 wounded.

Finding Osman Digna's force in position near the village and wells of Tamai, Graham marched out on 13 March with his whole force in two squares in echelon from the left, with Davis's 2nd Brigade leading and Buller's 1st Brigade on its right rear so that the two squadrons could support each other with fire. After marching for some time over a rough plain, Davis's square was suddenly assailed by fierce rushes from large parties of tribesmen. The men frantically opened fire and, despite bugle calls and orders from the officers, could not be persuaded to reserve their fire or to aim steadily. In a few minutes dense clouds of smoke hung on the still air, hiding the enemy and allowing him to creep up unseen. Those companies of the York and Lancasters and the Black Watch forming the front face of Davis's square had moved forward more quickly than the remaining companies forming the sides of the square so that gaps appeared in what should have been a solid wall of men. Under cover of the smoke, large bodies of the enemy burst out to rush upon the right-angle of the square, creeping and crawling beneath the bayonets and muzzles of the Gatling guns to enter the square and bear it back in wild confusion. Broken into small groups of men fighting for their lives, while officers strove to

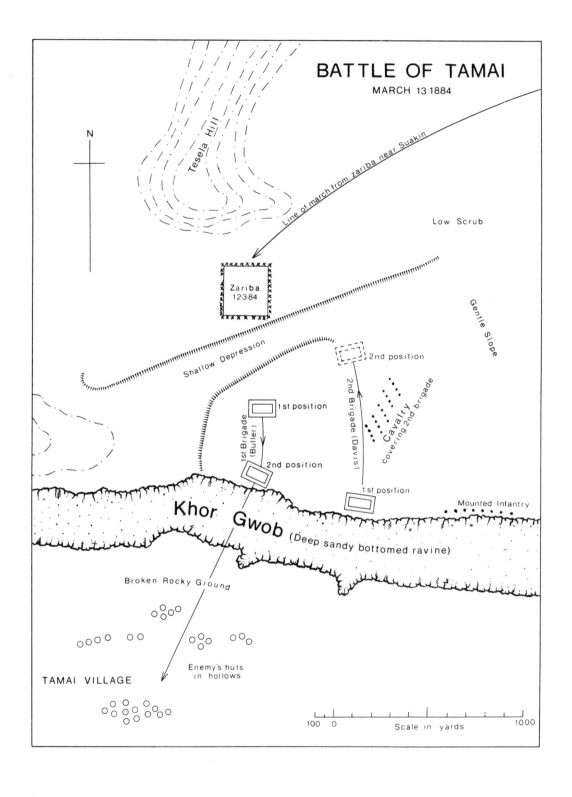

BATTLE OF TAMAI
MARCH 13 1884

Tesela Hill

N

Line of march from zariba near Suakin

Low Scrub

Gentle Slope

Zariba
12·3·84

Shallow Depression

2nd position

2nd Brigade (Davis)

Cavalry covering 2nd brigade

1st position

1st Brigade (Butler)

2nd position

1st position

Mounted Infantry

Khor Gwob (Deep sandy bottomed ravine)

Broken Rocky Ground

Enemy's huts in hollows

TAMAI VILLAGE

100   0   Scale in yards   1000

reorganise their men, the confused mass recoiled under the sheer weight of the attack. The machine guns of the naval brigade were captured but not before they had been locked by their crew who stood by them till the last. Left without protection, the gunners of the battery of four guns stood firm and mowed down the onrushing tribesmen with shrapnel. Highlanders, formed into small groups disputing every inch of the ground, gradually checked the retreat until the men began to rally and re-form to the shouted orders of officers and sergeants.

Five hundred yards to the right rear, Buller's square was being attacked in the same furious manner, but by sheer fire-power it literally blew away the enemy as he approached. Then the Gordons, Royal Irish and Rifles poured a steady fire across the open ground at the tribesmen attacking Davis's square. Stewart galloped his cavalry round to the left flank of the square and, dismounting his men, opened with their carbines and so caught the tribesmen between two fires. At last they wavered and ceased to advance. After fresh ammunition had been brought out, the 2nd Brigade formed in line and moved forward again to the attack to recapture the guns and turn them on the enemy. Large numbers of tribesmen attacked furiously from a broad and deep ravine where they had been lying concealed, but melted away as the troops, again in squares, poured in crashing volleys; they were finally routed by the cavalry who swept round their left flank and dismounted to pour volley after volley into their backs.

Amid wounded natives lying thickly in the scrub and firing or slashing at anybody who came within reach, Graham's force re-formed and began to advance on Tamai, about three miles from the battlefield. On occasions enemy groups seemed about to attack but they were turned back by artillery fire. Buller's brigade destroyed Osman's camp, while Davis's battered troops returned to the zariba occupied on the previous night. During the fighting the British had lost 109 killed and 102 wounded whilst beating off an estimated force of about 9,000 natives, of whom 2,000 were killed.

The victory at Tamai opened the road from Suakin to Berber on the Nile, still held by an Egyptian garrison. It was perhaps a fleeting opportunity to reach Khartoum but Graham's telegraphic request to do so was turned down by the government. On 28 March, after several skirmishes with the enemy, he received instructions that the campaign was to be brought to a close and so, leaving two British battalions to garrison Suakin, on 3 April he embarked the remainder of his force and sailed for Egypt.

Following Graham's withdrawal from Suakin, the British government belatedly decided to send an expedition under General Sir G. Wolseley to relieve Khartoum. He reached Cairo on 9 September 1884. Recalling his Red River Campaign, he decided that the force of 7,000 men should ascend the Nile in small boats manned by Voyageurs, boatmen hired from Canada. Eight hundred boats each 30ft long and 6ft 6in in the beam, were ordered from forty-seven British shipyards and within ten weeks arrived in Alexandria in nineteen separate ships. Contracted to transport the whole army as far as the Second Cataract, Thomas Cook's paddle-steamers towed lines of boats, like beads on a string, upstream to Wadi Halfa. Manned by two Voyageurs, each boat carried ten soldiers, sitting comfortably under awnings, smoking their pipes and trailing their hands in the water, together with their equipment. But from the Second Cataract onwards, the soldiers had to pull laboriously at the oars for many hours, hardly moving the boats against the strong current. The Royal Irish Regiment won the prize of one hundred pounds offered by Wolseley to the battalion making the quickest passage up to Korti. Thousands of natives struggled along steep and rocky banks, encouraged by Egyptian soldiers with whips, as the paddle-steamers, with steel hawsers slung under their hulls, were man-handled past the Second Cataract. By the middle of December the bulk of the expeditionary force was gathered at Korti, where a large camp was formed.

Wolseley divided his force into two separate columns — the River Column under Major-General Earle, consisting of 2,200 men with six screw-guns, was to proceed up the Nile by boat and then open up the desert road between Abu Hamed and Korosko, finally pushing on to Berber to co-operate with the second column. This column was commanded by Brigadier-General Sir Herbert Stewart and had the task of making its way straight across the Bayuda desert to Metemmeh to open up another and more direct road to Khartoum. Totalling 2,000 men with about 300 camel-drivers and native porters, it included a naval brigade under Lord Charles Beresford with a detachment of Royal Marines and a squadron of the 19th Hussars mounted on horses, together with the Royal Sussex Regiment, a company of the Essex Regiment, some Royal Engineers and half a battery of Royal Artillery. The most unusual part of the force was its Camel Corps.

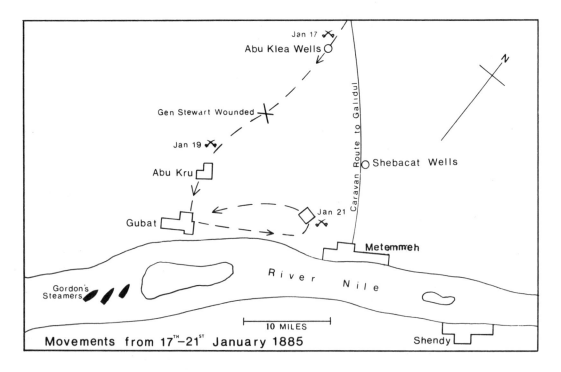

Movements from 17ᵀᴴ–21ˢᵀ January 1885

Proposed by Wolseley and accepted by the War Office, it consisted of specially picked men from the Grenadier, the Coldstream and the Scots Guards together with the Royal Marines, who formed the Guards Camel Regiment; the Heavy Camel Regiment of selected men from the Household Cavalry Regiments and other crack cavalry units; and the Mounted Infantry Camel Regiment composed of specially chosen men, most of whom had previously served in South Africa or Egypt, from various infantry regiments. Before the column could leave, the Camel Corps had to be trained to ride the camels. About thirty red tunics were taken to be worn by those who were to proceed on the first steamer from Metemmeh to Khartoum, with the idea of impressing and perhaps terrifying the Mahdi and his followers.

On 30 December Stewart moved out to occupy the wells of Gakdul. The great phalanx of camels, forty abreast, ambled forward in a solid column extending for half a mile, the centre composed of 800 baggage-camels driven by natives from Aden dressed in red turbans, blue jerseys and big brass identification labels. Three seven-pounder guns went with the column and thirty of Beresford's Blue Jackets were pulling a Gardner gun.

After a difficult journey with a considerable loss of camels the column reached Gakdul on 12 January and, leaving a detachment of the Sussex Regiment to hold the wells, the Desert Column moved forward to the Abu Klea valley. On the morning of 17 January 1885 Stewart formed his force of 1,500 officers and men, with three screw-guns and one

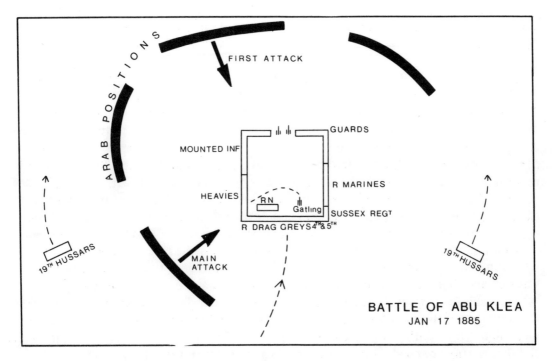

BATTLE OF ABU KLEA
JAN 17 1885

Gardner gun, into a huge square with the camels in the middle, and slowly marched off down the valley towards a row of coloured banners which stretched across it. It was a very hot day and going was rough. The square had frequently to halt for the doctors to attend to casualties from the harassing fire of the enemy, and in order to repair the form of the square so as to prevent its rear face being force out by the sluggish camels. Then the banners stirred as their bearers stood up and the Dervish army of 15,000 warriors lay before them in battle array. Suddenly and dramatically, the air was filled with shouting, screaming and the beating of drums.

Five hundred yards from the flags the square halted to dress its rear face. The shouting died away and a large part of the enemy army rushed forward in a serrated line, charging down in silence towards the left front corner of the square, the furious drumming of bare feet making the ground quiver. Although wave after wave went down before the fire of the Martinis and the Gardner guns, still the men came on. As they neared the square, the Dervishes changed their direction and came swiftly down on its most vulnerable point (the left rear corner where it had been bulged out by the camels and gapped by the Gardner gun) run out about 20 yards by the Naval Brigade. Even the massed volleys of rifle-fire did not turn back the Dervishes and in a few seconds this corner of the square was pressed back by sheer weight of numbers. The Gardner gun jammed and at least half the Naval Brigade was slaughtered as the men fought around it. Colonel Burnaby was killed while fighting outside the square and General Stewart was only rescued with considerable difficulty as his horse was shot from under him. Many of the infantry rifles jammed through heat and rapid firing, leaving the men with nothing but their bayonets, which frequently bent, with which to fight off the fanatical tribesmen.

Disordered and thrown into momentary confusion, the square was only saved by the stability of the Guards who held their ground on the two sides that were not attacked. Setting their feet apart and putting their rear rank about, the guardsmen shot down or bayoneted every native who approached them. As the left face of the square was gradually forced back to the rear of the front face, while the rear face was forced in, the camels formed a living traverse that broke the Arab rush and gave the defenders time to re-form. The centre of the square was a scene of desperate conflict, with camels, horses and men forming a slashing, hacking, surging mass. Lord Charles Beresford, trying to clear the jammed Gardner gun, was knocked down and carried against the face of the square by sheer weight of numbers. One flank of the formation was forced up a steep little mound; this enabled the rear rank to open fire over the heads of the men in the front-rank and thus to relieve the pressure. Finally the enemy troops momentarily wavered and then, in a dignified fashion, they slowly walked away from the square, turning their back upon it and leaving great piles of their dead behind them. In a battle that only lasted five minutes no fewer than 1,100 dead tribesmen were counted in the immediate neighbourhood of the square whilst the British lost 74 officers and men killed and nearly 100 wounded. Several Victoria Crosses were awarded for this action.

The muddy water at the wells of Abu Klea tasted like champagne, but the column spent a cold and miserable night as no stores or baggage had come up. Next morning, leaving the wounded behind in a small improvised fort with a guard of 100 men of the Royal Sussex Regiment, the column marched off to Metemmeh about twenty-three miles away. It was a very distressing march over rough ground and not until 7.30 am on the following day was a gravel ridge topped to reveal the Nile stretching ribbon-like before them, with a large force of tribesmen positioned between the column and the river. General Stewart said: 'First we will have breakfast and then go out to fight' and the column sat down on the sand to eat breakfast under a dropping shower of long-range bullets. It was at this point that Stewart was struck in the groin and mortally wounded; the command of the column was taken over by Sir Charles Wilson.

Leaving the 'Heavies', the 19th Hussars, the Royal Artillery and the Naval Brigade with their guns and the Gardner gun in a fortified redoubt made of boxes and rocks on a hillock, the rest of the column formed up in square and marched out at 2 o'clock in the afternoon. Reinforced from Omdurman, the tribesmen were in great strength and their banners rose out of the long grass on all sides. Whenever they revealed themselves, the guns in the zariba opened up and the Gardner gun kept grinding away. Then, as suddenly as at Abu Klea, the enemy came pounding down the hill with several horsemen in the lead. The square halted to receive the charge, and cheering spontaneously the men began to fire frantically. Then bugles sounded the cease fire and, surprisingly,

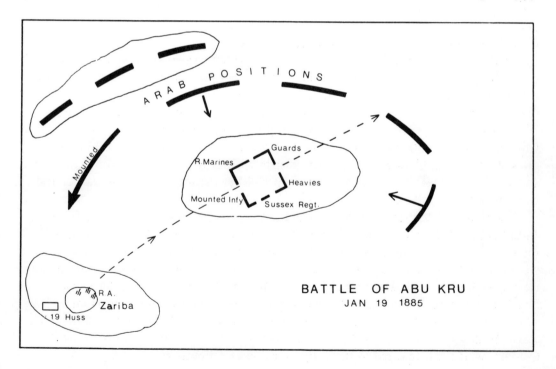

BATTLE OF ABU KRU
JAN 19 1885

the men answered the call. Steadied by the momentary rest, they began to fire again with deadly effect, so that not a single tribesman got within fifty yards of the square. In a few minutes the entire front ranks of the enemy were swept away and, hastily turning, the Dervishes disappeared. The British force had lost 1 officer and 22 men with 8 officers and 90 men wounded. When they reached the river, the men fell down like logs and buried their faces in the muddy water. They bivouacked on the river bank that night and early next morning formed up and marched back to the zariba, where there had been considerable fighting on the previous day. Reunited, the whole force marched away in columns of regiments carrying twenty-five wounded men on hand-stretchers because of shortage of camels. Although they hovered around the flanks, the enemy troops did not attack again in force and by nightfall, the column reached the river village of Abu Kru, where the wounded were placed in huts and the houses were loopholed for defence.

At dawn on 21 January, Sir Charles Wilson advanced with 1,000 men in double column to take the well-defended town of Metemmeh but after some fighting he retired leaving the town in enemy hands.

The force was joined by four armoured river-steamers sent down by Gordon from Khartoum, and the next two days were spent in overhauling the steamers, collecting wood for fuel, and reconnoitring. On the morning of 24 January 1885, *Bordein* and *Telahawiyeh* churned up the Nile towards Khartoum. The two steamers carried twenty men of the Royal Sussex, some naval personnel and about 200 Sudanese infantry; *Telahawiyeh* towed a barge laden with grain. Sir Charles Wilson was on *Bordein*. For three days the heavily laden vessels slowly made their way up river, moving only by day, frequently running aground, fighting skirmishes on the banks, and often stopping to pull down wooden houses to use as fuel. At first light on 27 January, the towers of Khartoum could be seen in the far distance and a heavy fire was opened on the steamers from four guns and thousands of rifles at a range of about six hundred yards. With boilers straining almost to bursting point, and running the gauntlet of guns and rifle-fire from batteries on both banks, the vessels, carrying their red-coated British infantry, pressed up-stream, to swing laboriously in sight of Khartoum. The lack of welcome was ample evidence that the town had fallen — it had been stormed two days earlier and Gordon had been killed.

Wilson ordered the steamers to turn and run full-steam down river, under fire from both banks, until 4 o'clock in the afternoon. With heavy hearts, the crews worked the steamers through the cataracts, sunken rocks and sandbanks, losing *Telahawiyeh* when it struck a sunken rock. On 31 January the last rapid was overcome, leaving a clear stretch of smooth water all the way to Metemmeh. In the afternoon *Bordein* too struck a sunken rock and had to be laid alongside a sandspit running out from an island where guns, ammunition and stores were quickly landed. Wilson entrenched his small force on the island and sent a ship's boat downstream to get help from the Desert Column, which was reached in the early morning of 1 February.

162

That afternoon Lord Charles Beresford took the small river-steamer *Safieh* up the Nile with a crew that included twenty picked marksmen of the Rifles, two Gardner guns and two four-pounders. On the third morning *Safieh* ran the gauntlet of Arab earth-works at Wadi Habeshi, passing within 80 yards of the entrenchments and pouring such showers of shells and bullets into them that the Arabs were unable to reply until the little steamer was 200 yards past them; then a well-directed shot from an Arab gun went through the stern and into one of the boilers. Beresford managed to get *Safieh* further upstream and anchored stern-on to the enemy at about 500 yards range. Through-out the day a firefight was carried on between the steamer and the Arabs on shore. At daybreak the next morning, with the boiler repaired, Beresford was able to embark Sir Charles Wilson and his party, who had descended on the right bank. Without further loss, *Safieh* reached the camp of the Desert Column on the evening of 6 February.

39 The Third Burmese War 1885

For some years after his accession in 1878 King Thibaw of Burma showed anti-British feeling which culminated in secret negotiations with France concerning rights in Upper Burma; this caused the alarmed British government to present an ultimatum in October 1885. It was rejected by Thibaw, and on 10 November 1885 General Prendergast left Rangoon by river for Thayetmyo, leading a force totalling 12,000 men. It included a naval detachment; the 2nd Battalions King's Liverpool Regiment; the 1st Battalion Royal Welsh Fusiliers; the 2nd Battalion Hampshire Regiment; Royal Artillery with sixty-seven guns and twenty-four machine-guns; native infantry and cavalry from India. This force was to oppose the Burmese army estimated at about 20,000 .

The only way to advance on Mandalay, the capital, was by 300 miles of easily defensible waterway, and so the advance up-river was a naval operation. Traversable only by narrow and tortuous tracks that were ideal for ambush, the country was extremely difficult, and natives and European alike suffered from heat-apoplexy, whilst malaria took a heavy toll — even the men's boots dropped to pieces in the heat, mud and water. River-forts fell with astonishing ease as troops landed and marched round to attack them from the land side at the same time as they were frontally engaged by the river-force. The collapse of resistance to the British advance was due solely to rapid preparation and adequate planning.

The only place where anything like a stubborn resistance was offered to the British advance was around the village of Minhla where the enemy, concealed in the thick jungle, fought fiercely against both land and water advances. The troops on shore moved forward under heavy fire from jungle and fort to carry the stockades with a rush as the garrison streamed out by a rear gate. British casualties were 3 killed and 23 wounded while the Burmese lost 170 dead and 276 prisoners. On 24 November Myingyan, a large and important town near the mouth of the Chindwin River was easily captured and on 26 November the king's state barge arrived with a flag of truce, bringing envoys to open peace negotiations. On 28 November, the force entered Mandalay unopposed, as the king surrendered himself and his kingdom to General Prendergast.

During the short three weeks' war, British casualties were 1 officer and 3 native infantry killed, 4 men drowned, 4 officers and 22 men wounded, while Burmese losses did not exceed 250. For various reasons the campaign was not decisively followed up and the army of occupation only secured its lines of communications, restricting its authority in the country to the range of its rifles, against the thousands of armed and unconquered Burmese soldiers turned loose on the country to become dacoits who devastated large tracts of the land. For the next two or three years a constant and unremitting struggle followed, as rebels and dacoits in all parts of the country were harried

164

and pursued by columns of native troops and British county regiments. Brigadier-General G. S. White took command of the Upper Burma Field Force in March 1886, reinforced by the Royal Artillery; the 2nd Battalion Royal West Surrey Regiment; the 1st Battalion South Yorkshire Regiment; the 1st Battalion Rifle Brigade; the 2nd Battalion Royal Munster Fusiliers, together with numerous Indian infantry and cavalry regiments. By October 1886 the total strength of troops in Burma was over 500 British officers and 31,000 British and native cavalry, infantry and artillery.

In January 1891 the town of Kawlin in Upper Burma was besieged. The relief force included the Devonshire Regiment; the Duke of Cornwall's Light Infantry; the Oxford and Bucks Light Infantry, together with native infantry, cavalry and artillery. In 1889 to 1890 Brigadier-General G. B. Wolseley mounted the Ponkan Expedition that was entirely successful at a cost of 51 killed and wounded. This and the Wuntho Expedition brought the third Burmese War to a close. Most of the leaders who had not surrendered or been killed were in hiding and their men had settled down to a peaceful life. The time it took to annex Upper Burma — five years — was just half that required for the pacification of Lower Burma after the second Burmese War.

40 The Battles around Suakin 1885

In order to build the railway from Suakin on the coast to Berber on the Nile, it was essential to crush Osman Digna's forces of 7,000 men at Tamai, 3,000 at Hasin (six miles west of Suakin) and a small garrison at Tokar. Lieutenant-General Sir Gerald Graham arrived at Suakin on 12 March 1885 to command a force of about 13,000 made up of the 1st Guards Infantry Brigade and a Line brigade formed of the East Surreys, the Shropshires, the Berkshires and the Royal Marines. There was a cavalry brigade of four squadrons of the 5th Lancers and the 25th Hussars; some mounted infantry; Engineer detachments and an Indian contingent formed of the 15th Sikhs, the 9th Bengal Cavalry, the 17th and 28th Native Infantry, with a company of Madras Sappers. Later, a force of 500 infantry and artillery arrived from New South Wales. There were also 11,000 camp-followers.

The port of Suakin was crowded with naval vessels, troopships, transport and hospital ships, and special vessels for condensing 85,000 gallons of water a day for the troops. 6,000 baggage and 500 riding-camels with their headmen and drivers were gathered together from India, Egypt and Aden, as well as mules from Gibraltar, Malta and Cyprus. The fighting men were almost lost in the multitudes of camp-followers and labourers working on the railway.

Leaving the Shropshires to garrison Suakin, Graham marched out on 20 March with his force, formed as three sides of a square, made up of over 8,000 officers and men with 1,192 horses, 210 mules, 735 camels and 10 guns, with cavalry covering the front and flanks. Graham's objective was the wells at Hasin; from here a force could threaten the right flank of any British column moving south-westwards. Over rough ground scattered with small boulders and prickly mimosa bushes, the troops made a most exhausting march on a very hot day until they debouched from a pass on to a spacious plain encircled by craggy hills. Banners waving and weapons flashing in the sunlight, the Arabs could be seen posted in great strength on a spur to their left front; the bushes were alive with riflemen who swarmed through the undergrowth, although the only signs of their presence were little puffs of smoke rising above the mimosa bushes. The Berkshires and the Marines dashed forward in gallant style, racing to assault the enemy's position on some hillocks to the right of the ridge occupied by the tribesmen. The Marines reached the crest first and covered the advance of the Berkshires with rolling volleys of musketry that re-echoed among the surrounding hills.

Forced from their position, the Arabs retired across the plain towards Tamai, harassed by two squadrons of Bengal Lancers; two more squadrons of Bengal Cavalry and the 5th Lancers completely scattered a body of enemy on the right who were trying to turn the British flank via the Hasin Valley. Through weight of numbers, the Bengal Lancers on

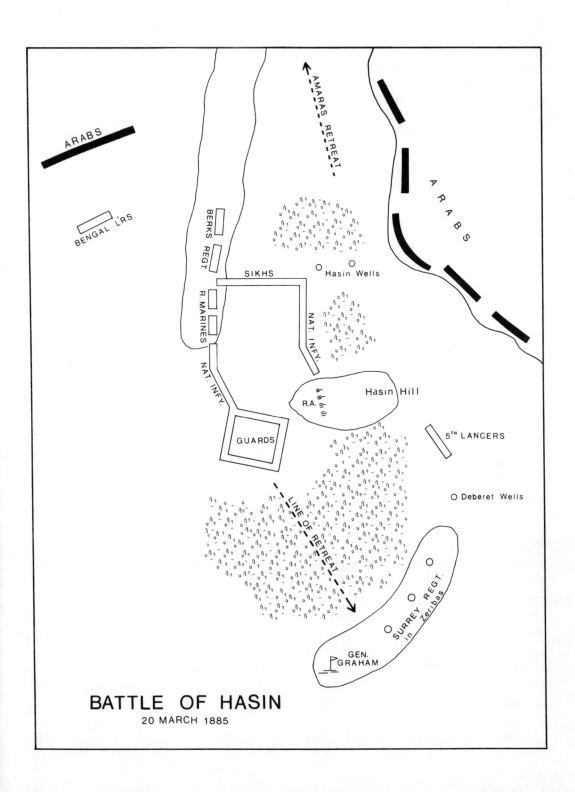

ARABS

BENGAL L'RS.

AMARAS RETREAT

ARABS

BERKS REGT.

SIKHS

Hasin Wells

R. MARINES

NAT. INFY.

NAT. INFY.

Hasin Hill

R.A.

5TH LANCERS

GUARDS

Deberet Wells

LINE OF RETREAT

SURREY REGT.
in Zeribas

GEN.
GRAHAM

BATTLE OF HASIN
20 MARCH 1885

the left were forced to retire on to the Guards' square which had been posted as a reserve in the rear. As they raced after the retiring horsemen, the Arabs suddenly came upon this square and attacked it without a moment's hesitation, but not one of their 3,000 spearmen and riflemen got nearer than fifteen or twenty yards before being beaten back by crashing volleys of musketry.

Leaving the East Surreys to hold the hill-tops that commanded the Hasin wells, Graham's infantry brigades retired in square, covered by the Horse Artillery, whilst parties of Arabs galled them with fire from the bushes. The British losses were 1 officer and 8 men killed and 3 officers and 36 men wounded, while the Arabs lost an estimated 1,000 men.

Then Graham sent out a force to construct and garrison two zaribas as intermediate supply posts in the desert. Led by Major-General Sir John McNeill VC, it consisted of a squadron of the 5th Lancers; the Berkshire Regiment; the Royal Marines; a detachment of the Naval Brigade with four Gardner guns; an Indian Brigade of Infantry with a large convoy of camels; and an Engineer detachment laying a telegraph line as the troops advanced. Formed in two squares, the force advanced slowly through dense scrub and mimosa bush and by noon had only reached Tofrik, 6 miles from Suakin. McNeill realised that he could not build the zariba at the arranged eight-mile point before dusk and so he telegraphed Graham for permission to make a zariba at Tofrik. He planned to form three separate squares of mimosa-thorn fence placed diagonally like a chess board, the large central square housing the transport animals and stores, the two smaller flanking squares were to hold the fighting troops and Gardner guns. Under the protection of a screen of infantry pickets and cavalry, who reported that the enemy to their front was in small parties retiring towards Tamai, the flanking squares were built and the surrounding bush was cleared in oppressive heat. The Marines were working on the northern flanking square with two Gardner guns and the Berkshires were in the southern flanking square with the other two Gardners, both with their arms piled. At 2 o'clock, when the men fell out by half battalions to eat their dinner, there was no proper field of fire around the incomplete defences. The Indian infantry was in the area of the unfinished central square where the camels and mules were collected after off-loading.

At 2.30pm, cavalrymen came galloping in to report that the enemy was advancing rapidly; on their heels came the cavalry outposts fleeing through the working-parties under a heavy fire from natives who seemed to have sprung, screaming and shouting, from the very earth. Thousands of Arabs had crept up unnoticed through the rocks and scrub while the shirt-sleeved infantry worked at the zaribas, their arms piled some yards away. With a hoarse roar, 5,000 black gleaming Hadendowas rose to their feet and flooded in, hacking and stabbing as they hit the bunched camels; the animals shivered, swayed, and then poured down upon the startled infantrymen like floodwater from a burst dam, throwing into disorder the native infantry who fired a volley and then broke and rushed towards the central square. The plain was covered with riderless horses, camels and mules tearing towards Suakin, as working-parties rushed for their arms. The

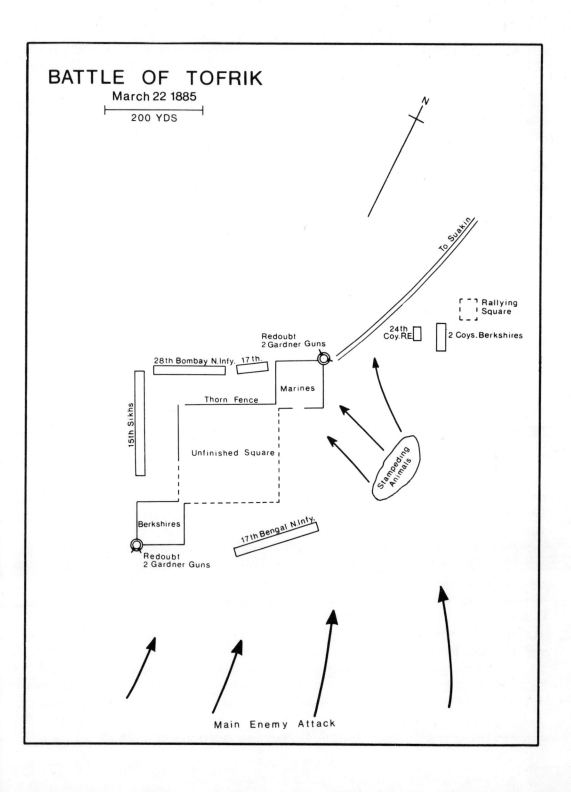

BATTLE OF TOFRIK

March 22 1885

200 YDS

N

To Suakin

Rallying
Square

24th
Coy.R.E.

2 Coys.Berkshires

Redoubt
2 Gardner Guns

28th Bombay N.Infy.   17th.

Marines

15th Sikhs

Thorn Fence

Unfinished Square

Berkshires

Redoubt
2 Gardner Guns

17th Bengal N.Infy.

Stampeding Animals

Main Enemy Attack

main attack was directed at the zariba of the Berkshires where General McNeill was lucky to escape with his life. A group of Berkshires outside the middle zariba formed a square and, holding their fire until the Arabs were within thirty yards, mowed down the tribesmen milling around the small formation.

In the first rush, some sixty Arabs penetrated the Marines' square and were instantly shot or bayoneted; but an avalanche of Arabs, Indian Infantry in flight, camp-followers and animals burst through the central square, carrying away many of the formed soldiers. Because the tribesmen were amongst the transport animals, the Berkshires and Marines were forced to fire heavy volleys into them. Camels reared their great bodies into the air before slumping into shapeless tawny masses on the blood-soaked sand. The space marked out for the central zariba was a hideous chaos of shouting demoralised men, frantic camels and plunging, kicking mules, while the Hadendowa warriors flitted amid clouds of dust, cleaving paths through the mass with their long razor-sharp swords.

The 15th Sikhs and the 28th Bombay Native Infantry remained firm, however, and maintained an intact line to receive and repulse successive assaults. Thrown back, large bodies of the enemy milled around in all directions, charging at the zariba fence, slashing at the helpless camp-followers, gashing and hamstringing camels and mules until at last, turned back by the concentrated fire from the Marines and Berkshire squares, the surviving Hadendowas slowly and sullenly retreated from the area.

The twenty minutes that the battle had lasted were crowded with instances of cool bravery, wild bewilderment and fanatical desperation. As the smoke and dust cleared away, a shambles of bodies of men and animals was revealed. The British lost 100 men killed and 140 wounded; 900 camels were destroyed while at least 1,000 of the enemy dead lay around and within the zaribas.

The night was very dark and the tense troops were prevented from sleeping by the moans and cries of the wounded and by the bullets that came whizzing into the camp, fired by the tribesmen who still infested the bush around them. Next morning, General Graham came up with the Brigade of Guards and for the next eight days the men were kept busy clearing the battlefield and rebuilding the zariba to suit a garrison of one battalion. Water was scarce and men collapsed in dozens from sunstroke, but the tribesmen's confidence had been shaken by their reverse and the campaign was tailing off into a series of marches and counter-marches, convoy-escorting, zariba building and skirmishes. The men of the New South Wales contingent comporting themselves with gallantry in one such affair at Dhakdul.

Observation was kept by a captive balloon filled from gas cylinders and towed by a rope attached to a wagon drawn by horses in the centre of the moving square of men. At a height of 300-400 feet, it was possible to have a perfect observation of the surrounding country and messages were sent down on pieces of paper tied to a long string.

On 3 April Graham advanced unhindered towards Osman Digna's headquarters at Tamai, he found the villages deserted and the wells almost dry. Most of the tribes had deserted Digna, and defensive operations were now practically at an end.

41 The End of the Nile Campaign 1885

On 2 January 1885 Earle's River Column moved away from Korti. It consisted of a squadron of 19th Hussars; the Staffordshire Regiment; the Black Watch; the Gordon Highlanders; the Duke of Cornwall's Light Infantry; a battery of Egyptian artillery; and the Egyptian Camel Corps. With the Hussars on the left and the Camel Corps on the right bank, heavy whale-boats battled against rocks and cataracts — it took the burly soldiers of the Black Watch four days to work their way through a cataract 7 miles long. Frequently the boats had to be portaged and, with everything removed from them, carried along the rough rock-strewn banks for a mile or more; on other occasions, the crews of three boats hauled a single whaler through the rocks of the swift-flowing river.

Leaving the boats and marching through the desert towards Abu-Hamed, Earle found his path blocked by the enemy strongly positioned on the Kirbekan ridge. He decided to make a feigned frontal attack while sending six companies of the Staffords and the Black Watch, together with the Hussars, round the left flank to take the enemy in rear. He himself accompanied the flanking column which, although observed and under fire for much of its route, managed to get into position so as effectively to turn the enemy position by taking it in rear and overlapping it on the right flank. The guns of the false frontal attack could be heard as the Staffords and the Highlanders, with pipes skirling, stormed the heights at the point of the bayonet. Whilst searching the crest for Arabs hiding in holes or behind rocks, they came upon a stone hut, from which a tribesman shot and killed General Earle.

While the fighting on the heights was going on, the Hussars rode off and captured the enemy camp at the entrance to the nearby Shukook Pass. The whole operation cost 3 officers and 9 men killed, 4 officers and 44 men wounded, against an estimated Arab loss of hundreds.

For twelve more days the force struggled up-river towards Abu-Hamed, which it would probably have captured together with Berber, but on 24 February the men were ordered by Wolseley to return; on 8 March they arrived back at Korti, after taking only nine days for the down-stream voyage (although several lives were lost during its course), against thirty-one days to ascend the cataracts. During this period Redvers Buller's Desert Column had been effecting a masterly retirement from its position on the Nile near Metemmeh, the marching square repeatedly fending off small-scale Arab attacks.

On 2 May, Wolseley arrived in Suakin to announce that the government had suspended the building of the railway and that they were to retire from the Sudan altogether, leaving only a garrison at Suakin. By mid-May, Korti was completely evacuated, and its forts and large buildings were destroyed as the troops retired. Buller superintended the arrangements until 17 June when he handed over command of the rear-guard to General

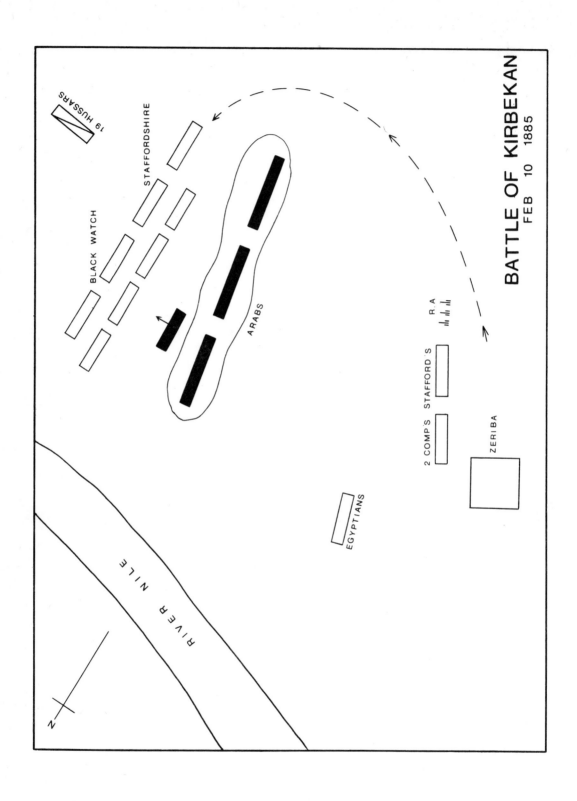

BATTLE OF KIRBEKAN
FEB 10 1885

19 HUSSARS

STAFFORDSHIRE

BLACK WATCH

ARABS

R.A

STAFFORD'S

2 COMP'S

ZERIBA

EGYPTIANS

RIVER NILE

N

Brackenbury. In June the Mahdi died of typhus as Wolseley returned to England, and the Nile Expedition was at an end.

Major-General Sir Francis Grenfell succeeded Sir Evelyn Wood as Sirdar of the Egyptian army and was now busily forming a Nile Frontier Force of British and Egyptian troops. Towards the end of November 1885, the Khalifa Abdullahi, the Mahdi's successor, appeared with a Dervish army a few miles south of Ginnis, and attacks were made on British posts at Kosha and Mograka. General Sir Frederick Stephenson, with two British brigades, attacked and defeated the enemy at Ginnis on the penultimate day of 1885 — it was the very last occasion on which British troops went into action wearing scarlet tunics. It was not a very great battle, but it was the first time that the Dervishes had been fought to a standstill by the Egyptian troops, backed by some English regiments, including the Cameron Highlanders. The surprised Mahdi retired with his army behind the Third Cataract.

Three years of raid and counter-raid ensued, with Egyptian troops gaining strength and confidence as the British regiments were withdrawn. On 28 April 1887 Lieutenant-Colonel Chermside led an all-Egyptian force on a night march to wipe out a strong Dervish army at Saras. This greatly raised the morale of the Egyptian army: it was the very first occasion on which Egyptian regular troops, without British support, had fought the Dervishes. In mid-1889, the Mahdi attempted to invade Egypt and isolate Wadi Halfa by sending a force through the Western Desert to the Nile, 25 miles north of Aswan. At Toski on 3 August 1889 the Dervishes under the Emir Wad en Nejumi were attacked by Grenfell with two brigades of Egyptian infantry, a regiment of British cavalry, and a brigade of British infantry. In this action, which marked the turning point in the tide of the Mahdist invasion, Kitchener was in command of the mounted troops and skilfully lured the Dervish force to destruction. Their leader was killed in the engagement. Kitchener was later appointed Sirdar of the Egyptian army and, with the Dervishes far away in the south and peace reigning in Egypt, began to prepare his forces for an attempt to reoccupy the Sudan.

42 Minor Operations on the North-West Frontier of India 1888-92

The Hazara Field Force

On 7 September 1888 a punitive expedition under Brigadier-General J. W. McQueen was sent into the Black Mountains to punish tribes for killing two British officers and four Gurkhas. Totalling nearly 9,500 officers and men, the expedition consisted of three mountain batteries, one company of sappers and miners; nine Battalions of native infantry; the Royal Irish Regiment; the Northumberland Fusiliers; the Suffolks; the Seaforth Highlanders, and the Royal Sussex, together with Gatling guns. No tents were taken and the only baggage allowed was half a mule-load for each officer and sixteen pounds for other ranks. Each man carried seventy rounds of ammunition with thirty rounds per rifle, loaded on to mules; five days food supplies were also carried.

Marching out in five columns on 3 October 1888, the force was fiercely engaged almost at once in rocky and mountainous country, over slopes and crags, with paths so steep that even the mules could not ascend them: fourteen of them were killed by falling over precipices, while one mile-long ascent took a column twelve hours to cover. Constant casualties were caused by tribesmen sniping at camps during the night and many villages were destroyed during hard and bitter fighting before the tribesmen submitted and were dispersed. British casualties were 2 officers and 23 men killed, 3 officers and 54 men wounded. The columns were back in British territory on 13 October.

Operations in the Black Mountains, 1891

On 12 March 1891 Major-General W. L. Ellis marched out with a force of 7,300 officers and men with 15 guns. The force included the Seaforth Highlanders; the Royal Welsh Fusiliers and the King's Royal Rifle Corps. Working in two columns, it was heavily engaged in the narrow streets of Kanar village, where the enemy fired from the flat rooftops. As the British occupied all the commanding ground within range, the tribesmen were forced to withdraw. Those tribes who did not make their submission had their villages burned and the British force returned by 9 June, having lost 9 killed and 39 wounded.

Expedition to the Zhoh Valley, 1890

Major-General Sir G. S. White led the Zhoh Field Force into the Zhoh Valley on 1 October 1890 to capture Dost Muhammad, a rebel leader but, as he was unable to find him or his band of outlaws, there was no fighting, and subsequently Sir George White decided to impress the natives by marching troops to the top of the celebrated Takht-i-Suliman, the highest part of the great mountain range, using paths up the precipitous eastern face which were considered impassable even to mountain cattle and sheep. Often scrambling up on hands and knees after lying sleepless under six degrees of frost at night, the men accomplished the hard climb. Writing in his dispatch General White said 'The ascent . . . was by far the most difficult physical operation I have ever called upon soldiers to perform, and the fact that the British soldiers and Baluchi sepoys, fully accoutred, scaled these dangerous heights, will not be lost on the Shiranis ' (the local tribesmen).

The Second Miranzai Field Force, 1891

Although not such fine men nor so formidable as the Afridis, the Ovakzai tribe were wiry mountaineers who had frequently been troublesome, and punitive expeditions of native troops had been sent against them in the past by Brigadier Neville Chamberlain in 1863, and Major Jones and Lieutenant P. Cavagnari in 1868. In 1869 two companies of the 36th Foot took part in an expedition under Lieutenant-Colonel Keyes. The first Miranzai Field Force under General Sir William Lockhart went out in January 1891, encountering light opposition but sustaining thirty-three cases of frostbite because of the night-time temperature of twenty degrees below freezing. After an apparently successful operation the force broke up, but a few days later further murderous and treacherous attacks were made on small parties of troops. Lockhart raised another force of about 7,400 men, including the King's Royal Rifles and half a battalion of the Manchester Regiment, and then marched out on 17 April 1891. The operations covered a lot of ground and were highly successful; they culminated in the blowing-up of defensive towers in the presence of tribal gatherings. Two powerful tribes had their countries traversed and mapped for the first time and the Afridis in the Khanki Valley were shown that the British had the power to reach them. Total British casualties between 4 April and 15 May amounted to 28 killed and 73 wounded.

Expedition against the Isazai Tribes, 1892

In 1892 there was a widespread coalition against the British among the tribes in the Chagarzai territory. The situation was almost without precedent on this border, and could be compared with the Ambela outbreak of 1863; for the unrest was stimulated by the quite unfounded belief that a British force was going to march through Chagarzai territory to Thakot. Consequently, Major-General Sir William Lockhart mounted an expedition of 6,250 men and 2 guns, which marched out in September 1892 to confront the Isazai tribes in Baio. Reaching the village without any opposition, the force destroyed the fort and then withdrew. The expedition is chiefly notable for the first recorded use of the Maxim machine-gun on the frontier and for the unusually indifferent health-record of the force, which lost 24 men through cholera.

43 Minor Operations in India 1888-94

Sikkim, 1888

Early in 1888 Tibetan troops occupied part of Sikkim on the borders of Tibet, an area over which Britain had treaty rights. With the objective of turning the Tibetan garrison out of Lingtu, Colonel T. Graham RA took the field, on 25 February 1888, with 200 men of the 2nd Battalion Derbyshire Regiment; 400 men of the 13th Bengal Infantry and 700 men of the 32nd Pioneers together with four guns of the Royal Artillery.

He was ordered not to invade Tibet, but told that, if he was attacked, he could pursue his attackers over the border: he was to try to effect surrender or dispersion of the Tibetan garrison without loss of life on either side. Hampered by thawing snow at 12,600 feet above sea level, his force advanced in two columns along a steep road through a bamboo jungle to attack and capture without loss some stockades and a rudimentary fort garrisoned by Tibetans armed with matchlocks, bows and slings. During the operation, archers in the trees fired large numbers of arrows without much effect. Later, in June, about 3,000 Tibetans attacked the base camp at Gnathong and were repulsed after three hours' heavy fighting with the loss of 100 men, against British casualties of 3 killed and 11 wounded. These operations were made unpleasant for the force through incessant rain — the average rainfall in this area is 140 inches and the rainy season lasts from May to November.

Graham was reinforced until he had 1,700 men with 4 guns and in September the force turned out to attack a wall 4ft high and 3 miles long, constructed by the Tibetans on a ridge near the Jelap-La-Pass. It was manned by about 7,000 Tibetans who ineffectively discharged jingals and smooth-bore cannon, but were soon demoralised by the artillery as Graham advanced in a heavy mist, with the Gurkhas, the Derbyshires and the Pioneers taking position after position. On the following day, in pouring rain, the advance continued, forcing the Tibetans to struggle back through the passes to their own land. In these operations the British lost 4 men wounded while the Tibetans were estimated to have lost 400 killed and as many wounded.

Manipur, 1891

In 1890 the ruler of Manipur State voluntarily abdicated and his brother was appointed regent in his place. The situation called for a demonstration of strength by the government of India, and a military mission was therefore sent to the area. 400 men of the Gurkha Rifles were sent as escort to the Chief Commissioner of Assam, but the force encountered difficulty and fought its way back to Cachar with some losses. In April 1891 a force of about 4,000 men, including the 4th Battalion King's Royal Rifle Corps with some artillery was sent out and, after encountering spasmodic but stubborn resistance, reached Manipur later in the month. Manipur State was then declared forfeit to the British Crown.

The Waziristan Field Force, 1894

A large force was mustered on the frontier to supervise the demarcation of the boundaries of Waziristan, but the tribesmen of that area caused heavy casualties in a sudden night attack on the camp at Wana, being beaten off only after hand-to-hand fighting with Gurkhas. Subsequently on 2 December, Lieutenant-General Sir William Lockhart formed the Waziristan Field Force, consisting of three brigades each made up of native infantry, cavalry and artillery, with the 2nd Battalion Border Regiment in the 1st Brigade. Moving in columns, the force marched into Mahsud country in December 1894 and, almost without opposition, carried out its task of extracting fines, destroying towers and fortifications and taking hostages, sheep, and cattle. The 2nd and 3rd Brigades were back in camp by 22 January 1895 while, under Colonel Gaselee, the Border Regiment with Gurkhas and Punjab Infantry went out as the demarcation party. By the end of February the new boundaries had been established and on 30 March the Waziristan Field Force was broken up.

44 The Siege and Relief of Chitral 1895

In March 1895 about 370 native troops, under Dr Robertson, the British Agent, were besieged by large numbers of frontier tribesmen in the small stone fort of Chitral. A relief expedition of 15,000 men under General Robert Low was assembled to relieve Chitral through the Swat Valley. The force consisted of the Buffs, the Bedfordshire Regiment, the King's Own Scottish Borderers, the East Lancashire Regiment, the King's Royal Rifle Corps, the Seaforth Highlanders, the Gordon Highlanders with Indian cavalry and infantry, together with two mountain-gun batteries. By 3 April they had reached the Malakand Pass and were attempting to force it.

As he did not know when they would reach Chitral, Lieutenant-Colonel J. G. Kelly, already in the area of operations, went out with a small relieving force of about 500 native infantry and two mountain-guns. The force left Gupis on 28 March, carrying only the barest necessities and with only enough sun-glasses for a small proportion of the men, so that practically everyone suffered from painful snow-blindness. The mules carrying the guns and stores found the going very hard, and half-tamed yaks requisitioned from villagers were no more satisfactory. After ten days of incredible hardships over wild and precipitous country thick with snow, the guns and ammunition having to be either carried on poles or towed on improvised sledges by men suffering from both snow-blindness and frostbite, Kelly's force had their first engagement with the enemy on 9 April. The tribesmen were in a very strong position, stretched across the narrow Chakalwat Valley, and their defensive sangars had to be put out of action by gunners who were so handicapped by snow-blindness that they were unable to lay the guns properly. Every shell counted: the guns, under very heavy fire, had to be brought up to within 400 yards of the sangars. Excellent co-operation between artillery and infantry turned the enemy out of his strong position, and Kelly's men were able to man-handle their guns across the fast-flowing river and move down to Mastuj. Here they relieved Lieutenant Moberly and some native infantry who had been besieged in a small stone fort. Kelly's men rested for two or three days until they received information by runner of the action fought by Low at the Malakand, when they calculated that if they hurried they could still arrive at Chitral before the larger force got there.

The siege of Chitral fort had been proceeding throughout this period, marked by a resolute and aggressive resistance by the small defending force. The stone fort, only 80ft square, with walls 8ft thick, had been vigorously attacked by the tribesmen who had even run a mine to within a few feet of the walls, covering the sound of digging by playing native bagpipes and tom-toms. A raiding party from the fort, about 100 strong, attacked the mine with the bayonet and blew it up at a cost of 8 killed and 13 wounded, whilst about 60 tribesmen were left for dead in the crater of the exploded mine.

178

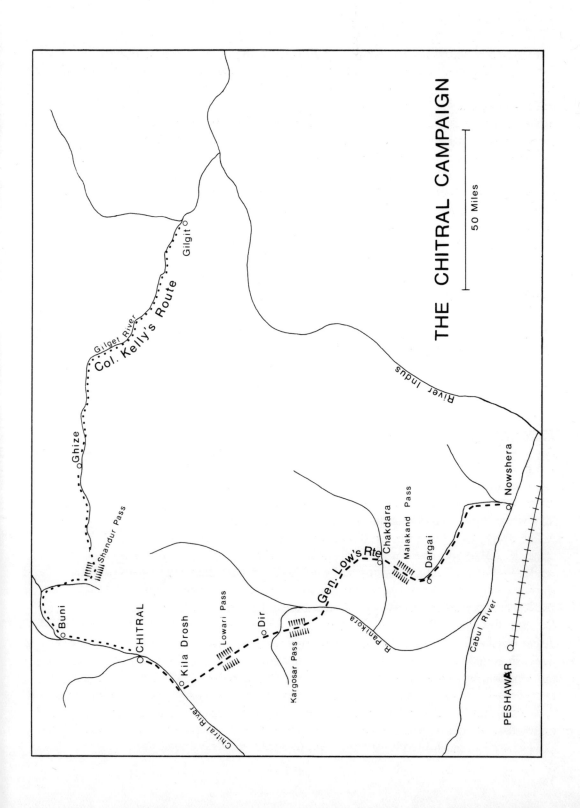

Gilgit

Col. Kelly's Route

Gilget River

Ghize

Shandur Pass

Buni

CHITRAL

Chitral River

Kila Drosh

Lowari Pass

Dir

Kargosar Pass

Gen. Low's Rte

R. Panjkora

Chakdara

Malakand Pass

Dargai

River Indus

Nowshera

Cabul River

PESHAWAR

THE CHITRAL CAMPAIGN

50 Miles

Eight miles below Mastuj, Kelly's small force came upon a large number of enemy tribesmen well positioned in one of the most famous natural defensive positions in the country, reputed to be impregnable. Again, the little mountain-guns did sterling work in destroying enemy sangars before Kelly's men finally put the enemy to rout after an attack involving the descent of ravines by improvised rope-ladders and the climbing of steep and slippery goat-tracks. Then followed five days of skirmishing in the rock-strewn defiles in front of Chitral until, on the night of 18 April, the besiegers stole quietly away. Two days later, Colonel Kelly's column marched into the fort. The siege had lasted forty-six days, and one fifth of the garrison had been killed or wounded.

Low's force arrived some four or five days later, after a great deal of very heavy fighting which began on 3 April, when the mountain-guns shelled the enemy positions along the crests bordering the Malakand Pass (the lowest of them was 3,000 feet above the valley). Then Sikhs and Guides carried the sangars on the left and worked their way along the crest to turn the enemy's flank; they were nineteen hours under arms and they lost many officers. The Scottish Borderers and the Gordon Highlanders worked up the centre of the Pass with the King's Royal Rifles, the Bedfords and native infantry in support. After a precipitous climb, when the men had to haul each other up, the village on the summit was carried with the bayonet and left in flames; the enemy was driven across the ridge into the Swat Valley beyond. British casualties were 8 officers and 61 men. It was estimated that the enemy massed about 12,000 men and had sustained some 5,000 casualties.

Next day the advance encountered the enemy on a high ridge. The guns came into action as the infantry advanced under fire from the heights and repeated attacks from large parties of tribesmen. Two companies of the Bedfords were attacked by vastly superior numbers of natives but magazine-fire at short range halted them in their tracks and sent the survivors scurrying for cover. Although they were working over most unsuitable country, the Guides cavalry distinguished themselves here against the tribesmen who would face magazine-rifle fire but did not like lances.

The Swat River had to be crossed under fire from a ridge of hills completely dominating the only ford. The Sappers who attempted to bridge the river were forced to withdraw but the mountain-guns and the Maxim gun of the King's Own Scottish Borderers did good work against enemy positions on the ridge. Finally, the Sikhs and the Borderers were committed while the Bengal Lancers and the Guides forced the fast-flowing river under heavy fire. Once the Lancers got on the far bank of the river they dispersed the enemy with the lance although invariably he put up a stout resistance. The Scottish Borderers, linked arm-in-arm, forded the Swat higher up and, covered by the mountain-guns, carried a small fort, while the Sikhs crossed lower down and occupied two villages. This arm-linking method of river-crossing was only possible with brass cartridges and breech-loading rifles; in the old days of paper cartridges the musket and pouch had to be held above water. Casualties at the crossing were few, considering that the enemy had assembled 4,500 men and had suffered heavy losses.

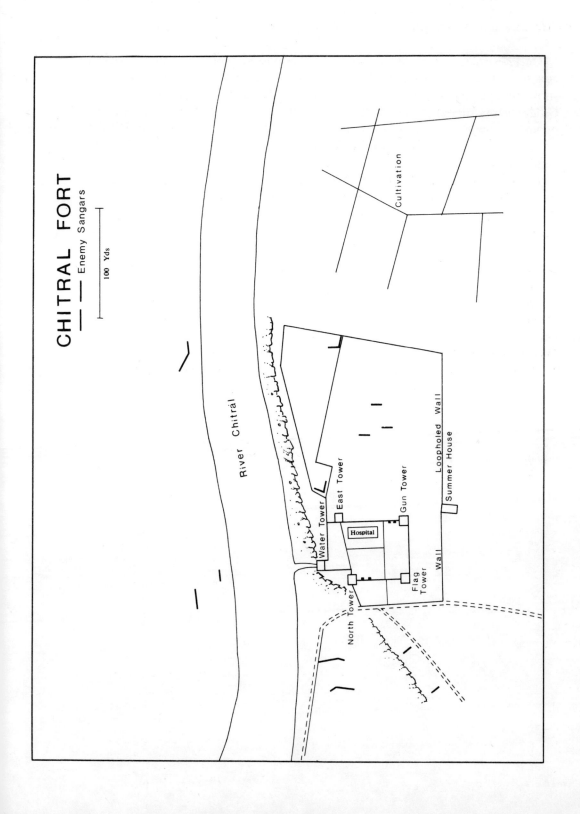

CHITRAL FORT

Enemy Sangars

100 Yds

River Chitral

Cultivation

Water Tower

East Tower

Gun Tower

Hospital

North Tower

Flag Tower

Wall

Loopholed Wall

Summer House

On 12 April Colonel Battye and his Guides passed over the Panjkora River to form a covering force on the right bank, but before daybreak the river, swollen with melted snow, rose suddenly and tribesmen sent down logs which swept away the bridge. The Guides were ordered to march down the right bank to a further crossing 2 miles lower down but, owing to a misunderstanding, they marched out of sight so that they could not be covered by the fire from the left bank. Dividing his force into three, Battye retired slowly down the river bank, himself remaining with the last party to cover the retreat until he was mortally wounded. The Guides, unable to cross the river that day, made a fortified camp on the river bank and spent a long night surrounded by at least 2,000 of the enemy who were discouraged from attacking them by star-shells fired across the river and the presence of some Sikhs and a Maxim gun that had been floated across the river on a raft made of inflated animal skins. At daybreak the tribesmen retired, leaving about 500 bodies behind while the Guides lost 2 officers and 3 men killed and 22 wounded.

Although there was constant skirmishing, no further major engagements took place as the infantry, cavalry and guns cleared the hills and slowly advanced towards Chitral. On 18 April General Gatacre, with the Buffs, Gurkhas, half a mountain battery, two Maxims and twenty days' supplies, was sent forward to make a dash for Chitral. When, on 21 April, news came that the fort had been relieved by Colonel Kelly he was ordered to halt and General Low, securing his communications as he marched, steadily advanced and a few days later entered Chitral.

45 The Mashonaland Field Force 1896

In June 1896 the natives of Mashonaland rebelled and, operating over a large area, murdered more than 120 white settlers. The district was in an alarming state of unpreparedness; its police had been taken for the Jameson Raid, and most of its available fighting men with their horses were in Matabeleland, where another rising was in progress. In response to a telegram sent by the British South Africa Company, a force of mounted infantry was sent to Salisbury by way of Beira to help the local forces to suppress the Mashona rising. Under Lieutenant-Colonel E.A.H.Alderson were four companies of mounted infantrymen fighting on foot, with every man a marksman or a first-class shot. They were reinforced by about 100 officers and men of the York and Lancaster Regiment and the Royal Engineers, disembarked while en route for Mauritius, and some 150 men of the West Riding Regiment together with 13 civilian scouts. Alderson soon had the rising under control. They marched warily and bivouacked each night in laagers with machine-guns and seven-pounder guns placed at alternate corners, after burning the grass all round the laager for about 150 to 200 yards so as to give no cover to an advancing enemy. Then they took by surprise the kraal of the biggest chief in Mashonaland and captured it inflicting some 200 casualties, losing 3 killed and 4 wounded and 'winkling out' natives who had hidden in deep and dark caves. A few days later a second action took place at another kraal formidably situated on a height going down sheer into the plain on three sides with a very narrow approach on the fourth side. The Mounted Infantrymen went along the slippery, sloping rock to an entrance strongly barricaded with logs. They were involved in a type of fighting peculiar to the Mashonas, whose kraals were backed by cliffs in which innumerable caves were dug, some of them extending underground beneath the huts of the kraals. The natives went to earth and then fired up through cracks in the rocks and earth under the feet of the troops above. Their old-fashioned large-bore elephant guns and muskets fired bits of iron, nails, brass, stones, even bottle-stoppers so that, at almost point-blank range, they made huge, often mortal wounds in the groin or abdomen of the men above.

By the end of November, after a considerable amount of manoeuvring around the countryside, Makoni, the rebel chieftain, was dead and his people scattered; his son and other sub-chieftains were fugitives, their kraals taken or burned. On 12 December 1896 the Mashonaland Field Force was broken up and returned to England to rejoin its own regiments. In difficult country against an elusive foe, and with a force that at no time exceeded 500 white men, the Mounted Infantry Corps had done extremely well at a cost of 3 officers and 4 men killed and 18 wounded.

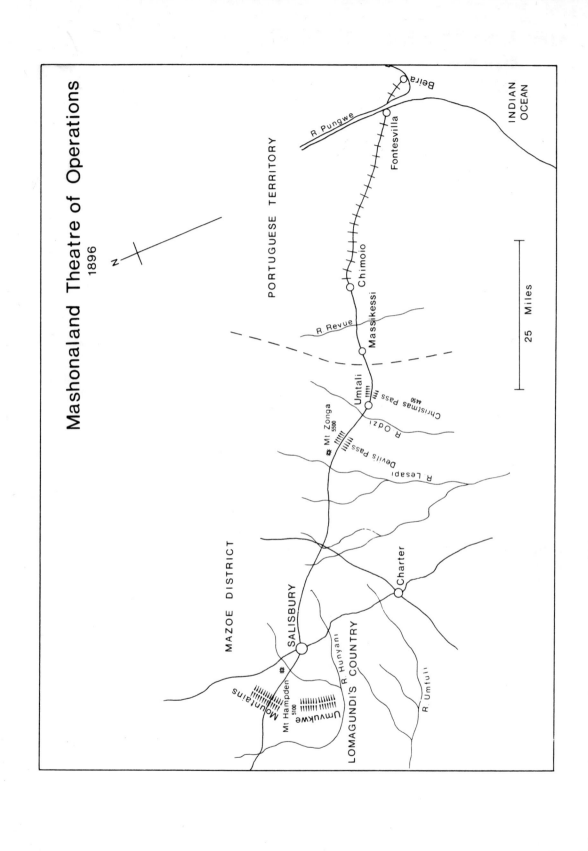

Mashonaland Theatre of Operations
1896

N

25 Miles

INDIAN OCEAN

Beira

R. Pungwe

Fontesvilla

PORTUGUESE TERRITORY

Chimoio

Massikessi

R. Revue

Umtali

Christmas Pass 4450

R Odzi

Mt Zonga 5500

Devil's Pass

R Lesapi

Charter

MAZOE DISTRICT

SALISBURY

R Hunyani

R. Umfuli

Umvukwe Mountains

Mt Hampden 5100

LOMAGUNDI'S COUNTRY

46 The Re-Conquest of Egypt 1896-8

In the years that followed Gordon's death at Khartoum the British public demanded insistently that he should be avenged. Moreover, France, Belgium and Italy were increasingly active in Africa and in March 1896 the British government instructed General H. H. Kitchener to undertake a campaign of re-conquest. This opened on 16 March 1896, when several Egyptian battalions were hurried up the Nile by rail and the river steamers of Thomas Cook and Sons, to garrison Akasha and the various posts between that and Wadi Halfa, which was to be manned by the North Staffords. A fortified camp was formed at Akasha to cover the railway construction, and here supplies for a further advance were to be accumulated by camel convoys following the river route, while reinforcements and supplies came up the Nile from Egypt.

Kitchener had solved the problem of supply for his Dongola Expeditionary Force by taking every advantage of river transport supplemented by camels, and by extending the railway as he progressed. By these means he intended to concentrate his striking force and drive the enemy from Firket. Then, when the Nile rose, the reserve troops and supplies accumulated at Firket would be carried in sailing boats up to Dongola in the wake of the army while the shallow-draught gun-boats assisted and guarded the river traffic and took part in the battles.

In the fourteen years that had elapsed since the British evacuation of the Sudan, an Egyptian army had been created that was capable of fighting alongside its British comrades and of holding its own against hitherto dreaded Dervishes. Many of the soldiers in these battalions had originally fought against the British for, after each victory, the best of the prisoners and deserters were enlisted in Egyptian battalions where British sergeant-instructors taught them to drill and shoot.

News of the rapid movement of the Egyptian army, and of reinforcements on their way from Suakin, reached the Khalifa at Omdurman and, under the Emir Hammuda, the Dervishes began to mass in great force at Firket and other places to the south. They had not altered appreciably since the battles of the early 1880s, retaining all their old dash and fire, although their spears and Remington rifles were no match for the hard-hitting Martini-Henry rifles of the new Egyptian army.

During May 1896 Kitchener consolidated his position at Akasha, bringing up more troops and improving his communications so that by the end of the month the railway line stretched 64 miles from Wadi Halfa and was only 25 miles from Akasha. Then Kitchener sent a force of Egyptian and Sudanese soldiers with British Maxim-gun teams by both river and desert routes to pounce upon Hammuda and his 3,000 tribesmen at Firket, 16 miles upstream from Akasha. With secrecy, silence and perfect timing, the force surprised the Dervishes at 5 am on 7 June 1896 and by 7.30 am, after very hard

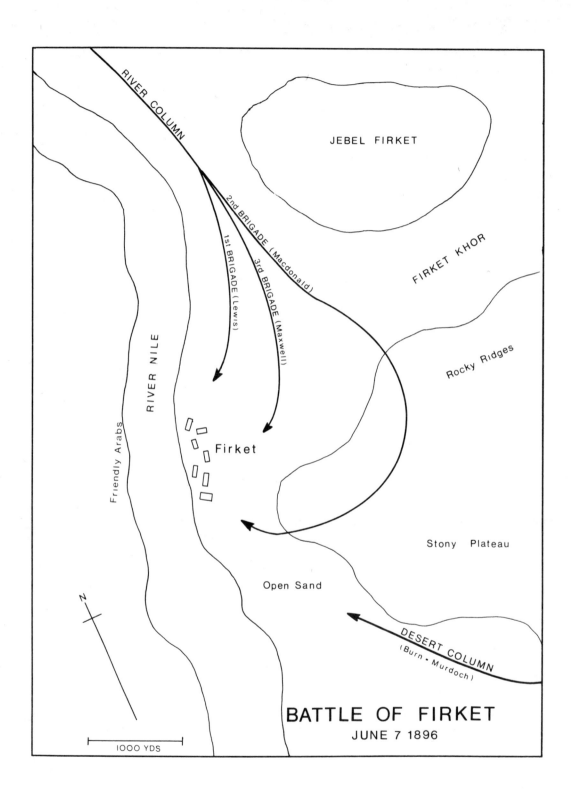

RIVER COLUMN

JEBEL FIRKET

FIRKET KHOR

2nd BRIGADE (Macdonald)

1st BRIGADE (Lewis)

3rd BRIGADE (Maxwell)

RIVER NILE

Rocky Ridges

Friendly Arabs

Firket

Stony Plateau

Open Sand

DESERT COLUMN
(Burn • Murdoch)

N

1000 YDS

BATTLE OF FIRKET
JUNE 7 1896

fighting, it had completely beaten them, taking more than 500 prisoners and killing or wounding over 1,000 men.

In the three months that followed this decisive victory, the advance was delayed by storms, floods and cholera. Nevertheless, in spite of the dreadful weather, advance parties of troops penetrated far up the river and, when Lewis's Egyptian Brigade was caught in a dust-storm, 1,700 men out of 3,000 collapsed and several died, overcome by heat, thirst and exhaustion.

Kitchener had a gun-boat, *Zafir*, brought out in pieces and reassembled at Kosha, but its boiler burst immediately after launching and it was not in action for some months.

Reinforced by the arrival of the North Staffords, the Dongola Expeditionary Force of nearly 15,000 men advanced southwards in brigade formations along the desert route and river-bank, some units making the journey in river steamers protected by gun-boats. On 18 September the Emir of Dongola transferred his force across the Nile to an entrenched position on the left bank at Hafir, forcing Kitchener to open the way to Dongola with nothing but gunboats and artillery, as the infantry was unable to cross the broad and swift-flowing Nile separating the opposing forces. Watched by battalions of Egyptian infantry sitting on the hot sand, the three-hour action took place on the following day, when the gunboats ran the gauntlet of the hostile batteries and steamed onwards to reach Dongola before sunset. The Emir evacuated Hafir; the Egyptian infantry crossed the Nile in boats abandoned by the Dervishes and Kitchener received the surrender of Dongola on the evening of 24 September. During this arduous six months' campaign, the Egyptian army had lost only 47 soldiers killed, 122 wounded and about 350 missing.

To maintain the successful momentum of the Dongola Expedition, Kitchener decided to build a railway across the uncharted and waterless Nubian Desert, from Wadi Halfa to Abu Hamed. The first sleepers were laid on 1 January 1897 and by 15 July the railway had been pushed almost half-way across the desert towards Abu Hamed. The work was now held up while a force was sent to throw the enemy out of that place. Commanded by Major-General Archibald Hunter with Lieutenant-Colonel Hector Macdonald, a flying column made up of an Egyptian and Sudanese infantry brigade, a mule battery of six Krupp twelve-pounder guns, four machine-guns, a few cavalry and 1,300 camels toiled painfully through a miserable wilderness of rock and ankle-deep white sand to cover 118 miles in seven and a half days at the hottest time of the year. The Sudanese infantry rushed the trenches with the bayonet and won a surprise victory over the Dervishes. Hunter had the Arab dead thrown into the river so that when, two days later, Kitchener at Merowe saw a procession of Arab corpses floating down-stream, he knew that a battle had been won.

Disheartened and perturbed by the sudden advance, the enemy evacuated Berber, strategically the most vital point between Wadi Halfa and Omdurman, which was occupied by Kitchener on 31 August. Holding a long line liable to attack at many points, with a small force at Berber and in front of him a large army of warlike Dervishes,

Kitchener realised that the time had come to ask for reinforcements of British troops. On 2 January the 1st Battalion Royal Warwickshire Regiment and the Cameron Highlanders at Cairo proceeded immediately to Wadi Halfa. The 1st Battalion Seaforth Highlanders at Malta and the 5th Battalion Northumberland Fusiliers at Gibraltar were also moved to Egypt. This British infantry formed a brigade under Colonel William Gatacre.

At the end of January 1898, the general situation was that the Egyptian army, composed of three infantry brigades, eight squadrons of cavalry and four batteries of artillery, held various posts along the Nile from Fort Atbara to Abu Hamed, while the British brigade under Gatacre was in camp 30 miles south of Abu Hamed. The Suakin-Berber route had been opened and its oases were held by armed posts. An Egyptian garrison defended Kassala, about 250 miles east of Khartoum, which the British had taken over from the Italians after their defeat at Adowa. Arrangements had been made with the Abyssinians to remain neutral. The main Dervish army, 40,000 strong, was with the Khalifa at Omdurman, and a further 20,000 men under Mahmud and Osman Digna were at Metemma.

In February the Khalifa allowed Mahmud to cross the Nile. He found himself in an angle formed by the Nile and the Atbara, from which he could not retreat without giving battle. So, short of supplies and with his force dwindling through desertions, he and his 12,000 followers entrenched themselves on the right bank of the Atbara and waited attack. The British brigade moved up and was bivouacked within 10 miles of Atbara Fort. Kitchener hesitated to attack. He was unable to tempt the Dervishes from their entrenched position; his army was nearly 1,400 miles from the sea and about 1,200 miles from its main base of supplies which had to come along a sand-banked river and a single line of rail which also carried the material for its own construction. The delay caused considerable hardship to the troops; they had only one blanket each and no overcoats, so that they suffered badly from the cold at night and the heat during the day. Poor food and inadequate sanitary conditions caused outbreaks of dysentery and enteric fever.

At last, however, Kitchener struck his camp and moved upstream to assault the Dervish position with a force consisting of about 14,000 men with 24 guns and 12 machine-guns; it included the British brigade; an Egyptian division of three infantry brigades; eight squadrons of Egyptian cavalry; six companies of the Camel Corps and a Rocket detachment, together with two British and two Egyptian Maxim-batteries. On 8 April, formed into four great brigade squares with the British leading, the force trudged under a bright moon across the desert until 4 am, when they deployed into attack formation. Advancing through the scattered bush and scrub, they reached open ground overlooking the shallow crater-like depression where, less than half a mile away, lay Mahmud's stronghold. At 6.20 am the first gun fired on the zariba, followed by a heavy cross-fire of shells and rockets that set trees, bushes and straw huts alight. Clouds of smoke rolled over the enemy's trenches; earth and stones flew in all directions.

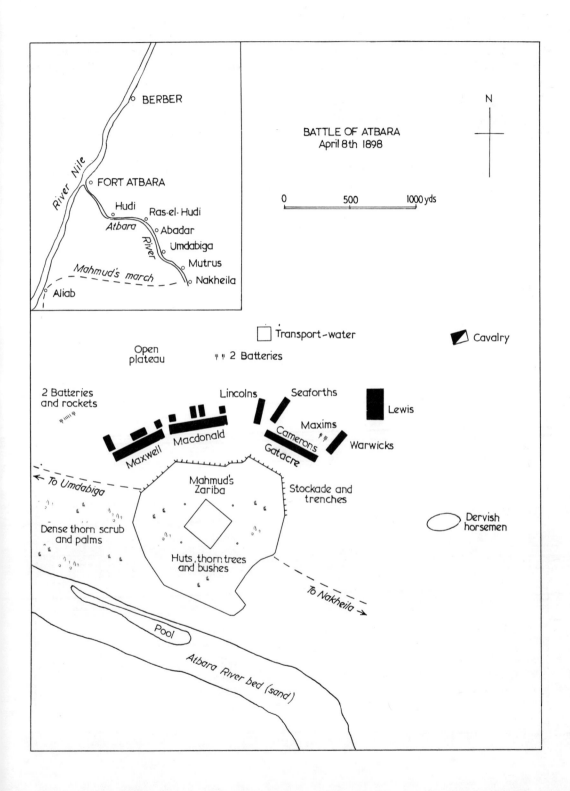

BERBER

River Nile

FORT ATBARA

Hudi
Ras-el-Hudi
Atbara
Abadar
River
Umdabiga
Mutrus
Nakheila

Mahmud's march

Aliab

BATTLE OF ATBARA
April 8th 1898

N

0   500   1000 yds

☐ Transport-water

◆ Cavalry

Open
plateau

⚲⚲ 2 Batteries

2 Batteries
and rockets

Lincolns

Seaforths

Lewis

Maxwell   Macdonald

Camerons
Maxims
Gatacre

Warwicks

← To Umdabiga

Mahmud's
Zariba

Stockade and
trenches

Dense thorn scrub
and palms

Dervish
horsemen

Huts, thorn trees
and bushes

To Nakheila →

Pool

Atbara River bed (sand)

Lying prone in their deep trenches, the Dervishes showed no signs of life except once, when hundreds of horsemen scrambled into the saddle and galloped out to the Egyptian left front where they were hotly engaged by the cavalry and machine-guns. At 7.40 am the bombardment ceased and the general advance was sounded. Then, with bands playing, pipes skirling and shouts of 'Remember Gordon!', the lines and columns of infantry bore down on the Dervish zariba. The British had the Cameron Highlanders in line along their whole front; then, in columns of their eight companies, came the Lincolns on the right, the Seaforths in the centre and the Warwicks on the left. All halted to volley-fire by sections and moved off again at the sound of the bugle.

Mahmud's position was said to be fronted by a dense and extremely prickly thorn hedge, but when the Cameron Highlanders came up to the position they found that there was only a loose, low barrier of dry camel-thorn that was easily tugged away. Inside the zariba were a stockade and a triple trench in the midst of bush thick with palm stem, mimosa thorn and scrub grass, and dotted with a honeycomb of holes and pits. When the infantry stormed into the zariba there was no sign of life. Suddenly out of the earth came running dusty, black figures, turning to shoot as they fell back before the advancing infantry. Leaving the ground behind them carpeted thickly with dead tribesmen, Camerons, Seaforths and Lincolns deployed right and left to sweep straight across the zariba to the rear entrenchment and beyond, through thick undergrowth, to the river. They thronged the river bank in double line and fired crashing volleys into

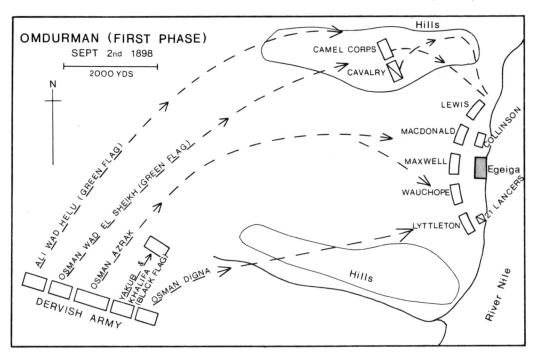

the fleeing natives until the intervening quarter-mile of dry sand-bed was spotted with black shapes. With some difficulty the troops were finally restrained from firing; there was a sudden silence followed by a loud burst of cheering, and the forty-minute battle was over.

The British Brigade lost 5 officers and 21 men killed and 99 officers and men wounded; the three Egyptian brigades lost 57 men killed and 386 wounded, including 10 British officers. The Dervish losses are unknown but they were estimated at 40 emirs and 3,000 men killed, and many captured, including Mahmud himself. Only Osman Digna and 4,000 out of the 12,000 who had garrisoned the position managed to rejoin the Dervish army at Omdurman.

The victorious force marched northwards to summer quarters along the Nile: here, during July and August, they were reinforced by a new British brigade formed of the 1st Battalion Grenadier Guards from Gibraltar; the 1st Battalion Northumberland Fusiliers and the 2nd Battalion Lancashire Fusiliers from Cairo, and the 2nd Battalion Rifle Brigade from Malta; the 21st Lancers were sent up from Egypt, together with considerable artillery reinforcements. The force now totalled over 22,000 men, with 44 guns, 20 Maxims and 3 new gun-boats which were put together immediately after the battle of Atbara.

On 24 August the army began to move southwards by successive divisions, preceded by the cavalry and the Camel Corps and marching on a two-brigade front in a formation well adapted for repelling a sudden assault. On 31 August they came to a hilltop and, looking down, saw Omdurman lying to their front, an extensive area of mud houses with the Mahdi's tomb rising above them. Before the city, noticeable at first only because of their banners, was a solid wall of motionless warriors drawn up in five immense masses on a three-mile front, eight or ten deep; it totalled perhaps 40,000 men.

Kitchener expected to be attacked, and ordered the searchlights of his gun-boats to be turned on the enemy's camp throughout the night, while the infantry lay down behind a low fence of thorn bushes in a shallow trench about a foot deep with a raised parapet in front. The mounted troops withdrew within the enclosure. Once again, this time at daylight, on 2 September the gun-boats and 5-inch howitzers bombarded Omdurman at over 3,000 yards range, throwing fifty-pounder shells that tore great holes in the dome of the Mahdi's tomb.

At the same time the cavalry and Camel Corps went out in a wide screen to reconnoitre, soon sending back messengers to say that the entire Dervish army was advancing. At first a few flags appeared over the crest; then came solid masses of spearmen and rifle-men led by horsemen. The muffled roar of a vast multitude reached the ears of the waiting Anglo-Egyptian army as the Dervishes spread themselves in a gigantic semi-circle round the front and left of the position. The Egyptian cavalry and the Camel Corps were ordered by Kitchener to draw the enemy across his front, and, with the Horse Artillery retired northwards towards the Karari Hills, to be followed by 20,000 Dervishes mustered under green flags. At 6.50 am the artillery opened fire at 2,700 yards range;

then the gunboats on the southern flank opened up and the Grenadier Guards fired section-volleys at 2,000 yards. As the Dervishes came within range, the Highlanders, the Lincolns and the Egyptian brigades took up the firing, standing in double rank behind their low zariba; they shot as fast as they could load and pull the trigger and the rifles grew so hot that men had to change them for others taken from the supports. As the guns bellowed, shrapnel whistled and Maxims growled savagely, the Dervishes advanced in a well-defined line divided into masses of about 4,000 men, covering the whole plain between the hills and all the ridge from Jebel Surkab to the river but the never-ending hail of bullets and shells prevented a single Dervish from getting closer than about 300 yards to the Anglo-Egyptian position, and at 8 am the survivors sullenly withdrew towards the west, leaving the ground white with the jibbahs of more than 2,000 dead.

The cavalry and the Camel Corps had taken up a position on the Karari Hills but, out-flanked by vastly superior numbers of enemy, they were now in great difficulty: the Camel Corps in particular showed itself quite unable to contend with a mobile enemy on rocky ground. The Dervishes pressed the attack, capturing two guns, and almost succeeded in isolating the Camel Corps, but at a critical moment a gunboat appeared from upstream and, assisted by the fire of the land artillery, drove the pursuers back with very heavy losses.

At 8.30 am Kitchener sent the 21st Lancers forward to reconnoitre and clear the ground, while the force broke up and expanded to march in echelon of brigades from the left to guard against an attack on the right flank or rear. It is possible that Kitchener was unaware that on his right front, hidden behind Jebel Surkab, lay the army of the Black Flag, 17,000 strong, under the Khalifa himself. Movement was slow as the 2nd British Brigade led along the river, with the 1st British on its right rear; then came the Egyptian Brigades of Maxwell, Lewis and Macdonald, with Collinson supporting. Wauchope's 1st British Brigade tried to overtake Lyttleton's 2nd British Brigade, with the result that Maxwell's 2nd Egyptian Brigade was out-distanced. Maxwell then attempted to close the widening gap between him and Wauchope, and Lewis hurried to reduce the interval between himself and Maxwell, leaving Macdonald, who had completed his move westwards towards the flank, nearly a mile from Lewis.

As Kitchener ordered Maxwell's brigade to storm Jebel Surkab, with the 2nd British Brigade on his left, the army of the Black Flag rushed out in a fierce attack on Macdonald's and Lewis's Egyptian Brigades. Kitchener immediately sent the 1st British Brigade hurrying back to Macdonald's assistance and so the army now faced west, with its right flank drawn back to the river. The Black Flag army attacking Macdonald was taken in flank by the fire of Lewis's brigade and also by Maxwell's brigade, who had captured the Jebel: it wavered and drifted back. Suddenly a howling storm of 12,000 unbroken fearless native warriors, the Green Flag army, came storming down from the Karari Hills to Macdonald's right rear, forcing him to form his Egyptian Brigade into an arrow-head as Wauchope came up rapidly with his brigade, sending the Lincolns to the right and the remainder of the brigade to the left of Macdonald.

Now began the fiercest fight of the day, as the Khalifa again brought up his own Black Banner warriors to surge forward with the Green Flag army. It was a grave moment. If Macdonald went, Lewis on his left, with Collinson and the supporting Camel Corps and the cavalry who had returned from a charge, must all go too. The 2nd British and 2nd Egyptian Brigades, advancing by the left of Surkab Hill, were too far away to help. The Egyptian, Sudanese and British infantry poured volley after volley into the attacking tribesmen and then Macdonald and his Egyptian infantry drove the army of the Green Flag back towards the hills, where a charge by the Egyptian cavalry changed their retreat into a rout. Then, in an imposing array of artillery, cavalry and camels, the whole army advanced westwards, driving the Dervishes before them into the desert.

Just before all this happened, the 21st Lancers, with four squadrons in line, came upon a force of about 300 Dervishes on an apparently open plain and swung into the first charge of their history. Suddenly between them and the Dervishes yawned a deep ravine filled with a solid mass of about 3,000 or 4,000 Dervishes. Too late to check, the Lancers surged down the steep side of the ravine, their horses plunging and falling, while Dervishes lay on the ground trying to hamstring them. Leaving behind 5 officers, 65 men and 119 horses, the cavalry went straight through and out on the other side,

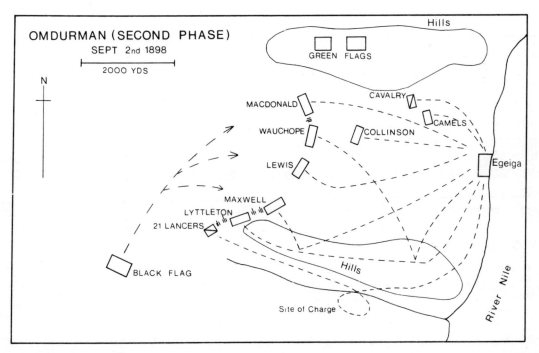

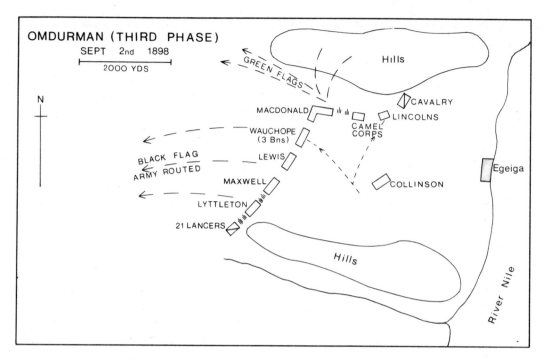

OMDURMAN (THIRD PHASE)
SEPT 2nd 1898
2000 YDS

dismounted and opened fire with their carbines at short range before getting themselves clear.

At 11.30 am the battle was over. The Dervish army was wiped out. It had lost 11,000 killed, 16,000 wounded and 4,000 prisoners from a total of about 40,000 men. The Anglo-Egyptian army, numbering perhaps 22,000 men, lost 48 killed and 382 wounded. It marched on, to meet very little resistance in the narrow, evil-smelling streets of Omdurman. The Khalifa escaped and remained at large until 24 November when a force of native infantry under Colonel Sir Reginald Wingate defeated the remaining Dervishes and found the bodies of the Khalifa and his brothers lying dead on the battlefield.

Immediately after the battle of Omdurman, on 4 September 1898, representatives of every regiment and corps paraded on the left bank of the Blue Nile in front of the ruin of Gordon's palace. National anthems were played, a twenty-one-gun salute was fired and a religious service was held. Gordon's favourite hymn, 'Abide with Me', marked the end of the campaign.

47 The Operations of the Tirah Expeditionary Force 1897-8

The general object of this expedition was to invade Tirah and exact reparation for the unprovoked aggression of the Afridi and Orakzai tribes; Tirah was their summer home and had never before been entered by a British force. The mountainous country was difficult and to a great extent unknown, and the men had to meet well armed and war-like tribes whose fighting men were numbered by tens of thousands — the Afridis alone were believed to be able to put 30,000 men into the field, at least half of them armed with modern rifles.

In October 1897 a force of 44,000 men, under the command of Lieutenant-General Sir William Lockhart, assembled at Kohat. In addition to fourteen battalions of native infantry and mountain artillery, the force included the Royal West Surrey Regiment; the Devonshire Regiment; the Yorkshire Regiment; the Royal Scots Fusiliers; the King's Own Scottish Borderers; the Dorsetshire Regiment; the Sherwood Foresters; the Northamptonshire Regiment; the Derbyshire Regiment; and the Gordon Highlanders. The Punjab was scoured for transport-animals and 60,000 camels, mules, bullocks and donkeys were assembled.

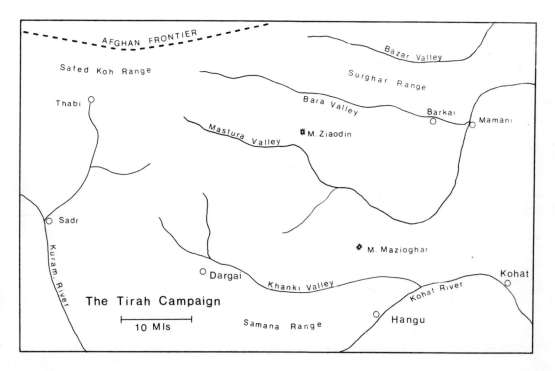

Lockhart's main column was to invade Tirah from Kohat by way of Sampagha and Arhanga Passes, while two subsidiary columns from Peshawar were to act in support. Before the main column moved off, it was necessary to make the road fit for their transport; this meant that tribesmen had to be dislodged from the village of Dargai and the ridges around it from where they could fire upon the road-parties. Dargai itself, 6,000 feet high, was only approachable over its last half-mile by a climb up sheer, broken and shelving cliffs over a narrow track with an entrance on the far side of a completely exposed coverless area of ground. The tribesmen were not in great strength on the position and British infantry and Gurkhas swarmed up the steep ascent and took the position at a cost of only 2 killed and 13 wounded. During mid-afternoon the position was abandoned because of difficulties of supply and water. The enemy closely pressed the rearguard and was only held off by mountain-guns, and in what turned out to be a difficult operation an officer and 7 men were killed; 5 officers and 29 men were wounded.

The main force left Kohat on 20 October, and had to retake Dargai, which was now strongly occupied by about 12,000 tribesmen. Covered by long-range fire from the Gordon Highlanders and the Maxim-gun detachment, together with mountain batteries, the Gurkhas formed up under cover about 500 yards from the cliff and then burst out on to the open ground in the face of extremely accurate and rapid fire. Reaching some broken ground about 100 yards on, after losing 3 officers and 50 men, they were

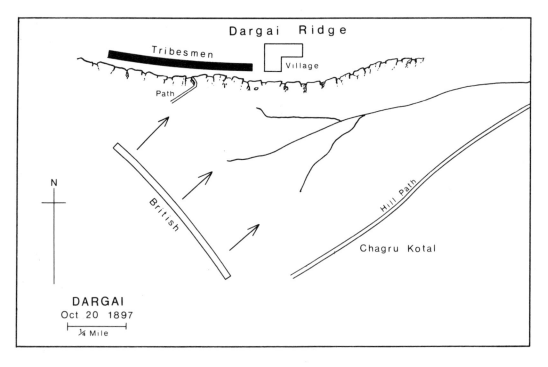

pinned down by heavy fire. The Dorsets and the Derbyshires were put in to try to rush the ridge and each lost between 40 and 50 men without succeeding. The Gordons and the 3rd Sikhs were ordered up and the artillery maintained a rapid, concentrated fire for three minutes; then the Gordons followed by the Sikhs and all the other troops dashed across the open ground. They swarmed up the steep slope so decisively that the enemy did not wait for the final assault but fled in all directions, followed by long-range volleys. Five Victoria Crosses were awarded for the Dargai action in which British casualties amounted to 4 officers and 34 men killed, 14 officers and 147 wounded.

On 29 October the Queen's and the King's Own Scottish Borderers stormed a ridge to take the Sampagha Pass and on 31 October, the Arhanga Pass was captured with little opposition. Throughout the advance, foraging parties and baggage were constantly under attack — on 25 October a man was killed and 36 wounded when a foraging party was attacked. On 1 November in a night attack on a convoy, the tribesmen captured thirteen boxes of ammunition and the Queen's Regiment's treasure-chest, and inflicted some losses. On 9 November, the Northamptons lost heavily as they retired from destroying enemy villages: they lost touch with their supporting Sikhs while they were carrying wounded down craggy cliffs. Trapped in a nullah under heavy fire, they were extricated by Sikhs and Gurkhas with total losses of 2 officers and 18 men killed, 4 officers and 44 men wounded. Sikhs and two companies of the Dorsets, who remained out in the darkness collecting stragglers, were cut off by Afridis and only managed to fight off the tribesmen at the bayonet point by capturing some partly burned houses and making a stand. The Dorsets were overwhelmed and lost their officers; the survivors were brought into camp by the senior sergeant. Total casualties in this affair were 4 officers and 25 men killed; 6 officers and 38 men wounded. On 22 November, a column which included the King's Own Scottish Borderers and the Yorkshire Regiment went out to explore the approaches to the Bara Valley and, as they returned, their rearguard became heavily engaged; they lost 1 officer and 4 men killed, 2 officers and 28 men wounded.

Because of the cold, the force was now obliged to evacuate the Tirah valley and the 3rd and 4th Brigades under Brigadier-General Westamacott, proceeding down the Shaloba defile to Dwa Toi down the Bara valley, experienced some of the heaviest rearguard fighting ever encountered in an Indian frontier campaign. Progress was slow for the roads were deep in mud, and, on the morning of 11 December, a thick mist allowed the Afridis to get in close and pour a heavy fire on to the crowded and helpless transport-animals and followers. As the transport tried to get off the track, it was bogged down in the fields and nullahs. The enemy attacked the rearguard with great boldness and the fighting continued throughout the day; casualties became so numerous that the fighting-line was seriously weakened by troops having to carry the wounded, for the dhoolie bearers were too terror-stricken to perform their duty. There was no water-supply at that night's camp after a day when over 70 men had become casualties during a relatively short march. The tribesmen only ceased their attacks on the next day, when the Peshawar force was met some four miles from Sawaikot.

On 29 January Lockhart sent out columns to capture the flocks of the Afridi tribes in the hope of bringing them to terms. All columns carried out their task without encountering any opposition, except the 4th Brigade from Mamanai, who had to fight one of the hardest actions of the campaign. 600 men of the Yorkshire Light Infantry and the 36th Sikhs with two guns advanced along a pass, occupying heights on either side as they moved forward. Then, through a misunderstanding, the native troops evacuated the heights on the west of the pass and these were immediately occupied by tribesmen who poured a heavy fire into the troops below. With difficulty the Yorkshire Light Infantry managed to cover the withdrawal until they were met at the mouth of the pass by a force sent out from camp. Owing to the hilly ground and the nature of the operation it was impossible to bring out the dead, but the rifles and the ammunition were saved. Total casualties were 5 officers and 28 men killed, 3 officers and 34 men wounded. This was almost the last fight of the campaign. The Afridis tendered their submission and by the end of June only a single brigade remained in the Khyber Pass. In 1900 regular troops were withdrawn and the Pass was handed back to the Khyber Rifles.

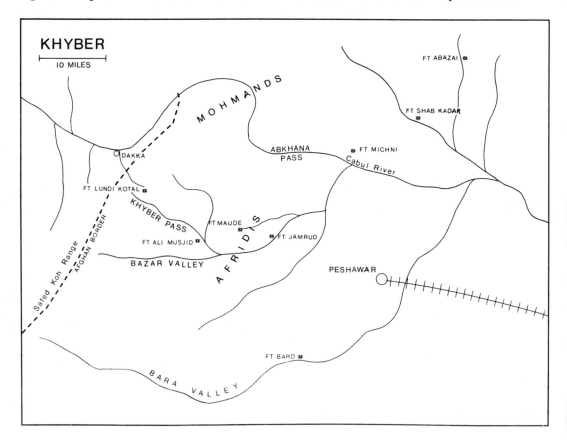

48 Operations on the North-West Frontier 1897-8

The Malakand Field Force

In July 1897 some 20,000 Afridi tribesmen suddenly attacked the Malakand Post. Beaten off with heavy loss after several days' hard fighting, the tribesmen then turned to the Chakdara Post, which survived several assaults before water and ammunition became scarce. Under Sir Bindon Blood the Malakand Field Force – 6,800 infantry, 700 cavalry and 24 guns – included the 1st Battalion West Kent Regiment; the 1st Battalion East Kent Regiment (The Buffs); the Royal Artillery, and native infantry and cavalry units. On reaching the Malakand camp, Sir Bindon Blood sent out a column which successfully relieved Chakdara after hard fighting. Then reinforced by the 1st Battalion Gordon Highlanders, the 2nd Battalion Highland Light Infantry, Punjab and Gurkha Infantry, he began his advance from Thana on 17 August encountering the enemy at Landaki where 5,000 tribesmen, holding a long flat-topped spur enclosing the valley like a great rampart, were kept occupied in front while Meiklejohn's brigade climbed the hills to threaten the enemy's left flank. The surprised and out-manoeuvred tribesmen fled from the spur, pursued by cavalry. It was here that in a misunderstanding two British officers were killed. Two Victoria Crosses were awarded, one to Viscount Fincastle who was with the party as war correspondent of *The Times*.

But as the Swat Valley quietened, tribal risings occurred in rapid succession in other parts of the frontier.

The Tochi Field Force, 1897

In June 1897 the Madda Khel tribe made a treacherous attack on a political officer and his escort of 300 native infantry and 2 guns. With only 16 rounds per gun, the artillery came into action at 100 yards range as the fighting retreat on foot began. Four white officers were wounded, two mortally, but all continued to lead their men as the small force retired by successive units while the guns, out of shell, fired blanks to discourage the enemy. Reinforcements arrived and the tribesmen withdrew, leaving a number of casualties behind them. Total casualties of the British force were 2 officers and 21 men killed and 28 wounded.

Subsequently the Tochi Field Force was formed. A punitive expedition under the command of Major-General Corrie-Bird was despatched, consisting of two brigades, and including the Argyll and Sutherland Highlanders and the Rifle Brigade in addition to native infantry and cavalry. Marching out on 20 July, the force engaged in sporadic skirmishing until October, when the tribes submitted and paid their fines. The Tochi Field Force was gradually broken up by January 1898: it had lost 6 men killed and 8 wounded in a campaign remarkable for the unusual amount of sickness amongst the

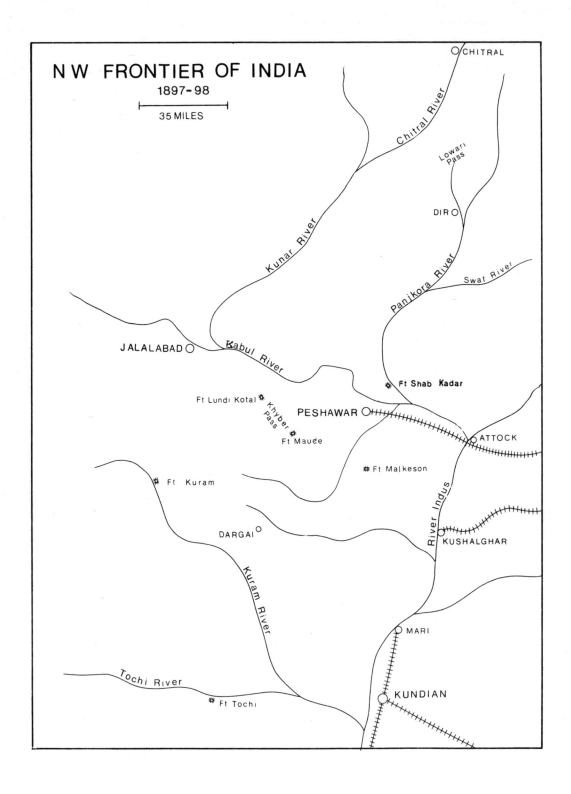

NW FRONTIER OF INDIA
1897-98

35 MILES

CHITRAL

Chitral River

Lowari Pass

DIR

Kunar River

Panikora River

Swat River

JALALABAD

Kabul River

Ft Shab Kadar

Ft Lundi Kotal

Khyber Pass

PESHAWAR

Ft Maude

ATTOCK

Ft Malkeson

River Indus

Ft Kuram

DARGAI

KUSHALGHAR

Kuram River

MARI

Tochi River

Ft Tochi

KUNDIAN

troops, for the climate of the Tochi valley is at all times trying and the hurried marches in the middle of the hot weather encouraged a severe epidemic form of dysentery.

Operations against the Ovakzais and Chamkannis, 1897

There had been smouldering discontent among these tribes since 1891 when the British had occupied the Samana posts, and in August 1897 the situation became serious enough for reinforcements to be sent to the area, among them the Royal Scots Fusiliers. On 27 August Major-General Yeatman-Biggs marched out with a force composed of 180 Scots Fusiliers, 487 Punjab infantry with artillery, and a squadron of Punjab cavalry. In an engagement that took place in intense heat, 86 of the Scots Fusiliers had to be carried back to Kohat in ambulances, prostrate with the heat, while the total casualties were 2 killed and 1 officer and 7 men wounded.

Reinforcements arrived at Kohat on the following day, including the 2nd Royal Irish Regiment and a field battery of the Royal Artillery; this force with difficulty relieved some British garrisoned forts, and for the next few days large numbers of tribesmen burned, raided and destroyed posts and villages and besieged many of the forts that dotted the area where the small British garrisons held out against large numbers of tribesmen until relief columns broke through. The operations concluded when the advancing British columns pushed back the tribesmen until the various tribes, one by one, made their submissions.

The Attack on the Shab Kadar Fort by Mohmands and Other Tribesmen, August 1897

On the afternoon of 7 August 1897 about 4,000 or 5,000 followers of the Hadda Mullah attacked the Shab Kadar Fort, looting and burning the village of Shankargarh. The attack on the fort was easily repelled by the garrison of 1 native officer and 46 border police and at dawn on the following morning the enemy drew off. Later a column under Lieutenant-Colonel Woon arrived from Peshawar. It included two companies of the Somerset Light Infantry, native infantry, two squadrons of Bengal Lancers and four guns of the Royal Artillery.

This force advanced on the following morning and found the enemy occupying a strong position on the undulating plateau at the foot of some hills, but the artillery did not open fire until an hour later than originally planned, owing to the difficult nature of the ground. This allowed the enemy to make a determined attempt to turn the British left flank. Colonel Woon was compelled to order a retreat in order to avoid being cut off from the Dakka Fort on which he was based. Brigadier-General Elles, commander of the troops in Peshawar, arrived and assumed command of the force, reorganising the infantry and artillery dispositions and sending cavalry to swoop down on the enemy's left rear, immediately putting the tribesmen to flight. It was estimated that the tribesmen lost more than 200 killed besides a large number of wounded, while British casualties were 9 killed, 4 officers and 61 men wounded.

The Mohmand Expedition, 1897

In August 1897 an expedition was mounted to punish the Mohmands and to prevent any violation of Dir territory which might imperil the safety of the Chitral road. The Mohmand Field Force under Brigadier-General Elles consisted of two brigades, including Somerset Light Infantry and Oxfordshire and Buckinghamshire Light Infantry, together with native infantry, Bengal Lancers, mountain artillery and a Maxim-gun detachment of the Devonshire Regiment.

After a long and unopposed march in conditions of intense heat, the troops met Sir Bindon Blood with the Malakand Field Force on 22 September and the two forces combined to take the Bedmanai Pass. It was thought that the pass was strongly held, but opposition was not very heavy and the British lost only 1 man killed and 3 wounded. On 24 September all the villages and towers in the Mitai Valley and the Suran Valley were destroyed, and on the following day in another action, involving the Somerset Light infantry and the Gurkhas, fortified villages in the Shindarra gorge were destroyed at a cost of 2 men killed and 17 wounded. On 27 September, a column moved against nine fortified villages occupied by the Koda Khel Baezai tribe. In the action that followed, the Oxfordshire and Buckinghamshire Light Infantry, together with the Gurkhas, played a prominent part in dispersing the enemy, while the sappers and pioneers demolished the towers and forts.

The march continued slowly. The tracks were difficult and needed a good deal of work, but by 4 October all the offending tribes had paid their fines and submitted. The object of the expedition had been accomplished.

Expedition against the Bunerwals and Chamlawals, 1898

In 1897, when the general uprising of Pathan tribes on the North-West Frontier of India was quelled, only the Bunerwals and the Chamlawals refused to submit. Accordingly, in January 1898, under the command of Sir Bindon Blood, the Buner Field Force was formed; it consisted of two infantry brigades and included the Royal West Kents; the Buffs (East Kents); the Highland Light Infantry; native infantry; the Bengal Lancers; Guides Cavalry, field artillery and mountain-batteries. It was estimated that the enemy totalled between 3,000 and 4,000 tribesmen.

In an attack on the Tanga Pass, the artillery opened fire at 2,200 yards range, covering the Buffs as they made a difficult climb on to a ridge; they began volley-firing at 1,500 yards range, while the rest of the infantry made a frontal attack up steep slopes against tribesmen positioned behind stone sangars; they made steady progress in the face of matchlock fire and avalanches of rocks rolled down upon them. The tribesmen soon became demoralised by artillery fire and long-range volleys from the Buffs, and took to their heels when the attacking infantry neared the top of the slope. Only 1 man was killed but the tribesmen lost at least 50. Meanwhile, the cavalry forced the Pusai Pass in an operation made extremely difficult by the rough conditions, and the tribesmen, finding the cavalry and infantry in their midst, submitted.

49 The Boxer Rising 1900-1

In 1900, nationalistic fervour swept China as the Boxers, a vast association of fanatical extreme nationalists, murdered and tortured Christians in an attempt to expel all foreigners from the country. Secretly encouraged at first by the royal family of China and the government, they were soon out of control and a regiment of Chinese troops sent to deal with them was routed and its officers put to death. On 6 June, in an action which in effect allied the Chinese forces with the rebels, an imperial decree was issued forbidding Chinese troops to fire on Boxers.

The danger to the European colony in Peking was increasing daily, and a small body of marines from the allied warships lying off Taku managed to get up to the city. On 6 June, Peking was cut off from the outer world. Telegraph and railway lines were destroyed as thousands of Boxers poured into the city to take up threatening positions around the Legation area just under the south wall of the Tartar City. The Europeans took refuge in the British Legation where, in an area of ground some 2,000 feet long by 600 feet broad, 400 military personnel — Americans, Austrians, British, French, Italians, Japanese and Russian — crowded together with more than 500 men, women

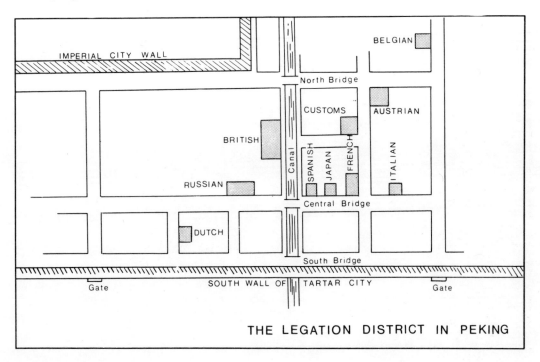

THE LEGATION DISTRICT IN PEKING

and children and 350 Chinese Christian refugees.

On 20 June the siege began as the Boxers and Imperial troops opened fire with repeating rifles, Krupp guns and smooth-bore cannon. Armed with makeshift weapons that included a home-made cannon, the small garrison resolutely held out, conscious that they would all be massacred if the Boxers broke in. On one day alone the Chinese artillery fired 700 rounds into the small area of the British Legation and their rifle-fire was continuous and heavy. On 9 June Vice-Admiral Sir Edward Seymour, Commander-in-Chief of the China Station, began to organise a relief column with all the men he could muster from his own ships lying off Taku, together with detachments of sailors and marines from the thirteen other warships of Austria, France, Germany, Italy, Japan, Russia and the United States of America. His force of just over 2,000 officers and men with 19 field-guns and machine-guns, entrained at Tientsin on 10 June. When they had reached Lang-Fang station, about halfway between Tientsin and the capital, they found the line and bridges completely wrecked; it was impossible to proceed any further by rail and reconnoitring parties had to fight their way desperately back to the main body. It was obvious that Seymour's situation was critical, and on 19 June his men began to retreat to Tientsin, marching along the river bank with the wounded and stores carried in four captured junks, which continually grounded on the shallow reaches of the muddy stream. Constantly harassed and under fire, they had to take several villages by rifle fire and at the point of the bayonet, but they were greatly handicapped when the

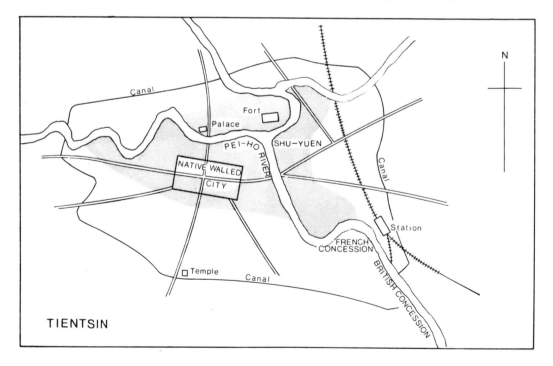

TIENTSIN

junk carrying the field-guns was sunk by Chinese shell-fire, leaving them with no weapons but their Maxim guns. On 22 June the force occupied the Imperial Chinese Armoury at Hsiku on the right bank of the Pei-ho River and there they fought off several very fierce attacks. On 25 June a 2,000-strong relief column of many nationalities, under the command of a Russian, managed to reach them and, after destroying the Armoury, the force withdrew, carrying 232 men in litters. They arrived at Tientsin on 26 June, having lost 69 killed and 207 wounded, 32 of them being British sailors and marines from *Centurion*.

After Seymour had left, tension mounted and landing-parties preceded by a bombardment captured the Taku Forts at a cost of 27 killed and 62 wounded. The Chinese put up a fierce resistance and suffered about 1,000 casualties. On 18 June communications between Taku and Tientsin were cut and the foreign settlements in the city, with only 25 British marines to defend them, were in an even more precarious position than those at Peking. On 20 June a mixed force of Russians and Americans landed in an attempt to reach the city but were turned back. On 23 and 24 June strong relief columns from Taku managed to reach Tientsin and nearly 12,000 troops of all nations were assembled for the defence of the city. By far the larger proportion of the force was Russian and Japanese, but the Royal Welsh Fusiliers had arrived from Hong Kong to supplement the British contingent. Guns in position all round the city bombarded it heavily and the Chinese carried on the siege with increasing boldness, constantly receiving reinforcements of Boxers and imperial troops. Naval twelve-pounder guns brought up by HMS *Terrible* were shifted around the defensive perimeter to meet various demands made upon them, but the defenders suffered from the obvious disadvantages of eight different allied commanders trying to act in concert.

At last, realising that it was essential to clear the area to the south-west, on 9 July Brigadier-General Dorward led out a mobile column consisting of Welsh Fusiliers, 400 bluejackets with their guns; a battery of Japanese horse artillery and 1,000 Japanese infantry and cavalry; 400 Russians and 100 United States Marines. In the face of stubborn resistance, the force achieved its objective with only light casualties. Two days later the enemy made a strong assault on the railway station garrisoned by 300 British, Japanese and French troops and was only driven off after four hours' fighting in which the allied forces suffered heavy losses. On 13 July, covered by the concentrated fire of 42 guns from the ships at Taku, two allied columns moved out against the Chinese; one column was made up of 12 companies of Russians and 2 companies of Germans, with 2 Russian field-batteries and a French mountain-battery; the second column assaulting the West Arsenal and the native quarter, of 2,000 Japanese, 700 British, 200 French, 60 Austrians, a few Italian seamen and 3 battalions of Americans commanded by a Japanese general. At nightfall the allies had not achieved their objective and had lost 775 killed and wounded, most of them Russian and Japanese; the British had 20 men killed and 93 wounded. Next morning, after bivouacking under the walls, the Japanese mined and blew up the gate of the native city and the troops swarmed in

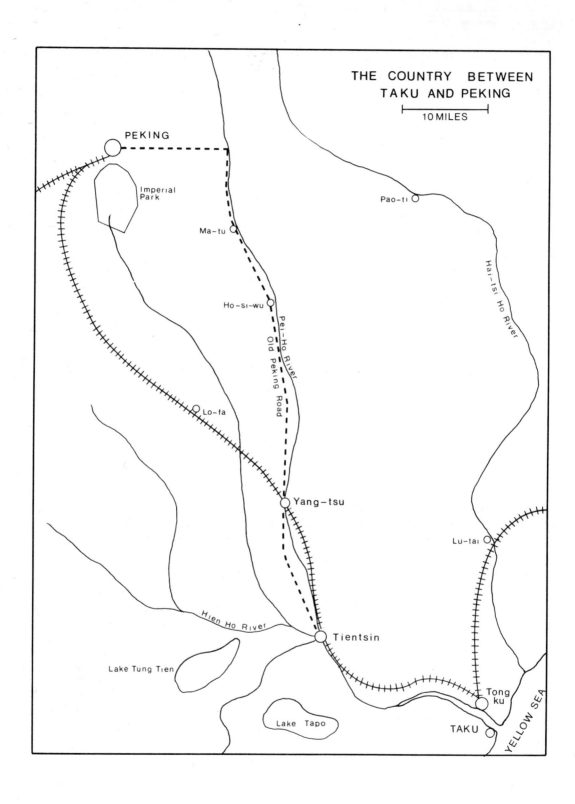

THE COUNTRY BETWEEN
TAKU AND PEKING

10 MILES

PEKING

Imperial
Park

Pao-ti

Ma-tu

Ho-si-wu

Pei-Ho River

Old Peking Road

Hai-tsi Ho River

Lo-fa

Yang-tsu

Lu-tai

Hien Ho River

Tientsin

Lake Tung Tien

Lake Tapo

Tong
ku

TAKU

YELLOW SEA

over the debris. Soon the whole of the native quarter, the Citadel and the Arsenal were in possession of the allies, together with 65 pieces of artillery. After much heavy fighting, the foreign settlements at Tientsin had been relieved.

Strong reinforcements arrived and a force of over 20,000 men was assembled under the command of Field-Marshal Count von Waldersee of the Imperial German army. It was formed of 10,000 Japanese with 24 guns; 4,000 Russians with 16 guns; 3,000 British with 12 guns; 2,000 Americans with 6 guns; 800 French with 12 guns; 200 Germans; and 100 Italians. The British detachment included Royal Marine Light Infantry, Royal Engineers, Royal Welsh Fusiliers and Indian native infantry and cavalry. Impatient with the delays inevitable in such a mixed force, the British General Gaselee told the other allied commanders that if they did not move he would advance alone, with the Anglo-Indian contingent and on 4 August, the force marched out to relieve Peking. At 3 am on the following morning a strong assault was made on Pei-tang, where the Japanese particularly distinguished themselves, their infantry losing 200 killed and wounded as they swarmed forward, covered by their artillery firing with remarkable precision at 3,000 metres. Most of the Chinese dead were wearing the uniform of the imperial army and they were armed with the new Mannlicher rifle that, with a range of 2,500 metres, was a better weapon than any possessed by the allies. No prisoners were taken on either side, Boxers and Chinese soldiers being summarily executed after inter-rogation.

With the temperature over 100°, the march went on, harassed by artillery and rifle-fire. Men were constantly falling from bullets and sunstroke. For many miles the road ran through 12ft-high fields of millet that completely shut off any breeze; at every step the feet of men and animals sank deep into the dust which hung in a cloud over the line of march, whilst the sun burned down upon them. Staggering along under their blanket-rolls and full marching-equipment they could only cover 8 miles in a day, while the nights were made difficult by mosquitoes swarming in dense clouds around the camp.

By 13 August the allies were outside the walls of Peking and next morning they moved against the city. In the face of a stubborn resistance, they showed dash and gallantry in forcing gates and scaling walls, until they were warmly greeted by Sir Claud Macdonald, Her Majesty's Minister at Peking, and his garrison, emaciated after eight long weeks of siege. The city had been relieved by a force composed of a greater number of different nations than had ever gone to war together since the Crusades.

For days on end, an orgy of looting went on and the British troops, forbidden to pillage, stood by and saw jewels and other objects worth a fortune taken by the troops of other nations.

A few more small engagements took place — on 11 September the walled city of Liang-hsain was stormed by Germans and the Bengal Lancers and on 20 September the Pei-tang Forts near Taku were bombarded by the allied fleet. On 18 October Pao-ting-fu was captured by a mixed force, and in early January 1901 the Chinese agreed to the allied terms and a note was signed which brought hostilities to an end.

Epilogue

Five days after the conclusion of the Boxer Rising, on Friday, 18 January 1901, a court circular, in cautious words, solemnly warned a shocked Britain that Queen Victoria was gravely ill. The Queen's sons, daughters and grandchildren hastened from all corners of Europe to Osborne, where silent crowds besieged the gates by day and by night. A hush settled over the nation.

Surrounded by her family, her mind quite clear, and in no pain, the aged Queen drifted slowly from sleep into death. At 6.30 on 22 January 1901, death came. The court physicians stated that death was due to the gradual decay of the bodily powers in a ripe old age . . . it might have been aggravated by overwork and mental distress.

When the nineteenth century faded out nobody was heart-stricken, but the end of the Victorian era produced a great blank. In an unprecedented sense, the Queen had mothered not only her own subjects but also those of other nations. All over the world the name of Victoria had had a magical ring, and by sheer force of character, she had endowed the principle of monarchy with a moral authority it had never before possessed.

With her reign had coincided the widest spread of British rule and all that the members of the British Empire knew of civilisation. The passing of her name from the symbols of their allegiance was an unparalleled shock to the imagination.

Meanwhile in South Africa, De Wet, the Boer commander, was concentrating his forces in preparation for a fresh invasion of Cape Colony.

Appendix I

LOCATIONS OF THE COLONIAL CAMPAIGNS

Abyssinia 1868	Jubaland 1898
Aden 1838	Levant 1840
Afghanistan 1838; 1841; 1878; 1879	Lushai (India) 1871
	Malay 1875
Ambela (India) . . . 1863	Malta 1878
Ashanti 1874; 1900	Manipur (India) 1891
Australia 1854	Mashonaland 1896
Bengal (India) 1857-9	Mombasa 1896
Benin 1897	Natal 1879
Bhutan (India) 1864	New Zealand . . . 1861; 1863; 1864
Buner (India) 1898	Niger 1898
Burma 1852; 1884	Oudh (India) 1857-9
Canada 1837; 1870	Persia 1838; 1856
Chilas (India) 1892	Punjab 1845-6; 1848
China 1840; 1859; 1860; 1900-1	Sikkim (India) 1861; 1888
	Sind (India) 1843
Chitral (India) 1895	Somaliland 1890
Egypt 1882-5; 1896-8	South Africa 1846; 1847; 1848; 1851; 1852; 1877; 1879; 1881; 1898-1902
Gwalior (India) . . . 1843	Sudan 1884; 1885; 1896-8
Hunza (India) 1891	Tibet 1888
India – North-West Frontier 1848; 1849; 1850; 1852; 1853; 1854; 1858; 1864; 1866; 1867; 1877; 1878; 1879; 1880; 1881; 1884; 1888; 1890; 1891; 1892; 1897	Transvaal 1881; 1898-1902
	Waziristan (India) 1894
Japan 1864	Zanzibar 1896

Appendix 2

LINE BATTALIONS

Before 1881: Old Numbering	After 1881: Abbreviated Territorial Title	Before 1881: Old Numbering	After 1881: Abbreviated Territorial Title
1st Foot	Royal Scots	33rd Foot	1st Bn West-Riding Regiment
2nd Foot	Queen's Royal West Surrey Regiment	34th Foot	1st Bn Border Regiment
		35th Foot	1st Bn Royal Sussex Regiment
3rd Foot	Buffs, East Kent Regiment	36th Foot	2nd Bn Worcester Regiment
4th Foot	King's Own Royal Lancaster Regiment	37th Foot	1st Bn Hampshire Regiment
		38th Foot	1st Bn South Stafford Regiment
5th Foot	Northumberland Fusiliers		
6th Foot	Royal Warwickshire Regiment	39th Foot	1st Bn Dorset Regiment
7th Foot	Royal Fusiliers	40th Foot	1st Bn South Lancashire Regiment
8th Foot	King's Liverpool Regiment		
9th Foot	Norfolk Regiment	41st Foot	1st Bn Welsh Regiment
10th Foot	Lincolnshire Regiment	42nd Foot	1st Bn Royal Highlanders
11th Foot	Devonshire Regiment	43rd Foot	1st Bn Oxford Light Infantry
12th Foot	Suffolk Regiment	44th Foot	1st Bn Essex Regiment
13th Foot	Somersetshire Light Infantry	45th Foot	1st Bn Derby Regiment
14th Foot	West Yorkshire Regiment	46th Foot	2nd Bn Duke of Cornwall Light Infantry
15th Foot	East Yorkshire Regiment		
16th Foot	Bedfordshire Regiment	47th Foot	1st Bn North Lancashire Regiment
17th Foot	Leicestershire Regiment		
18th Foot	Royal Irish Regiment	48th Foot	1st Bn Northampton Regiment
19th Foot	Yorkshire Regiment	49th Foot	1st Bn Royal Berkshire Regiment
20th Foot	Lancashire Fusiliers		
21st Foot	Royal Scots Fusiliers	50th Foot	1st Bn Royal West Kent Regiment
22nd Foot	Cheshire Regiment		
23rd Foot	Royal Welsh Fusiliers	51st Foot	1st Bn Yorkshire Light Infantry
24th Foot	South Wales Borderers	52nd Foot	2nd Bn Oxford Light Infantry
25th Foot	King's Own Scottish Borderers	53rd Foot	1st Bn Shropshire Light Infantry
26th Foot	1st Bn Scottish Rifles		
27th Foot	1st Bn Royal Inniskilling Fusiliers	54th Foot	2nd Bn Dorset Regiment
		55th Foot	2nd Bn Border Regiment
28th Foot	1st Bn Gloucester Regiment	56th Foot	2nd Bn Essex Regiment
29th Foot	1st Bn Worcester Regiment	57th Foot	1st Bn Middlesex Regiment
30th Foot	1st Bn East Lancashire Regiment	58th Foot	2nd Bn Northamptonshire Regiment
31st Foot	1st Bn East Surrey Regiment	59th Foot	2nd Bn East Lancashire Regiment
32nd Foot	1st Bn Duke of Cornwall Light Infantry	60th Foot	King's Royal Rifle Corps

Line Battalions

Before 1881: Old Numbering	After 1881: Abbreviated Territorial Title	Before 1881: Old Numbering	After 1881: Abbreviated Territorial Title
61st Foot	2nd Bn Gloucestershire Regiment	85th Foot	2nd Bn Shropshire Light Infantry
62nd Foot	1st Bn Wiltshire Regiment	86th Foot	2nd Bn Royal Irish Rifles
63rd Foot	1st Bn Manchester Regiment	87th Foot	1st Bn Royal Irish Fusiliers
64th Foot	1st Bn North Stafford Regiment	88th Foot	1st Bn Connaught Rangers
65th Foot	1st Bn Yorks and Lancs Regiment	89th Foot	2nd Bn Royal Irish Fusiliers
		90th Foot	2nd Bn Scottish Rifles
66th Foot	2nd Bn Royal Berkshire Regiment	91st Foot	1st Bn Argyll and Sutherland Highlanders
67th Foot	2nd Bn Hampshire Regiment	92nd Foot	2nd Bn Gordon Highlanders
68th Foot	1st Bn Durham Light Infantry	93rd Foot	2nd Bn Argyll and Sutherland Highlanders
69th Foot	2nd Bn Welsh Regiment	94th Foot	2nd Bn Connaught Rangers
70th Foot	2nd Bn East Surrey Regiment	95th Foot	2nd Bn Derbyshire Regiment
71st Foot	1st Bn Highland Light Infantry	96th Foot	2nd Bn Manchester Regiment
72nd Foot	1st Bn Seaforth Highlanders	97th Foot	2nd Bn Royal West Kent Regiment
73rd Foot	2nd Bn Royal Highlanders	98th Foot	2nd Bn North Stafford Regiment
74th Foot	2nd Bn Highland Light Infantry	99th Foot	2nd Bn Wiltshire Regiment
75th Foot	1st Bn Gordon Highlanders	100th Foot	1st Bn Leinster Regiment
76th Foot	2nd Bn West-Riding Regiment	101st Foot	1st Bn Royal Munster Fusiliers
77th Foot	2nd Bn Middlesex Regiment	102nd Foot	1st Bn Royal Dublin Fusiliers
78th Foot	2nd Bn Seaforth Highlanders	103rd Foot	2nd Bn Royal Dublin Fusiliers
79th Foot	The Cameron Highlanders	104th Foot	2nd Bn Royal Munster Fusiliers
80th Foot	2nd Bn South Stafford Regiment	105th Foot	2nd Bn Yorkshire Light Infantry
81st Foot	2nd Bn North Lancashire Regiment	106th Foot	2nd Bn Durham Light Infantry
82nd Foot	2nd Bn South Lancashire Regiment	107th Foot	2nd Bn Royal Sussex Regiment
		108th Foot	2nd Bn Royal Inniskilling Fusiliers
83rd Foot	1st Bn Royal Irish Rifles	109th Foot	2nd Bn Leinster Regiment
84th Foot	2nd Bn Yorks and Lancs Regiment	Rifle Brigade	Rifle Brigade

Recommended Reading

A bibliography for this book would necessarily cover the literature of every campaign, battle and expedition involving British troops throughout the entire sixty-four years of Queen Victoria's reign. Such a monumental list could easily form a book in its own right; indeed *A Bibliography of Regimental Histories of the British Army* by Arthur S. White (1965) is such a volume. The following list of books is not a bibliography in the real sense, but rather recommended reading.

Every 'Small War' of the nineteenth century, however minor, was described in the *Illustrated London News* and given added impact by woodcut pictures that frequently owed much to the imagination of the artist. Reports were sent home by men on the spot — war correspondents like William Russell, G. A. Henty, Vulliamy, Villiers, Archibald Forbes, G. W. Steevens and others who shared danger and hardship with the soldiers in order to obtain material for their despatches. Sometimes their vivid descriptions changed the course of the war itself or forced concessions for the army from reluctant governments. All the newspapers of the day carried their stories, while *Black and White*; the *Graphic* and *Punch* are rich with accounts of battles and expeditions. Other publications, both Victorian and contemporary, that contain valuable information include the *Cornhill Magazine*; the *Army and Navy Gazette*; the *Army Quarterly*; the *Soldier Magazine*; *Blackwood's Magazine*; the *United Services Magazine*; the *Cavalry Journal* and *Journal of the Society for Army Historical Research*. Nor should we forget the magazines of individual regiments, who are rightly proud of the men who went before them.

All campaigns were recorded in official publications — every colonial war had its official account, besides being documented in:

London Gazette
General and Regimental Orders
Statements and Order Books, Nominal Rolls etc of Cavalry, Infantry and Artillery
Parliamentary Papers
Foreign Office Drafts and Despatches
Regimental and Colonial Records

The various editions of the *Encyclopedia Britannica* contain much valuable information on the men and events of the time. The *Dictionary of National Biography* is helpful for many of the commanders penned their own stories or were covered by other biographers.

Many of the campaigns described here were fought on the frontiers of India. They are fully documented in *Frontier and Overseas Expeditions from India.* Intelligence

Recommended Reading

Branch, Army HQ, India (1910).

INDIA

Cork, Barry J. *Rider on a Grey Horse* (1958)

Roberts, Field Marshal Lord *Forty-one Years in India* (1900)

Singh, Brigadier R. *History of the Indian Army* (1963)

Toy, Sidney *The Strongholds of India* (1957)

FIRST AFGHAN WAR

Macrory, P. *Signal Catastrophe* (1966)

THE LEVANT

Williams, N. *The Life and Letters of Admiral Sir Charles Napier* (1917)

CHINA — 1841

Rait, R. *The Life and Campaigns of Hugh, 1st Viscount Gough* (1903)

SIND

Anglesey, The Marquis of *Sergeant Pearman's Memoirs* (1968)

Lawrence, R. *Charles Napier: Friend and Fighter 1782-1853* (1952)

Swinson, A. and Scott, Donald, eds. *The Memoirs of Private Waterfield* (1968)

GWALIOR WAR

Rait, Robert *The Life and Campaigns of Hugh, 1st Viscount Gough* (1903)

THE SIKH WARS

Bajwa, Farya Singh *The Military Systems of the Sikhs during the period 1799-1849* (1964)

Bruce, G. *Six Battles for India* (1970)

Rait, Robert *The Life and Campaigns of Hugh, 1st Viscount Gough* (1903)

AFRICA — KAFFIR WARS

Moore-Smith, C.G. ed. *Autobiography of Sir H. Smith* (1901)

BURMA

Laurie, Colonel W.E.B. *The First Two Burmese Wars (nd)*

AUSTRALIA

Currey, C.H. *The Irish at Eureka* (1954)

CHINA — 1859-60

Hurd, D. *The Arrow War* (China 1856-60) (1967)

NEW ZEALAND

Holt, E. *The Strangest War (The Story of the Maori Wars in New Zealand 1860-1872)* (1962)

THE AMBELA EXPEDITION 1863

Forrest G.W. *Life of Field-Marshal Sir Neville Chamberlain* (1909)

Recommended Reading

JAPAN
James, D.H. *The Rise and Fall of the Japanese Empire* (1951)
ABYSSINIA
Moorhead, Alan *The White Nile* (1960)
Myatt, F. *The March to Magdala* (1970)
THE RED RIVER EXPEDITION
Lehrman, J.H. *All Sir Garnett* (1960)
ASHANTI 1874
Lloyd, A. *The Drums of Kumasi* (1964)
SECOND AFGHAN WAR
Diver, M.*Kabul to Kandahar* (1935)
Hanna, Colonel H.B. *The Second Afghan War* (1910)
Macmunn, Lieutenant-General G. *Afghanistan* (1929)
ZULU WAR
Binns, C.T. *The Last Zulu King — The Life and Death of Cetshwayo* (1963)
Furneaux, R. *The Zulu War* (1967)
Morris, D.K. *The Washing of the Spears* (1966)
FIRST BOER WAR
Ransford, O. *The Battle of Majuba Hill* (1967)
THE NORTH-WEST FRONTIER
Callwell, Major-General Sir C.E. *Tirah 1897* (1911)
Churchill, W.S. *Frontiers and Wars* (1962)
Durand, Colonel A. *The Making of a Frontier* (1910)
Fincastle, Viscount and Elliott-Lockhard, P.C. *A Frontier Campaign/Operations of the Malakand and Buner Field Forces* (1897)
James, L. *The Indian Frontier War. The Mohmud and Tirah Expeditions 1897-8* (1898)
Robertson, Sir G.S. *Chitral — The Story of a Minor Siege* (1898)
Swinson, H. *North West Frontier* (1967)
Younghusband, Sir F. *The Relief of Chitral* (1910)
Younghusband, G.J. *The Story of the Guides* (1911)
EGYPT AND THE SUDAN
Churchill, W.S. *The River War — An Account of the Reconquest of the Soudan* (1933)
Moorhead, A. *The White Nile* (1960)
Moorhead, A. *The Blue Nile* (1962)
Slatin, R.C.and Wingate, F.R. *Fire and Sword in the Sudan* (1898)

Recommended Reading

Symons, J. *England's Pride* (1963)

MASHONALAND

Alderson, E.H. *With the Mounted Infantry and the Mashonaland Field Force* 1896 (1898)

BOXER RISING

Fleming, Peter *The Siege at Peking* (1959)

Index

Index